THE GOSPEL OF ETERNAL LIFE

THE GOSPEL OF ETERNAL LIFE is one of the IMPACT BOOKS, a series designed to bring the modern reader the significant achievements of scholars, both Catholic and non-Catholic, in the fields of Scripture, Theology, Philosophy, Mathematics, History, and the Physical and Social Sciences. Among the titles in the series are:

The School Examined: An Essay on the Curriculum by Vincent Smith

Catholic Thought in Crisis by Rev. Peter Riga

Introducing the Old Testament by Frederick L. Moriarty, S.J.

This Good News: An Introduction to the Catholic Theology of the New Testament by Quentin Quesnell, S.J.

Maturing in Christ: St. Paul's Program for Growth in Christ by George Montague, S.M.

Seven Books of Wisdom by Roland Murphy, O.Carm.

New Testament Essays by Raymond Brown, S.S.

God and Contemporary Man by Robert J. Kreyche

With the Eyes of Faith by Rev. John L. Murphy

Catechetics by Alfred McBride, O.Praem.

The God of Exodus by James Plastaras, C.M.

The Biblical Meaning of Man by Dom Wulstan Mork, O.S.B.

The Word Dwells Among Us by William E. Lynch, C.M.

The Person and the Group by John Thornhill, S.M.

Christ and Original Sin by Rev. Peter De Rosa

An Existential Approach to Theology by G. M. A. Jansen, O.P.

The Gospel of Eternal Life

REFLECTIONS ON THE THEOLOGY OF ST. JOHN

DOMINIC CROSSAN, O.S.M.

THE BRUCE PUBLISHING COMPANY
MILWAUKEE

IMPRIMI POTEST:
Terence M. O'Connor, O.S.M.
Provincial
Eastern Province of Servites

NIHIL OBSTAT:
Richard J. Sklba, S.S.L., S.T.D.
Censor deputatus

IMPRIMATUR:
✠ William E. Cousins
Archbishop of Milwaukee
April 3, 1967

for
Aileen and Tom
for
Pat and Daniel

"The time is come . . .
for destroying the
destroyers of the earth"
(Ap 11, 18).

Preface

THE function of this book is to offer to the interested reader an example of continuous exegesis and personal reflection on a major section of the New Testament. The tremendous interest in the thought of the Bible in recent years has already furnished excellent introductions and survey works but not, as yet, too many works of verse by verse interpretation directed to English-language audiences. And yet, since neither general introduction nor even particular survey can ever replace the thoughtful reading of the text in the continuous sequence of its own presentation, this volume directs itself at this latter need. It is presumed that the reader will have always before his eyes the text of the Bible itself, since the purpose of a commentary is but to open its message to his present situation. The text used in this commentary and therefore recommended for the reader's use is the Oxford edition of the Revised Standard Version.*

There is one point on which the serious reader must be warned and indeed invited to meditate for himself. It would seem comparatively easy to explain these ancient writings combined together under the general title of the "Johannine literature." Presuming a knowledge of their original language, Greek, and a general familiarity with the milieu of origin, etc., one has simply to interpret what the author was saying. Yet behind this apparent simplicity there is a yawning chasm whose presence is only slowly being admitted by exegesis, the science of interpret-

---

ing such works.[1] We are not dealing, however, with what John
was saying to first-century believers alone; we are dealing with
the word of God which endures forever. It cannot suffice for the
modern reader to know just what John intended for long ago,
since even John himself considered he had a message of transtemporal validity and abiding urgency. The problem is how this
message can become alive again for the modern reader as a challenge of ultimate significance. For example, the Greek words we
correctly translate as "love" or "life" or "light" may have had
immediate intellectual or emotional reactions from that first audience which these translations, although philologically accurate and
grammatically impeccable, do not have for us. The difficulty is
not just translation as a linguistic exercise but communication as
a human mystery. The present writer does not believe one has
even done exegesis of John's writings until the reader has received, as a vital reality, the message of the work and has felt its
impact in his own life and his own existence. Within the living
framework of the Church's life, John had no hesitation in completely rephrasing Jesus' message to make it more relevant for a
wider audience than that encompassed by a Galilean hillside.
With all due proportion, and within the same Church's continuing life and faith, the exegete has not adequately fulfilled his
function until he has also rephrased John in terms of immediate
relevancy for his own readers.

It is clear that such exegesis requires two steps. First, the
reader must be able to understand exactly what John was saying
in his own language to his own people for his own time. Second,
he must see this message as ultimate concern for his own generation and his own time and place. Recently, a theologian whose
training in literature had rendered him especially sensitive to this
problem in the theory of interpretation discussed the problem
as follows:

> The solution is a double movement: a centripetal movement of
> transporting the literary work into my language, my epoch and
> mentality; and a centrifugal movement of transporting myself
> into the language, epoch and mentality of the writer.

[1] For a history of recent debates on this subject, cf. R. E. Brown, "After
Bultmann, What? — An introduction to the Post-Bultmannians," CBQ, 26
(1964), 1–30; P. J. Cahill, "Rudolf Bultmann and Post-Bultmann Tendencies," id., 153–178. Cf. also J. M. Robinson, "Scripture and Theological
Method," CBQ, 27 (1965), 6–27.

We must perfect our scientific equipment so that we can trans-
port ourselves into the intellectual world of the Old and New
Testaments; but we must also be able to bring this world to our
own, that it may be an active force in our Christian life. A full
exegesis must include both elements, and, in my opinion, the
name of exegesis should not be given to a consideration of a
biblical text purely as an object of study, although this is, of
course, an indispensable part of the whole exegesis; the personal
meaning, the relevance to Christian life, must form part of Catholic exegesis, considered in its integrity.[2]

Such an attempt to restate the message of John in another
language is also quite dangerous. One can misjudge the language,
or one can distort the message. But while such attempts may fail,
not to make them is a greater failure. Let me be specific. We are
aware that many people could find little spiritual vitality in a
theology that discussed God in the technical vocabulary of scho-
lastic thought. But with all due respect, it is not sufficient to talk
of the relations of God and man in the biblical category of, say,
covenant. Once the allure of its novelty has evaporated, one will
begin to seek a fuller understanding of the reality behind the
term, and then a word that adequately restates that reality in
terms of modern existence. If the exegete is in contact with his
own age and has some understanding of his own generation's
thought and anguish, he should find himself rephrasing the
ancient message in his own mind almost necessarily and un-
consciously.

In this book I am trying, quite deliberately and consciously, to
express my own understanding and interpretation of the Johannine literature in language more meaningful than that of mere
translation. It may be unfortunate, but when the Greek word
phōs is translated as "light," this writer thinks automatically and
viscerally of an electric switch and a glowing bulb. To say that
God is light leaves such a person somewhat unimpressed. Such
terms, and they are frequent in the Johannine writings, cannot
simply be translated; they must be reinterpreted and rephrased.
What is offered in this volume is, then, an "interpretation" of
the Johannine literature. I believe that it is true to the mind and
intention of John. It is hoped that, although a personal evaluation,
it is not a subjective nor an arbitrary one. Its success must be de-

2 L. Alonso-Schökel, "Hermeneutics in the Light of Language and Literature," CBQ, 25 (1963), 371–386; cf. 381, 383.

termined by one question. At the conclusion, has the reader
been touched deeply and vitally and existentially by the message
of John and the challenge of Jesus? If he has not, then the
author has probably failed them both.

Dominic M. Crossan, O.S.M.
Jerusalem
27 December 1966

Contents

PREFACE   vii

ABBREVIATIONS   xv

I. GENERAL INTRODUCTION TO THE
JOHANNINE LITERATURE   1

  A. The Identity of the Johannine Author   1
    1. The Possibility of a Common Author   1
    2. The Identity of the Common Author   3

  B. The Character of the Johannine Author   5

  C. The Sequence of the Johannine Literature   8

II. PROLOGUE TO THE GOSPEL OF ETERNAL LIFE   9

  A. Introduction to the Letter   9
    1. The Purpose of the Letter   9
    2. The Plan of the Letter   11

  B. Interpretation of the Letter   12
    1. The Theme of the Letter (1:1–4)   12
    2. The First Movement: Christian Life Is Light
      (1:5–2:27)   15
      a) Statement (1:5–7)   15
      b) Negative Development (1:8–2:2)   16
      c) Positive Development (2:3–11)   16
      d) Application to the Heresy (2:12–27)   18

    3. The Second Movement: Christian Life Is Fidelity
      (2:28–4:6)   21
      a) Statement (2:28–3:3)   21
      b) Negative Development (3:4–10)   23
      c) Positive Development (3:11–24)   24
      d) Application to the Heresy (4:1–6)   26

    4. The Third Movement: Christian Life Is Love
      (4:7–5:12)   27

a) Statement (4:7–16)   27
b) Negative Development (4:17–18)   28
c) Positive Development (4:19–5:4)   28
d) Application to the Heresy (5:5–12)   29

5. *The Conclusion of the Letter (5:13–21)*   30

III. THE GOSPEL OF ETERNAL LIFE   32

A. INTRODUCTION TO THE GOSPEL   32

1. *The Gospel and History*   32
   a) The Gospel Rejected as History   33
   b) The Gospel Accepted as Metahistory   36
2. *The Gospel and Jesus*   38
3. *The Gospel and Its Structure*   41

B. INTERPRETATION OF THE GOSPEL   44

1. *The Overture to the Gospel (1:1–18)*   44
   a) Structure of the Overture   44
   b) The Meaning of the Overture   46

2. *The Challenge to Rebirth (1:19–4:42)*   49
   a) Structure and Theology   49
   b) The New Creation (1:19–2:11)   50
      1) *The First Day (1:19–28)*   51
      2) *The Second Day (1:29–34)*   52
      3) *The Third Day (1:35–39)*   53
      4) *The Fourth Day (1:40–42)*   54
      5) *The Fifth Day (1:43–46)*   55
      6) *The Sixth Day (1:47–51)*   56
      7) *The Seventh Day (2:1–11)*   56
   c) The New Temple (2:12–25)   59
   d) Into the New Creation (3:1–36)   61
   e) In the New Temple (4:1–45)   65

3. *The Victory Over Death (4:43–5:47)*   67
   a) Life Against Death (4:43–54)   68
   b) Life Against Paralysis (5:1–9)   70
   c) The Source of Life (5:10–47)   71

4. *The Promise of Life (6:1–71)*   74
   a) The Multiplication of Bread (6:1–13)   77
   b) The Reaction of Misunderstanding (6:14–15)   78

c) The Gift of Understanding (6:16–21)   78
d) The Meaning of the Bread (6:22–59)   79
e) The Result of Misunderstanding (6:60–66)   82
f) The Reply of Understanding (6:67–71)   83

5. *The Crisis of Decision (7:1–8:59)*   83
   a) The Setting for the Dialogues (7:1–13)   86
   b) The Seven Dialogues (7:14–8:59)   86
     1) *Moses and Jesus (7:14–24)*   87
     2) *The Decision Is Now (7:25–36)*   87
     3) *The Offer of Life (7:37–44)*   88
     4) *Division Among the Authorities (7:45–52)*   90
     5) *The Offer of Light (8:12–20)*   90
     6) *The Decision Is Now (8:21–30)*   91
     7) *Abraham and Jesus (8:31–59)*   92
   c) Appendix: The Woman Taken in Adultery
     (8:1–11)   92

6. *The Promise of Light (9:1–10:42)*   93
   a) Healing and Judgment (9:1–38)   94
   b) The Meaning of Judgment (9:39–10:42)   96

7. *The Victory Over Death (11:1–54)*   100
   a) Prologue (11:1–4)   101
   b) The Seven Dialogues (11:5–44)   101
   c) Epilogue (11:45–57)   103

8. *The Challenge to Rebirth (12:1–36)*   103
   a) The Advent of Death (12:1–11)   104
   b) The Promise of Glory (12:12–16)   105
   c) The Faith of the World (12:17–22)   105
   d) The Price of Victory (12:23–36)   106

9. *Summary and Sorrow (12:37–50)*   106

10. *The Consummation of the Gift*   107
   a) The Words of Consummation (13:1–17:26)   108
     1) *Dialogue With Betrayal (13:1–35)*   109
     2) *Dialogue With the Apostles*
       (13:36–16:33)   112
     3) *Dialogue With God (17:1–26)*   121
   b) The Works of Consummation (18:1–20:31)   122
     1) *The Passion of Jesus (18:1–19:42)*   122
     2) *The Resurrection (20:1–10)*   131

3) The Ascension (20:11–18)   131
4) The Gift of the Spirit (20:19–23)   132
5) The Community of the Spirit
   (20:24–31)   133

Appendix I: On the Relative Chronology
of the Passion   133
   i) The Problem   134
   ii) The Proposed Solution   134
Appendix II: On the Post-Resurrection
Apparitions of Jesus   139

11. Postscript (21:1–25)   144

IV. EPILOGUE TO THE GOSPEL OF ETERNAL LIFE 146

A. INTRODUCTION TO THE APOCALYPSE   146
   1. The Literary Form of Apocalypse   147
      a) From Prophecy to Apocalypse   150
      b) The Message of Cosmic Hope   150
   2. The Structure of the Apocalypse   154

B. EXPLANATION OF APOCALYPSE   156
   1. Introduction (1:1–8)   156
   2. Message to the Seven Churches (1:9–3:22)   157
   3. Announcement of the Day of the Lord
      (4:1–16:21)   158
      a) The Scroll Vision (4:1–5:14; 10:1–11)   158
      b) First Announcement of the Day (6:1–11:9) 159
      c) The Conflict Vision (12:1–17)   162
      d) The Second Announcement of the Day
         (13:1–16:21)   163

   4. Advent of the Day of the Lord   166
      a) The Day of Rome (17:1–19:10)   166
      b) The Day of all the Earth (19:11–22:5)   167

   5. Conclusion (22:6–21)   169

GENERAL BIBLIOGRAPHY   171

SCRIPTURAL INDEX   175

SUBJECT INDEX   179

Abbreviations

OLD TESTAMENT

Gn	Genesis	Lam	Lamentations
Ex	Exodus	Jer	Jeremiah
Lv	Leviticus	Ez	Ezekiel
Nm	Numbers	Dn	Daniel
Dt	Deuteronomy	Ho	Hosea
Jos	Joshua	Jl	Joel
Jgs	Judges	Am	Amos
Ru	Ruth	Ob	Obadiah
1 Sm	1 Samuel	Jon	Jonah
2 Sm	2 Samuel	Mi	Micah
1 Kgs	1 Kings	Na	Nahum
2 Kgs	2 Kings	Hb	Habakkuk
1 Chrn	1 Chronicles	Zph	Zephaniah
2 Chrn	2 Chronicles	Hg	Haggai
Ezr	Ezra	Zch	Zechariah
Neh	Nehemiah	Mal	Malachi
Est	Esther	Tb	Tobit
Jb	Job	Jdt	Judith
Ps(s)	Psalms	Wis	Wisdom
Prv	Proverbs	Sir	Sirach
Eccl	Ecclesiastes	Bar	Baruch
SS	Song of Songs	1 Mc	1 Maccabees
Is	Isaiah	2 Mc	2 Maccabees

NEW TESTAMENT

Mt	Matthew	1 Tm	1 Timothy
Mk	Mark	2 Tm	2 Timothy
Lk	Luke	Ti	Titus
Jn	John	Phlm	Philemon
Acts	Acts of the	Heb	Hebrews
	Apostles	Jas	James
Rom	Romans	1 Pt	1 Peter
1 Co	1 Corinthians	2 Pt	2 Peter
2 Co	2 Corinthians	1 Jn	1 John
Gal	Galatians	2 Jn	2 John
Eph	Ephesians	3 Jn	3 John
Phil	Philippians	Jd	Jude
Col	Colossians	Ap	Apocalypse
1 Th	1 Thessalonians		(Revelation)
2 Th	2 Thessalonians		

PERIODICALS

AER	American Ecclesiastical Review
Bib	Biblica
Bz	Biblische Zeitschrift
CBQ	Catholic Biblical Quarterly
ClR	Clergy Review
EB	Etudes Bibliques
ETL	Ephemerides Theologicae Lovanienses
ExpTimes	Expository Times
Heth J.	Heythrop Journal
HPR	Homiletic and Pastoral Review
IER	Irish Ecclesiastical Record
JBL	Journal of Biblical Literature
JTS	Journal of Theological Studies
Mar	Marianum
MarStud	Marian Studies
NTA	New Testament Abstracts
NTS	New Testament Studies
RB	Revue Biblique
Scr	Scripture
TD	Theology Digest
TS	Theological Studies
tr.	translated by

THE GOSPEL OF ETERNAL LIFE

CHAPTER I

General Introduction to the
Johannine Literature

THE purpose of this book is to present an understanding of the entire "Johannine literature," a general term which includes the three Epistles of John, the Gospel itself, and Revelation or the Apocalypse. Before beginning with the actual text of these writings, it will be necessary to explain and to justify summarily their unification in one volume. It will also be necessary to obtain some appreciation of the theological and literary genius which lies behind their creation. These works represent a way of thinking and of writing which is not that of our western and Graeco-Roman tradition of thought and literature. We cannot become accustomed to them without some preparatory awareness of the principles involved.

A. THE IDENTITY OF THE JOHANNINE AUTHOR

1. *The Possibility of a Common Author*

It is not necessary for the beginning student to know all the ramifications of recent debates on the Johannine writings, but he should have at least a general idea of why these five writings can be grouped together, and especially how modern scholarly endeavors are reversing many of the conclusions considered firmly established at the turn of the century. For fuller background he may refer to relevant literature on the subject.[1] Past criticism has

---

[1] A glance at the annotated bibliography at the end of this volume shows the change in critical discussion on authorship for the Johannine literature. The two extreme positions, namely, that St. John the apostle wrote all five

often denied any intrinsic connection between these works and has questioned even the possibility of a common author for them all. Most especially, it has argued that the apostle John is not their common author. The opinion followed in these pages is that advocated by F.-M. Braun. This theory seems to explain all the internal (texts) and external (traditions) evidence on authorship in the most convincing manner. He has argued that the apostle John stands behind the five writings traditionally associated with him — the Apocalypse, the three Epistles of St. John, and the Gospel according to St. John. Differences in vocabulary, style, theological expression, etc., are to be explained, according to this theory, either by the change in situation and occasion of the writing, or by the use of different secretary-disciples to whom different degrees of creative liberty were accorded. Most likely the Gospel according to St. John was "published" after his death by his disciples, to whom, for example, we owe the addition of the last chapter of that Gospel.

The order of their appearance, according to this scholar, was: the Apocalypse, the third Epistle of St. John, the second Epistle of St. John, the first Epistle of St. John, and finally the Gospel itself. We can summarize the main steps to this conclusion, but it must be remembered that this is no more than a sketch. There are five points to be established. (1) The literary unity of the Gospel must be shown by noting how certain literary characteristics, words, expressions, turns of phrase, etc., so pervade the entire work as to postulate one mind behind its present state. (2) The unity of authorship for the Gospel and for the first Epistle is shown in somewhat the same manner. (3) The unity of the first

---

works associated with him, or that St. John never saw any of them, have both given way to a much more nuanced central position which thinks of St. John and a group of scribe-disciples, of a long life of catechesis, and of editing and redaction after his death by his pupils. For discussion, cf. R. C. Fuller, "The Authorship of the Fourth Gospel," *Scr*, 5 (1952), 8–11; A. Valentin, "The Johannine Authorship of the Apocalypse, Gospel and Epistles," *Scr*, 6 (1954), 148–150; J. N. Sanders, "St. John on Patmos," *NTS*, 9 (1963), 75–85; J. Edgar Bruns, "John Mark: A Riddle Within the Johannine Enigma," *Scr*, 15 (1963), 88–92. For the medial position adopted here, cf. F.-M. Braun, *Jean le théologien et son Évangile dans l'Église ancienne* ("Études Bibliques"; Paris, 1959). The term "author" is here used in the widest possible sense, as the common source (a school, perhaps) from which all five writings originated. For a recent and definitive discussion of the whole authorship problem cf. Raymond Brown *The Gospel according to John (i–xii:)* (Garden City, N. Y., 1966).

and second letters of St. John can be argued from the similar expressions and ideas found in both. (4) The connection in over-all form and specific expression between the second and third letters is demonstrated. (5) Finally, and here with greatest difficulty, the common theological mentality behind the Apocalypse and these other writings is explained. In conclusion, according to this theory, it seems best to see one dominant and indeed brilliant mind behind all the works attributed traditionally to St. John; the differences are to be explained by theological development, by change in type of literature, by divergent occasions, and finally by the use of different secretaries.

2. The Identity of the Common Author

If a common author, at least in the sense of a dominant theological mind operating at the center of a school of disciples, can be maintained for these five writings, is there any possibility of discovering who that person might be? It was once maintained that the thought patterns, vocabulary, style, etc., of the Gospel according to St. John proved that it could not have been written before well into the second century, and therefore could not have been written by St. John himself, then long dead. This theory is no longer tenable because of recent discoveries in archaeology. There are three main points to be considered in this regard.

First, W. F. Albright[2] has consistently argued that the total breach in historical continuity, which the terrible destruction inflicted by the Roman armies on Palestine in A.D. 66 to 70 effected, necessitated the export before that date of all precise topographical and geographical data in the Gospel tradition. He has shown, and others continue to do so, that such data in the Gospel of John are constantly correct as checked by archaeology. Therefore, the tradition imbedded in this Gospel must stem originally from a Palestine milieu prior to A.D. 70, at the latest.

The discovery of early papyrus copies of John has rendered

---

[2] From the Stone Age to Christianity (2nd ed.; Baltimore, 1957), pp. 388–390; The Archaeology of Palestine (London, 1954), pp. 238–249; "Recent Discoveries in Palestine and the Gospel of St. John," The Background of the New Testament and Its Eschatology ("Dodd Festschrift"; Cambridge, 1956), pp. 153–171.

physically impossible an original of that Gospel much later than the year A.D. 100. For example, in 1935 C. H. Roberts discovered in the John Rylands Library at Manchester a tiny papyrus fragment which contained the text of Jn 18:31–35 and 37–38. This fragment had reached mid-Egypt by A.D. 150 and that small fragment made many ponderous volumes on the Gospel of John outdated. The original, of which this fragment represented a forlorn descendant, could scarcely have been written much after the year 100. Besides this lone fragment, called Papyrus Rylands 457, there has recently been discovered a papyrus codex containing about two-thirds of John and written about the year A.D. 200; it probably stemmed from Egypt and is named Papyrus Bodmer II.[3] It is still possible that even earlier papyri may yet be discovered, but even now a date for John much after A.D. 100 is impossible.

Finally, the discoveries at Qumran[4] have shown a Palestinian milieu contemporaneous with Jesus and the apostle John into which much of the specifically Johannine vocabulary and thought can fit quite well. For example, the tension between light and darkness in John finds resonance in this sectarian background and thus renders a first-century date by no means impossible.

These three points then — the archeology of John's topography, the new papyri of the Gospel, and the Qumran background — render John the apostle at least a possible author, and at this point it seems sheer hypercriticism not to accept the candidate for authorship which the earliest tradition has always offered us, i.e., the apostle John himself. This hypothesis actually fits in quite well with one significant internal fact in the Gospel itself, namely the complete silence concerning James and John, the sons of Zebedee, who play such a large role in the

[3] E. R. Smothers, "Papyrus Bodmer II: An Early Codex of St. John," TS, 18 (1957), 434–441.

[4] M. Burrows, The Dead Sea Scrolls (New York, 1955), and More Light on the Dead Sea Scrolls (New York, 1958); G. Vermès, Discovery in the Judean Desert (New York, 1956); F. M. Cross, Jr., The Ancient Library of Qumran and Modern Biblical Studies (New York, 1958); J. T. Milik, Ten Years of Discovery in the Wilderness of Judaea ("Studies in Biblical Theology," 26; London, 1958); J. Daniélou, The Dead Sea Scrolls and Primitive Christianity (Baltimore, 1958); R. E. Murphy, The Dead Sea Scrolls and the Bible, (Westminster, 1956); R. E. Brown, "The Qumran Scrolls and the Johannine Gospel and Epistles," CBQ, 17 (1955), 403–419; or New Testament Essays (Milwaukee, 1965), pp. 102–131.

Synoptic tradition. These two men accompanied Jesus on the first Galilean synagogue tour (cf. Mk 1:35–38, as against Lk 4:42–43) and were presumably the only ones, with Peter and Andrew of course, of the later Twelve to do so. This early association is apparent in the special favor shown to them by Jesus, for example, at the vivification of Jairus' daughter (cf. Mk 5:37 = Lk 8:51, as against Mt 9:23); at the transfiguration (cf. Mk 9:2 = Lk 9:28 = Mt 17:1); at the discourse on the temple (cf. Mk 13:3, as against Lk 21:7 = Mt 24:3); and finally at the agony in the garden (cf. Mk 14:33 = Mt 26:37, as against Lk 22:40). This would be understandable reticence if the "disciple whom Jesus loved" was John, son of Zebedee, brother of James. One can also notice the relations between the author of the Gospel according to St. John and Peter within that writing, for example, in 13:23–24; 18:15–16; 20:1–10; 21:20–23; compare these with the relations between the apostles John and Peter in Acts 1:13; 3:1–4, 11; 4:13, 19; 8:14. There is also the emphasis on Samaria in John 4:1–42 and the activity of the apostle John in that region in Acts 8:14–17. In summary, then, it seems reasonable and likely to accept the external tradition which has attributed the Gospel according to St. John and the other Johannine writings to John the apostle ever since Irenaeus (d. ca. 202–203) in *Adversus Haereses* III, 1, 1. This means that all five works traditionally associated with John the beloved disciple can quite justifiably be considered as a unity, as they will be in this volume. These five works represent products of the same theological school at whose center stands the apostle John.

B. THE CHARACTER OF THE
JOHANNINE AUTHOR

The question of authorship is not the most important one. For example, whoever wrote the Shakespearean plays is known to us most fully from these plays themselves and whatever we name him is surely secondary to appreciation of his genius and study of his work. A correct response to the Johannine literature demands two things of us. We must be constantly aware, first, that we are dealing with a poet, and a Hebrew poet at that; second, that we are reading the work of a brilliant theologian and not just a letter writer or a biographer. Even if we never knew the author's name these facts would still be clear from the writings themselves. Therefore it will be necessary first to say something of how a Hebrew poet thinks and writes before we consider the text itself, for to misunderstand structure and form can only end in mistakes in comprehension of content and teaching.

In discussing John as poet the point is not the sustained imagery and symbolism which is the heart of all poetry, and which traditions of meter and rhyme, line and stress serve but to discipline. Rather it is to note that the specific poetic techniques of Hebrew poetry are so deeply imbedded in the mind of John as to appear time and time again in the overall structure and form of large sections of his prose compositions.

In 1753 Robert Lowth, who was later to be bishop of London, delivered a series of lectures at Oxford University. The Latin text of these addresses was later translated as "Lectures on the Sacred Poetry of the Hebrews." They constituted the virtual rediscovery of "parallelism" as the basic poetic technique of biblical verse. Although parallelism is found in many ancient poetics, and in certain excellent modern speeches, it is only in biblical and Ugaritic verse that it reaches the pervasive application which Lowth established once and for all as characteristic of biblical prosody. The parallelism used in Ugaritic poetry was only discovered during the excavations at Ras Shamra in Syria in 1928, and the years following. The use of this technical method in biblical verse would be an example of a tradition of the Syro-Palestinian bards adopted completely by the Hebrews after the conquest of Canaan. Lowth's thesis was that biblical verse was characterized primarily by a parallelism of thought and line so that its basic units were pairs of lines synonymous both in form and in content, the same idea expressed twice in parallel terms.

The two main types of parallelism to be considered can be designated as "consistent" parallelism and "varied" parallelism, and it is hoped that these terms in some way approach the way the poet himself would have seen his activity. In consistent parallelism the words, be there two, three, four, or more, are in perfect consecutive balance in the two lines. An example of this, with two words per line in the original Hebrew, is Isaiah 21:3.

> I am bowed down so that I cannot hear,
> I am dismayed so that I cannot see.

The second major type of parallelism uses any device which works a variant on this basic scheme of consistent parallelism. It is obvious that the consistent form could get rather monotonous and do little to test the poetic imagination of the artist. Accordingly, various technical methods were used to vary the basic type of parallelism. This was done by making changes in the second line, and the most important example of this is parallelism "varied by reversal." In this technique the order of the words is reversed in the second line. An example can be found in Proverbs 2:4 which reads literally:

> If you seek her as silver
> and as for hidden treasure search for her.

These two cases are very simple examples of the fundamental literary devices used in Hebrew poetry; but what exactly is the relevance of this to the writings of John? Behind the written Gospel is a long tradition of oral catechesis in which the techniques of Israel's poetry would frequently have been used if only because they rendered the work of memorization easier for both preacher and audience. Take one of the two devices mentioned above and replace the words in the lines of poetry with ideas expressed at some length in prose. If we wished to preach five points we might well arrange them so that the climactic point comes last and the others lead gradually up to it. But the Hebrew preacher will more likely mention the five points in consistent parallelism so that each of the five points appears twice. Or again, he might use parallelism varied by reversal, so that his five points will be structured in the sequence: one, two, three, four, five, five, four, three, two, one. In this last case the most important and climactic point would appear in the center and not at the end of the construction. If we failed to appreciate the influence of poetic technique on the ordering of such a prose sermon we might miss the content completely. Very often the difficulties experienced by the reader of John arise from the fact that he is seeking to infuse an Aristotelian logic into a chapter which was fashioned according to Hebrew artistry. Both are disciplines, but each must be accepted on its own terms. As we read the five works of John it will be quite clear that we are dealing with a consummate thinker, but we must never forget that he is a theologian whose mentality and writing are deeply imbued with and affected by the oral techniques of Hebrew poetry, and that these quite frequently dictate the structure and sequence of what appear to us on the surface to be ordinary prose narratives and discourses. John is a theologian-poet, and that combination can be ignored only at the risk of frequently missing both content and message.

C. THE SEQUENCE OF THE JOHANNINE LITERATURE

In discussing the theory of F.-M. Braun on the authorship of the Johannine literature it was stated that he maintained the following chronological order for the five works; Apocalypse, 3 John, 2 John, 1 John, and finally John itself. For reasons of clarity we shall not follow this chronological sequence of the writings. John itself is of course the center of the entire discussion. But the first part of the book will be concerned with 1 John, which serves as an excellent prologue to this work. In that letter the great themes of the Gospel are sketched and considered in résumé. Such Johannine motifs as life and death, light and darkness, love and sin can be introduced and explained by considering this letter first, and most especially the dominant Johannine theme of love can be firmly established as the heart of the entire literature. After studying 1 John, the Gospel itself can be explored. Because of the importance of form in determining content it seems best to interpret it according to the given sequence of the chapters, rather than by accumulating isolated texts around central themes. Only sequential study of the text can open John's message to our own minds and our own lives. Then, as an epilogue, we shall discuss the Apocalypse, that great and majectic vision of hope which points the Christian challenge of love not only into the personal present but also into the cosmic future.

CHAPTER II

Prologue to the Gospel of Eternal Life

THE first letter of John serves as a magnificent prelude to the Gospel itself, for it delineates the great themes of light, fidelity, holiness, and especially of love, which stand at the center of the latter writing.

A. INTRODUCTION TO THE LETTER

Before any of the inspired writings of the Bible can grasp us today in our historical time and place, before they can strike us today as the sharp two-edged sword of God's word, two steps must be taken. We must be quite clear to whom the writing was first addressed. Knowing this, we must see the enduring word spoken to them in the relativities of their own situation. Then we must carefully rephrase that message in terms of contemporary relevance so that it meets us at the point of our own historical ordeal and our own existential anguish. Thus, the first step in our study of 1 John will be a discussion of the purpose, and then the plan, of the letter.

1. The Purpose of the Letter

It is clear that 1 John was written to combat some form of Christological heresy. It was a circular letter intended no doubt for the many churches of Asia under the guidance of John, who was probably living at Ephesus.[1] We shall see some of these same daugh-

---

[1] For a fuller discussion of this problem cf. J. A. T. Robinson, "The Destination and Purpose of the Johannine Epistles," NTS, 7 (1960), 56–65.

ter-churches again in reading Apocalypse 2–3. This same heresy appears, presumably in a more advanced state, in the writings of Ignatius of Antioch (d. 103), who sought to combat it. He writes in his letter *To the Trallians*, 9–10:

> And so be deaf when anyone speaks to you apart from Jesus Christ who was of the race of David, the Son of Mary, who was truly born and ate and drank, who was truly persecuted under Pontius Pilate and was really crucified and died. . . . Moreover he was truly raised from the dead by the power of the father. . . . If, as some say who are godless in the sense that they are without faith, he merely seemed to suffer — it is they themselves who merely seem to exist. . . .

The same heresy is mentioned in another letter of St. Ignatius, *To the Smyrnaeans*, 2, where he writes, "and he suffered truly, and just as truly, raised himself from the dead. He did not merely suffer in appearance as some of the unbelievers say. . . ."

Later, in *Adversus Haereses* (I, 26, 1), St. Irenaeus specifically places John in opposition to the heretic Cerinthus at Ephesus and sums up this latter's doctrine thus:

> And a certain Cerinthus, too, in Asia taught that the world was not made by the first God but by a certain power far separated and distant from the Royalty who is above all, and which knows not the God who is over all. And he added that Jesus was not born of a virgin (for that seemed to him impossible) but was the Son of Joseph and Mary, like all other men, but had more power than man in justice, prudence and wisdom. And that after his baptism there descended on him from the Royalty which is above all, Christ in the figure of a Dove, and that he then declared the unknown Father and did mighty works, but that in the end Christ again soared back from Jesus, and that Jesus suffered and rose again, but Christ remained impassable as being spiritual.

Even if it was not specifically Cerinthus himself that John had to oppose, it was certainly some incipient seeds of his heresy which were of concern in the first Epistle of John. This explains, on the one hand, the lack of any standard personal opening and conclusion to the letter, since it was intended for all the churches under John's jurisdiction, and yet, on the other hand, the deep personal commitment in the general tone of the letter itself which bespeaks profound love and concern for the recipients. The danger was from within the Christian churches themselves. But the constant emphasis on the reality of Christ in the flesh goes hand in hand with a complete lack of actual historical details of Christ's life. These can be presumed and it is their meaning, not just their actuality, that interests John. He is opposing the false teachers, who deny the reality of the incarnation, by building up the truth about the Christian mystery and letting the heresy shrivel in comparison with it. It is, then, a polemic of positive portrayal. The heretics denied the reality of the incarnation, that Jesus of Nazareth was fully man and fully God. John opposes this strenuously but not in tones of mere negative criticism. Rather, he depends on a positive exposition of truth as the best strategy, and only within such a frame of reference does the negative polemic appear.

2. The Plan of the Letter

John writes in a completely Hebrew manner and not in the style of logical development to which we are accustomed in the West. His method of development is closer to the musical than to the literary. There is one major theme which is advanced in various "movements" and studied from every angle. Within the three main movements there are many cross-references and allusions to what has gone before or is yet to come. The total effect is not obtained by the inevitable conclusion to well-prepared premises, but by the repetition of the same ideas over and over again, ever the same and ever different. If we can think of 1 John as a symphony in three movements, with the dominant theme given immediately in 1:1-4, it may be easier to appreciate the work. John is interested in refuting the heresy with a vision of the absolute beauty and truth of the Christian revelation and life, and he develops his ideas in a quasi-musical structure. The letter must be read slowly; then the total cumulative effect becomes operative.

The following are the main literary elements of the structure. There is, first of all, the dominant theme which appears throughout the entire writing and can be described as the beauty of the Christian life. This is stated immediately in 1:1-4. Second, this dominant theme is developed in three separate movements. (1) The Christian life is light; this appears in 1:5-2:27. (2) The Christian life is fidelity; this appears in 2:28-4:6. (3) The Christian life is love; this appears in 4:7–5:12. Third, each of these three movements follows four major points of development. There is first of all the "statement" of the way the dominant theme is handled in that specific movement; hence, for example, the three key statements: "God is light" in 1:5; "God is righteous" (i.e., faithful) in 2:29; and "God is love" in 4:8. After the "statement" comes the "negative development" which usually emphasizes sin. This is followed by the "positive development" which stresses the commandments and especially the great commandment of love. And finally there is the "anti-heresy application" which specifically attacks heresy. Putting all these literary elements together as the raw materials of the letter, and quite aware of the fact that John's thought processes overflow our divisions at every point, we can see the following main structure in 1 John.

Theme	Three Movements	Statement	Negative Development	Positive Development	Anti-heresy Application
Beauty of the Christian Life	as light	1:5–7	1:8–2:2	2:3–11	2:12–27
	as fidelity	2:28–3:3	3:4–10	3:11–24	4:1–6
	as love	4:7–16	4:17–20	4:21–5:4	5:5–12

Within the broad framework of the outline above, John's central theme of the magnificent beauty of the Christian life continually grows, expands, and deepens, but the vision of the Christian life in its three facets as light, as fidelity, and as love is always first developed both negatively with regard to sin and positively with regard to the commandments before any anti-heresy application is made.

B. INTERPRETATION OF THE LETTER

1. The Theme of the Letter

Read 1 John 1:1–4

These four verses serve as a statement of the theme. All that John has to say is here in résumé. In the parable of the wicked vineyard keepers (Mk 12:1–12 = Mt 21:33–46 = Lk 20:9–19), Jesus spoke of the messengers God had sent throughout the centuries to challenge his people with the divine will for their destiny. Finally, God sent his own Son as the ultimate messenger from the depths of divinity. The same idea is used by the author of the Epistle to the Hebrews who opens his letter with:

> In many and various ways God spoke of old to our fathers by the prophets; but in these last days he has spoken to us by a Son, whom he appointed the heir of all things, through whom also he created the world. He reflects the glory of God and bears the very stamp of his nature, upholding the universe by his word of power.

The present text uses the same idea but on an even grander scale and with a universal vision.

In the Old Testament the term "word of God" was frequently used to express the divine control of all reality, making it the sign of God's presence, the external manifestation of his own being. It was by his word that God called being from chaotic nothingness into the gathering tension of the evolutionary process and pointed it toward mankind. The beautiful prayer of Wisdom 9:1–3: illustrates this.

> O God of my fathers and Lord of mercy,
> who hast made all things by thy word,
> and by thy *wisdom* hast formed man,
> to have dominion over the creatures thou hast made,
> and rule the world in holiness and righteousness,
> and pronounce judgment in uprightness of soul,
> give me the wisdom that sits by thy throne,
> and do not reject me from among thy servants.

This recalls the serene omnipotence of the creative "Let there be" in Genesis 1 (cf. also Ps 33:6); it also repeats man's destiny from Genesis 1:26–28, his role as divine image, continuing creation in love.

The divine word spoke not only in creation but also in Israel's election and throughout her history as God's people. At God's word she was liberated from Egyptian bondage and doom. Once again we can read the majestic lines of Wisdom 18:14–16:

> For while gentle silence enveloped all things,
> and night in its swift course was now half gone,
> thy all-powerful *word* leaped from heaven, from the royal throne,
> into the midst of the land that was doomed,
> a stern warrior carrying the sharp sword of thy authentic command,
> and stood and filled all things with death,
> and touched heaven while standing on the earth.

From this moment onward, prophet after prophet molded and interpreted Israel's history in accordance with the divine word which came to him from God. These two facets, God's word in creation and in history, are joined together in Psalms 147:18–19:

> He sends forth his word, and melts them;
>   he makes his wind blow, and the waters flow.
> He declares his word to Jacob,
>   his statutes and ordinances to Israel.

In modern terminology we would unify creation and history under the title of evolution and confess the word of God at work within its finality.

But most especially did God's word confront Israel in the law. Indeed what we call the Ten Commandments, she termed the ten words:

> The Lord said to Moses, "Cut two tables of stone like the first; and I will write upon the tables the words that were on the first tables, which you broke" (Ex 34:1).

These were not external compulsions placed on Israel by ruthless divine power; they were rather creative words of God specifying clearly what it meant to be "My people" (Ex 19–20). By these words they were created as "My people," and by these alone could they be continually formed to authentic life (Ex 34:28).

All this rich biblical background lies hidden in John's choice of the expression "Word" to describe Jesus. In him all of creation and of history, all of divine law and of human destiny have reached climactic perfection. He is the ultimate Word from God. He is the truest manifestation which God can offer mankind and in him man sees most fully what it means to be man. In Jesus, as terminal manifestation of God, man is revealed to himself. Revelation could be described as God's proclamation of God to man; but such a statement might tend to obscure the fact that it also reveals man to himself. Indeed it might be safer to define revelation as God's revealing man to himself since this necessarily includes also the revelation of God to man.

The announcement of the apostolic witness to Jesus as God's Word is summed up by John in four points. The eternal life hidden in the heart of God "from the beginning" has become audibly, visibly, tangibly present to the world in the advent of Jesus who was, John insists, a true human being, one whom we "touched with our hands." The community continues to witness this reality to the world, that those who have not seen may yet believe and receive the gift of authentic life as well. This eternal life, this authentic human existence now and forever, is life in a community of love whose vital center is the presence of the Trinity as community of love in their midst. Finally, the result of such life is joy, complete joy in the acceptance of existence charged with meaning and challenge, in love now and hope hereafter.

These four short verses sum up all John has to say and the rest of this book will be little more than commentary on them, and development of them. They are a statement of thesis both for the Epistle itself and for the entire Johannine literature. This overture establishes the polemic of the letter on the highest and most positive level. The glory and joy of Christian life is deeply embedded in the reality of Christ's humanity; and the suggestion that Jesus was not really and truly a human being is automatically excluded.

2. The First Movement: Christian Life Is Light
Read 1 John 1:5–2:27

a) Statement (1:5–7)

The vision of eternal life offered to mankind in 1:2 is first considered as light. The key phrase of the first movement is found in 1:5: "God is light." God is clear, shining, refulgent, and perfect knowledge of himself and of all being. He approaches man as such refulgent light to show mankind what it means to be human by showing him what it means to be divine. God is light and in him we see ourselves. Since the structure of the Johannine writing is so alien to our literary methods it might be useful to note the construction of 1:5–7 as an example of what was said earlier about the influence of Semitic oral poetry on his writing style. In 1:5 the same point is asserted twice, first positively and then negatively. "God is light" (positive), "and in him is no darkness at all" (negative). "If we say we have fellowship with him while we walk in darkness, we lie and do not live according to the truth" (double negative): "but if we walk in the light, as he is in the light, we have fellowship with one another, and the blood of

Jesus his Son cleanses us from all sin" (double positive). Thus
the structure of 1:5–7 is an example of that parallelism varied by
reversal which was mentioned earlier. Many sentences in 1 John
which appear very convoluted to our literary taste become clear
and straightforward when read with an awareness of Semitic
form and pattern.

b) Negative Development (1:8–2:2)

God as revealing light forces man to face himself and to admit
that he is a sinner. This is not merely a question of actual sins,
be they of commission or omission, but also of that radical unconcern, that primordial unlove, wrapped in which we all enter
a world in ancient alienation from its Lord. When man denies
this birth-state of unconcern, out of which baptism releases him
even as a child by acceptance into the community of concern and
love, he denies the mission of Jesus. Even afterwards, if he re-
lapses again into actual sin, there is still forgiveness in contrition
before a merciful Father who cannot refuse the pleading of
Christ for us.

c) Positive Development (2:3–11)

The man who lives in the God who is light turns from sin to
love; this the very touchstone of his passage. Not names or titles or
slogans, but the lived reality of love approves the one who walks
in God's revelation and assures him that he is with God. John
plays with the words "new" and "old" for the commandment
of love and once again his typical syntax structures itself in the
sequence new–old–old–new in 2:7–8. This reversed parallelism
weaves itself into the entire fabric of the Epistle and gives it a
unique, characteristic style. The modern reader, who does not
encounter this pattern in contemporary writing, may have great
difficulty in discerning its presence. The commandment of love,
the revelation that the depths of man's being demand love and
concern for his fellows, is no innovation of Christianity. Long
before, Israel had the words of God:

"You shall not hate your brother in your heart, but you shall
reason with your neighbor, lest you bear sin because of him.

You shall not take vengeance or bear any grudge against the sons of your own people, but you shall love your neighbor as yourself: I am the Lord" (Lv 19:17–18).

Jesus himself cited this very passage, along with Deuteronomy 6:4–5, to sum up the challenge of life in Luke 10:25–28. Israel also knew that in the great "Day of Yahweh," when God would establish among his people a kingdom of peace and justice and mercy, this love for fellow members of God's people would flow out to all the world. In the stately poetry of Isaiah 2:2–4:

It shall come to pass in the latter days
　　that the mountain of the house of the Lord
shall be established as the highest of the mountains,
　　and shall be raised above the hills;
and all the nations shall flow to it,
　　and many peoples shall come, and say:
"Come, let us go up to the mountain of the Lord,
　　to the house of the God of Jacob,
that he may teach us his ways
　　and that we may walk in his paths."
For out of Zion shall go forth the law,
　　and the word of the Lord from Jerusalem.
He shall judge between the nations,
　　and shall decide for many peoples;
and they shall beat their swords into plowshares,
　　and their spears into pruning hooks;
nation shall not lift up sword against nation,
　　neither shall they learn war any more.

This reign of peace and love was then promised to all mankind. So John does not coin any new commandment any more than did Jesus before him. The God of Israel was always a God of love. What is new is that the moment of fulfillment has now arrived. God has already established the firstfruits of his rule of love in the life and death of Jesus, and this abides forever in the presence of the risen Lord. The new commandment is the old commandment lived out at last in perfect obedience, in the obedience of Christ even unto death on the cross, forgiving those who had so condemned him. The man who accepts in faith this vision of authentic human existence incarnated in the mission of Jesus possesses true self-awareness; the man who still hates does not even know what it means to be a human being on this earth. Such a man still walks blinded in darkness.

d) Application to the Heresy (2:12–27)

Only at the very end of each of the three movements does John directly attack the heresy itself. This heresy is mentioned in 2 John 7:

> For many deceivers have gone out into the world, men who will not acknowledge the coming of Jesus Christ in the flesh; such a one is the deceiver and the antichrist.

The warning is here addressed to his readers as "little children." This title of love is used quite regularly in the letter, previously in 2:1 and later in 2:18, 28; 3:7; 4:4; and 5:21. The only other passage where it appears is in John 13:33 when Jesus so addresses his own after the departure of Judas. In 2:12–14 we are dealing with an admonition addressed to the entire Christian audience, who are termed "little children" (2:12) and "children" (2:13c). The audience is then broken down into "fathers" and "youths" in 2:13a–b and 2:14a–b. The "fathers" are those of the first generation, eyewitnesses of Jesus himself or at least hearers of many who were. The "youths" are the second generation, those who must believe without ever having seen Jesus or even heard those who did.

John uses the term "world" (2:15) in two very different senses. The word can denote the physical universe and all its inhabitants, and it is this that "God so loved" in John 3:16. But it is often used as a synonym for all the forces of hate opposed to Jesus' revelation of love at all times and in all places. It is a very serious mistake to confuse the two senses and to conclude that the physical universe is not God's sacrament but a realm of evil. Centuries of Christian writing, all too often infected with variants of the very heresy opposed here by John, have used such texts as 2:15–17 to demand unconcern for this world and its pain even though it is our very destiny to control and eliminate such anguish and disorder out of love for one another. But not so easily do we shrug off our mission to take responsibility for the future of evolution out of concern for each other. Not so easily can we annul our destiny given irrevocably in Genesis 1:26–28:

> Then God said, "Let us make man in our image, after our like-ness; and let them have *dominion* over the fish of the sea, and over the birds of the air, and over the cattle, and *over all the earth*, and over every creeping thing that creeps upon the earth."

So God created man in his own image, in the image of God he created him; male and female he created them. And God blessed them, and God said to them, "Be fruitful and multiply, and fill the earth and subdue it; and have dominion over the fish of the sea and over the birds of the air and over every living thing that moves upon the earth."

John intends to sum up in three categories the forces of hate and unlove, evil and unconcern, which are opposed to God (2:16). Man betrays his God, betrays himself, and thereby betrays his place in the divinely planned evolutionary process, by accepting as his god either passion ("lust of the flesh"), or possession ("lust of the eyes"), or power ("pride of life"). These "gods" represent the three great areas of archetypal betrayal open to man.

The Old Testament offered man only two possibilities: the living God or the gods who are made by the hands of man. The choice was between Yahweh, the God who was really the ultimate center of existence, or any golden calf who was but the external projection of man's hopes and fears, his terrors, his insecurities, or his desires. Never does the Bible offer a third possibility: neutrality, atheism, the absence of any god, for it knows that man always lives from a central thrust of being, and whatever that dynamism is, that is his god. But only the living God who is love will sustain a man as the center for authentic existence. Passion, possession, or power as focal points of ultimate concern and deepest commitment betray the living God and also the living man, for they betray the God-given meaning of the three areas in which man must exist: the realm of "I" (power); the realm of "thou" (passion); and the realm of "it" (possession). Man is destined to find God in, and only in, these three areas. But it is a fundamental betrayal of being to substitute any part or even the entirety of the three arenas of destiny for Yahweh, the community of love. On the first entrance of God's people into their promised land, Joshua had challenged them (24:15):

And if you be unwilling to serve the Lord, choose this day whom you will serve, whether the gods your fathers served in the region beyond the River, or the gods of the Amorites in whose land you dwell.

Centuries later Jesus reiterated this basic choice, the eternal either/or forever facing mankind and rooted in the existential fact that he is free to accept or reject God, but not to be God.

He is free but still within the frame of divine evolution. Here also John warns his readers that if their god is not the One Who Is, they will have some other god, be it passion or possession or power.

The more general admonition against the abiding danger of the golden calf, the god made by our own hands (2:15-17), leads directly into the more specific attack on the heresy which is the present golden calf facing John's readers (2:18-27). It is from within the Christian community itself that these false teachers, and "Antichrists," and "liars" have arisen. John reminds his readers that they are in the last age of human evolution in which Christ and Antichrist face one another. It is the age in which the reality of Jesus of Nazareth, perfectly human and perfectly divine, is the protagonist of the ancient struggle of God against Ungod. One very important positive point in this section is the fact that John does not merely appeal to external authority to confirm his statements or to sanction his warnings. The writer could easily have appealed to his power or at least his dignity as having known:

> That which was from the beginning, which we have heard, which we have seen with our eyes, which we have looked upon and touched with our hands, concerning the word of life — the life was made manifest, and we saw it, and testify to it, and proclaim to you the eternal life which was with the Father and was made manifest to us (1 Jn 1:1-2).

But he does not do so. Instead he appeals to their own Christian being and experience, to the Spirit who stirs in the depths of their own spiritual existence. He appeals to the fact that "You have been anointed by the Holy One, and you all know" (2:20-21). Again, in 2:26-27, he says:

> I write this to you about those who would deceive you; but the anointing which you received from him abides in you, and you have no need that anyone should teach you; as his anointing teaches you about everything, and is true, and is no lie, just as it has taught you, abide in him.

John's admonitions are made only to stir up their Christian consciences and their intuitive response to his words will be his sanction. He simply seeks to open their hearts to the force of the Spirit dwelling within the community, and so within each one of them.

This terminates the first movement of the letter in which the stress is on God as revealing light, on God showing mankind in Jesus what it means to be human and in that vision what it means to be divine.

3. The Second Movement: Christian Life Is Fidelity

Read 1 John 2:28–4:6.

a) Statement (2:28–3:3)

The second movement in the symphonic structure of 1 John will have a four-point development similar to the first. Once again the key phrase for the section appears in a statement about God in 2:29 and repeated again in 3:7. God, the God who has revealed himself in final clarity through Christ, is *dikaios*, and only in Christ is this fully manifested. What exactly does the Greek word *dikaios*, an adjective, and its corresponding noun, *dikaiosynē* mean in 1 John? The word is variously translated in modern English editions of the Epistle. It appears as just, holy, upright, righteous, and their appropriate noun forms. The primary problem is not what these words mean for us today, where they have all too often been hedged in by centuries of religious controversy, but what *dikaios* meant for John and his readers. For the moment we can accept the translation of "righteous" and see how it fits the reality hidden behind the word in the Old Testament and its equivalent in the New Testament. The root in the Hebrew Old Testament is *sdq* and its derivatives; and in the Greek New Testament it is *dikaioō* and its various forms. What do these words mean?

In ordinary usage we think of "the righteousness of God" as vindictive justice, that whereby he punishes sinners, or distributive, that by which he rewards the just. This is not, however, the biblical understanding of the expression. The use of parallelism in Old Testament poetry often makes it quite clear what words these writers consider to be synonymous. Thus, for example, in the consoling message of Deutero-Isaiah, righteousness and salvation appear together quite frequently. In Isaiah 46:13:

> "I bring near my righteousness, it is not far off,
> and my salvation will not tarry."

In the Psalms the "righteousness" of God is often paralleled or associated with God's salvation, God's truth, or God's mercy. In Psalm 71:15 we read:

> My mouth will tell of thy righteous acts,
>   of thy deeds of salvation all the day,
>   for their number is past my knowledge.
> With the mighty deeds of the Lord God I will come,
>   I will praise thy righteousness, thine alone.

In both the books mentioned above, for example, in Psalm 98:2 or in Isaiah 56:1, God's "righteousness," equivalent by parallelism to his salvation, is described as something to be revealed.

In the Old Testament, then, the "righteousness of God" is neither vindictive nor distributive but salvific, and is based upon God's covenantal commitment to Israel. God is righteous in that he is abidingly faithful to his freely made promises of deliverance and salvation for his people. Hence such terms as justice, righteousness, salvation, fidelity, and truth are interchangeable in the Old Testament with regard to God.

The important point in all this background is that to say God is *dikaios* is to state that he is utterly faithful to his ancient promises of salvation for his people and, in the final analysis, it is to affirm his absolute fidelity to his own inner being. When the term is used for men as being *dikaios*, or when we talk of the *dikaiosynē* of mankind, we mean man's total fidelity toward that to which he has committed himself. When we say he receives this from God we mean that such dedication is to the destiny given by God to man in gratuitous love. Proximately, to be *dikaios* means to be faithful to one's baptismal commitment or, more remotely, it means to be faithful to our own inherent being, to be what God wants us to be. To be holy, upright, righteous, or just, or any other translation for *dikaios*, means to become what we are called by God to be. The best English translation would seem to go beyond any of the words, and as a suggestion we might choose "fidelity" (noun) or "faithful" (adjective). To be holy, etc., is not primarily to obey some external command of God forcing us from without, but to be absolutely faithful to the exigencies God has forged at the very center of our being. To be holy is to be human; to be just is to be ourselves; to be righteous is to accept our being; to be upright is to accept what God has called us to be and which he has written forever upon our hearts.

We can now see the connection between the first two movements of this Epistle, and the progression in overall thought from one to the other. God is light and has shone upon us in Christ with full awareness of what he has destined us to be. This revelation of our own being has come to completion in Christ, as God had always promised his people from of old. He has been faithful to his ancient covenant; we must now accept this revelation, this light, and live our new being in active fidelity to the light in which we know ourselves. There is thus only one point left for the final movement. If God as light has revealed us to ourselves; if he did this in fidelity to himself, so must we be faithful to ourselves; but what then does it mean to be God and what then does it mean to be man?

God's revelation of man to himself gradually gathered intensity until it reached its planned and promised culmination in Christ. So also man's struggle to be faithful to this full understanding of his own being, to his own promised commitment to God as light, will also be an ever deepening process. This is true not only on the personal level as each believer lives out his own life. It is true also on the wider cosmic level until the final manifestation, the climactic victory of Christ's presence in the world, takes place. This moment when Christ's one and only coming reaches total victory is here described in 2:28 and again in 3:2. As individuals we are going into the fullness of our own being, and so also is the cosmos thrusting forward toward the fullness of Christ's coming when mankind will eventually become in truth what it was destined to be from the beginning.

b) Negative Development (3:4–10)

John again turns first to a consideration of sin. God has communicated his own righteousness, his fidelity to himself, to us in Christ. He has brought us to live as his children in his Son. We have the power to remain faithful to this new being now fully revealed to us. This will appear outwardly in "right" works. On the other hand the devil, the symbol and sum of all the forces of evil, has his own children also, and they too are known by their

works. In the final phrase John says briefly and without development that the evil are those who do not love one another. Sin is
unlove. It is not merely hate that is sinful, but the very lack of
love itself.

c) Positive Development (3:11–24)

After the negative aspect, sin, the positive side again appears:
God's commandments summed up in love for one another. As
in 2:7–8, John recalls to them that love is no new commandment
from God. It was built into man's heart from his creation and was
there already to condemn the action of Cain (Gn 4:1–16), the
archetypal example of both hate (murder) and unconcern ("Am
I my brother's keeper?"). The inner being of evil, the life of
Satan, appears incarnated in Cain, who abides in death. His existence cannot truly be termed life, for it is inauthentic human existence. This life-in-death is the lot of all the men of Cain, both
those who dwell in unconcern ("He who does not love" in 3:14)
and those who dwell in murder ("He who hates" in 3:15). On
the other hand, God has incarnated his own being as love in
Jesus who remains the Lord of the community of faith through
the Spirit "which he has given us." God not only spoke, he showed
tangibly his love for us. We cannot simply talk of loving one
another or of loving God; we must likewise show this forth
visibly: "Let us not love in word or speech but in deed and in
truth" (3:18). To understand what this means we shall have to
go back for a moment to the teaching of Jesus himself.

Very many of the parables of Jesus speak of a division into two
groups within the imagery of the narrative. In the following
three cases which we can take as examples, these two groups are
explained in some detail:

1) *Parable of the Servants* (Mt 25:14–30). In this story there
are only two categories. There are first of all the servants who in-
vest their master's money wisely, making a gain equal to their
capital, and are praised by him as being profitable administrators.
The other side is represented by a servant who keeps his capital
safely but, since he does nothing with it, is dismissed and condemned as an unprofitable servant. The only categories are profitable and unprofitable. Jesus does not even mention the third
possibility — the servant who might waste his master's money in

evil living. He only considers response as against unconcern.

2) *Parable of the Sheep and the Goats* (Mt 25:31–46). In this great image of judgment, the good are those who respond adequately to the pain of human existence: to its hunger, thirst, loneliness, insecurity, injustice, and disease. The evil ones are condemned, on the other hand, for doing nothing in response to this anguish. Once again they are not those who steal bread from the starving, who strike the cup from the thirsty lip, who cast out the stranger, who rob or imprison or wound their fellows. They are those who do nothing when faced with the needs of others. The third possibility is once again ignored; the only classes mentioned are those who respond to need and those who do not respond, those who live in unresponse and unconcern.

3) *Parable of the Good Samaritan* (Lk 10:30–37). This example is the most important of all. Jesus is finally challenged to explain exactly what "love your neighbor," about which he talks so often, really means in practice. The story shows three categories. First, there are the robbers who are also, in effect, murderers. Second, there are the vested representatives of official religion. These men do not harm the wounded wayfarer, but neither do they help him. Possibly they are afraid of legal impurity from approaching a corpse. But, in any case, "they passed by on the other side." Finally, there is the good Samaritan. What does this man do? He responds as fully as possible to the stranger's needs. He cleans his wounds as best he can, takes him to shelter, pays for his care as the man has no money left, and finally makes allowance for his convalescence. He does no more and no less than respond perfectly to the man's human need. But in the climax of the parable Jesus ignores the action of the robbers and simply asks: "Which of these three, do you think, proved neighbor to the man who fell among the robbers?" The only categories to be discussed are the unconcern of the Priest and Levite as against the love of the Samaritan. Love in this case means exact response to another's need.

This word "love" has, on the one hand, been used to cover almost every variety of abuse of another's personal dignity through the centuries and, on the other hand, has frequently become so smothered with metaphysical discussion and distinction as to destroy almost completely the naked simplicity of Jesus' teaching. In 3:17 John recalls this simplicity to us: "But if anyone has the world's goods and sees his brother in need, yet closes his heart against him, how does God's love abide in him?" But he also goes deeper. To love is to respond as perfectly as possible to the human need of the other; and to love God is to respond to the need of *all* others. It is easy to *speak* of loving God, but what exactly does it mean in practice or indeed even in theory? John answers that to love others is the only certain sign and assurance we have that God is present to us. We cannot love him in distinction from loving all others; and the one who so loves has found God even if he never knows his name. With words one can distinguish the love of God and the love of others, but in reality, they have but one and the same manifestation.

There is a statement in 3:20 that deserves some comment: "God is greater than our hearts." Man is free and must respond to God freely. To do otherwise is not to act as a man. He must be allowed to follow his conscience or, in John's more Hebrew expression, his heart. But he must also be warned with terrible urgency that sincerity alone is not an adequate basis for authentic existence. It is God who speaks to us. He holds in his hands the very core of our being and it is in him alone that the ultimate basis for full human life resides. Since this God is love, only in love can full life be found. We must certainly follow our "heart," that is, let our decisions come from within us and not see them as forced, overriding our freedom. But we must also make certain, and use all the assistance we can find to do so, that our "heart" is that of God. In Jesus, God has challenged our freedom with a vision of what is within us, that from which we can never escape. Jesus is the great response of God to the need of evolution for complete fulfillment. He himself offers forgiveness to sin, sight to blindness, health to disease, bread to hunger, knowledge to ignorance, and assurance to insecurity. He confronts every human need he meets with the response due to it. This is to love, and this is our irreversible destiny.

d) Application to the Heresy (4:1–6)

Once again the movement terminates with a specific attack on the heresy which denied the reality of the incarnation. This is again discussed as being the present manifestation of the "world," the forces of evil opposed to God in Christ. The same principle of discernment is invoked as previously in 2:20 and 2:26–27. God dwells within the entire community of love and they recognize the voice of his Spirit, the promptings of his presence. They know it cannot deny the reality of Christ's humanity.

4. The Third Movement: Christian Life is Love
Read 1 John 4:7–5:12

a) Statement (4:7–16)

The theme now moves into its final movement. God is light in that he reveals man to himself. God is faithful in that this revelation has reached its promised perfection in Christ. Finally, "God is love." John states it in 4:8 and this is the chief phrase of the last movement. Most of the points in this section have been touched upon already in 3:11–24, an indication of how the rhythmic recapitulation of John's style refuses to fit into our airtight divisions. God is not a single person enthroned in icy olympian loneliness. God is a dynamic tension of communal love, an intense interpersonal relationship, a community of love. This fact means that all of evolution tends onward and upward toward the perfect externalization of this divine love at its center. Not in creation alone, nor even in man alone, but within the community of love welded together around the risen Lord, does this evolution reach its fulfillment. Our love for all men is, therefore, the most perfect sign, the ultimate sacrament of God's presence as love among us.

The Hebrew word "to know" means a vital, living contact with another; thus in Genesis 4:1: "Now Adam knew Eve his wife, and she conceived and bore Cain." So also in 4:7–8, in typical Johannine balance of positive and negative, we read: "He who loves is born of God and knows God. He who does not love does not know God."

To love others is the external sign of vital communion with God; not to love others is a sign of his absence. As God externalized his love for us in the sacrament of evolution which reached its perfection in Christ, so also we encounter the divine in the sacramentality of our universal love for others. Only in this way are we in living contact with God, the God whom "no man has ever seen" (4:12).

It should be quite clear from all this that to love, or even to commit oneself to total love, does not furnish us with a detailed program for life. Love as response to another's need is open to whatever that need may be and only closes when we know exactly what is required. This love is universal and narrows inward from this universality toward the other who here and now confronts me in need. And in an age of technology, of mass communications, and of increasing cosmic unity, love so conceived and accepted works through far more sophisticated forms than the wine, the oil, the donkey, and the inn of the good Samaritan. But however technological society may become, such efficiency is but our lengthened fingers. To love is still to respond to need, and its opposite is not only to hate, but also to be unconcerned.

b) Negative Development (4:17–18)

The negative section here concerns itself with fear and condemnation, and is very brief. The believer has no fear of judgment because he knows that his life is united with that of the One who judges. Even here on earth he is living by love and has entered the life of God. To paraphrase the poet: already with You, now is our eternity. Even "in this world" we are "as He is."

c) Positive Development (4:19–5:4)

"We love, because he first loved us," states the metaphysical trap in which God has caught us all. Since he himself is love, he created mankind, the peak of evolution's upward thrust, capable of human fulfillment only in love. We can, then, only be perfectly happy in unselfish concern for others; to love others totally and absolutely is to love ourselves most fully. God's "commandments," or God's "rewards" and God's "punishments," are but halting and indeed primitive methods of expressing the absolute finality built by him into the depths of our being, as this absolute meets the changing relativities of situation and circumstance. They are external vocalizations of what is actually internal and ontological. For example, when we were children we saw ourselves in terms of parental command and we thought and acted because of parental punishment or parental reward. But we became adults and accepted the responsibility of our freedom to think and act from within, in willed response to the known exigencies of our being situated in time and space and matter. So also our lives as individual believers, and the cosmic life of the community which walks in faith, must experience the same growth to adult-hood so that we eventually put away the ways of children and face God as adults — in thought and word and deed.

Our faith, which "overcomes the world," that is, all the forces of evil, is a faith that God is love and that therefore love alone can save us now and forever. This is a question of faith because all the experiential data for a documented conclusion on how to live one's life are not available until one's life is over, and that is a little too late. Faith must confront experience and direct it, but meanwhile we are thrust into existence and cannot withdraw from it temporarily while we investigate its meaning. By faith we accept from the depths of the creative divinity the meaning of our lives and, in living according to this, find through experience its truth. There are many who come to such faith, however inarticulate and unconscious it may be, only through bitter experience, but the scars can then be very deep and sometimes it is even too late to live.

d) Application to the Heresy (5:5-12)

Once again the movement terminates with a direct application to the heresy which would deny the reality of the "Word become flesh." This is the present manifestation of the forces of evil called by John "the world" or the "Antichrist." John argues in 5:10, as previously in 2:20, 26–27 and 4:4, to the eternal witness of faith within the heart of the believer. The reality of Jesus' humanity is known in that he was baptized by John the Baptist in solidarity with sinful mankind ("came by water"); in that he died a real death upon the cross ("came by blood"); and in that the Spirit of the risen Lord now dwelling in the community speaks of the reality of this life begun in water and ended in blood. All "three agree" that Jesus of Nazareth is Son of God and true man. The argument actually moves on two levels. The believer also receives this testimony internally: by the Spirit dwelling in his heart, initially through his baptism (water) and continually through the Eucharist (blood). Notice the reversal of parallelism in the sequence: water, blood, Spirit in 5:6–7 followed by: Spirit, water, blood, in 5:8. Historically (5:6–7) and sacramentally (5:8) faith knows the reality of Jesus the Christ.

Older English versions based on the Clementine Vulgate read our text in 5:8 as follows:

> There are three witnesses (in heaven: the Father, the Word, and the Holy Spirit; and these three agree. And there are three that bear witness on earth): the Spirit, the water, and the blood, and these three agree.

The words in parentheses are usually called the "Johannine Comma," and their history would seem most likely to be as follows. The words themselves are orthodox but undoubtedly not authentic. They are absent from all the Greek lectionaries, that is, the translations used in the liturgy; from all the independent Greek manuscripts; from all the ancient oriental translations; from the Fathers, who surely would have cited them in the great Trinitarian controversies. Among the Fathers they do not appear before Priscillian, Bishop of Avila (ca. 380). They are not even found in the most ancient manuscripts of the Vetus Latina or of the Vulgate itself. It is a case of an allegorical marginal gloss which crept into the later edition of the Vulgate in the fourth century. Besides John's three witnesses (Spirit, water, blood) another three (Father, Son, Spirit) were added in the margin in Spain or Africa during the fourth century and eventually worked themselves into the text itself. It is thus an uninspired marginal gloss and is to be omitted from the authentic text.

To deny the reality of Jesus as Incarnate Word renders God a liar, Christ a deceiver, and leaves mankind without access to, or possession of, the eternal life which God communicates only in Christ.

5. The Conclusion of the Letter

Read 1 John 5:13–21.

The concluding words in 5:13 are almost exactly those which conclude the Gospel of John in 20:31:

> These are written that you may believe that Jesus is the Christ, the Son of God, and that believing you may have life in his name.

The following section in John 21 is considered by many to have been adopted by John's secretary-disciple after his death, when the text was being put into its final form by the community. It is possible that 1 John 5:14–21 is a similar appendix by members of John's school. These words sum up many of the basic ideas of the letter and use the standard Johannine vocabulary. Like John 21, these verses are part of the inspired text which the community of faith brought forth as an authentic declaration of its own self-consciousness of God's presence within it and of what flowed therefrom in their crisis of faith and love.

The distinction between "sin which is mortal" and "sin which is not mortal" in 1 John 5:16–17 requires some comment. It is not our theological distinction of mortal and venial sin. The "sin which is not mortal," and from which one must pray God to restore life to the sinner, is the sin of weakness, however serious, to which the flesh or the spirit falls heir. But the sin which begets death eternal, which is truly mortal, is that of the heresy itself. By denying that God has confronted mankind climactically in the sacrament named Jesus of Nazareth and has shone the light of his love upon us in his salvific life and death, the sinner loses the only avenue of authentic existence open to him. Having lost this, he can no longer see the exigency of total love for others and absolute concern for the needs of others and he walks in death forever.

CHAPTER III

The Gospel of Eternal Life

A. INTRODUCTION TO THE GOSPEL

JOHN's first Epistle has served as a prologue to the Gospel in a double sense. It has given some indication of his main stylistic devices: a balance of negative and positive discussion of a theme; the use of Hebrew parallelism, both consistent and varied, in handling large sections of material; and above all the careful construction, born no doubt of catechetical necessities, which characterizes the writing of John. It has also introduced the most characteristic Johannine concepts and furnished some understanding of their content: for example, the Word, love, light, life, and the corresponding negatives: Satan, hate and unconcern, death, and darkness.

Before proceeding to the interpretation of the Gospel itself, in which these ideas are grounded even more deeply in the reality of Christ, we shall discuss the relationship of this writing to the actual historical events of Jesus' ministry and also investigate the overall plan which John followed in assembling the book in its present form. Once again form serves to elucidate content.

1. The Gospel and History

The discussion on the historicity of the Gospel accounts has always been most intensive with regard to John. In reaction to the denial of historicity by some critics, others have sometimes ended up by talking as if John were nothing except ordinary history. It is necessary, then, to consider the relationship between Gospel and history.[1]

[1] The literature is voluminous and this list is but a sample of it. For general theoretical problems of history and Gospel cf. H. Butterfield, *Chris-*

a) The Gospel Rejected as History

Our modern historical thinking has become dominated by one historical method to such an extent that any other methodology is often deemed invalid or impossible. This is especially unfortunate in that the method in question is a scant one hundred and fifty years old; it was conceived in Germany as the child of classical philology and empirical science around the start of the nineteenth century. The school was founded by Leopold von Ranke (1795–1886), who was to be professor of history at the University of Berlin for almost fifty years. It has been termed "positivistic" as it was a product of the nineteenth century's rational and empirical attitude toward reality. His school took its inspiration from the high ideals of precision and accuracy established by the classical philologists of the German universities and from the example of scientific exactitude set forth by the natural sciences, and declared that the function of the historian was to reconstruct a perfect picture of what had happened in the past, "exactly as it happened." Naturally, such a demanding ideal of history forced upon Von Ranke and his school a search for first-class historical sources. It was easy for him to take various renaissance authors who had written histories of their times and to prove their lack of historicity and so undermine their credibility. His first works contained a critical exposé of the inaccuracies of the historians of that earlier period. Having destroyed the value of such earlier

tianity and History (London, 1960); H. E. W. Turner, Historicity and the Gospels (London, 1963). On the past sequence of the debate itself cf. D. M. Stanley, "Rudolph Bultmann: a Contemporary Challenge to the Catholic Theologian," CBQ, 19 (1957), 347–355, and for its early period, J. M. Robinson, A New Quest of the Historical Jesus ("Studies in Biblical Theology," 25; London, 1959). For the later period, cf. the two articles cited, p. vii in this book. Excellent analyses of the present state of research can be seen in T. W. Manson, "The Life of Jesus: Some Tendencies in Present-Day Research," The Background of the New Testament and Its Eschatology ("Dodd Festschrift"; Cambridge, 1956), pp. 211–221; F. J. McCool, "The Preacher and the Historical Witness of the Gospels," TS, 21 (1960), 517–543; B. Vawter, "The Historical Theology of the Gospels," HPR, 62 (1962), 681–691. For a popular summary cf. H. Zahrnt, The Historical Jesus (New York, 1963). Works to be consulted with special reference to historicity and the Gospel of John are R. C. Fuller, "The Fourth Gospel, an Objective Record?" Scr, 5 (1952), 27–32; R. E. Brown, "Incidents That Are Units in the Synoptic Gospels but Dispersed in St. John," CBQ, 23 (1961), 143–160; "The Problem of Historicity in John," CBQ, 24 (1962), 1–14, or New Testament Essays (Milwaukee, 1965) pp. 143–167, 192–213.

works, Von Ranke claimed that he had found the ideal historical source, not in the works of earlier contemporary historians, but in the archives of the chancellories of Europe, and especially in the Venetian archives. These were the reports that the ambassadors of Venice had sent back to that Adriatic metropolis in its heyday and which were then "preserved" at Vienna. Money grants from the Prussian government and the favor of Metternich afforded Von Ranke time and opportunity for combing these records, which he considered his *Urkunden* (prime sources). They were accurate, detailed, and dispassionate accounts of affairs based on personal observations or agents' reports; they were written by men who were formally trained to observe critically the passage of events and their connections in the foreign posts to which they were assigned. Today we would be careful to check even such "pure" historical sources as these, but for the moment the magnificent histories which Von Ranke produced led this type of historical source to be canonized as the *only* one worthy of consideration.

All this historical ferment occurred in a Germany whose religious circles were ripe for a campaign against dogma. The success of Von Ranke's work brought into question the very possibility of ancient history. Archaeology was still of scant scientific help at that time. Immediately the Gospel records were questioned as historical sources. Were they not openly tendentious? Did they not admit they were born in faith and written for faith? Were not their writers far too deeply and personally involved in the events to be objective about them? Were their writers trained observers? It was this somewhat arrogant assumption that one type of historical source is the only one worthy of scientific consideration which was to dominate biblical exegesis up to recent times. It is absolutely necessary that we recognize this root cause of the eventual total bankruptcy of Gospel exegesis if we are not ourselves to repeat it. It must be admitted that this prejudice dominates many minds who are hardly even aware of its presence.

In all this it is only fair to mention that Von Ranke's historical ideals and their scientific exactitudes constituted a great stride forward for the science of history, but it could not render a social science into a physical one. Also, the great advances in literary criticism of the Gospel which arose in the course of the old quest of the historical Jesus cannot be discounted; it discovered many valuable things before it found itself at its own tomb.

Critics imbued with a positivistic historical bias immediately found the fourth Gospel completely unacceptable to the scientific historian. It was not history but symbolic theology based on certain themes borrowed from the Synoptic Gospels. The words of Jesus are really those of John and the narration is saturated with Johannine Christ-mysticism and speculation. The illusion that the Gospel was written by an intimate of Jesus and an eye witness of the recorded events is merely a literary fiction. With such sentences and judgments, John was the first to be dismissed as historically irrelevant. But the work of Luke and Matthew was soon found to be questionable as well. Neither of them seemed to be writing "pure" history, and the scientific historian could pay attention only to Mark as a serious source for the life of Jesus. But in 1901 the liberal school of German exegesis was shaken to its foundations by the advent of W. Wrede's *Das Messiasgeheimnis in den Evangelien*, which showed conclusively that faith had also played a part in the portrait of Jesus painted by Mark. In his own way, Mark was as much a theologian as Luke or Matthew or John. Accordingly, all the written accounts available to the historian were unworthy objects for any serious scientific consideration. Many scholars were skeptical that scholarly study could ever penetrate behind the faith-accounts of the early community to see and hear Jesus of Nazareth as scientific history would like to find him.

It was at this point that the method of "Form Criticism," as it is commonly called, appeared on the scene with the possibility of an escape from the dead end. It was born in Germany after World War I in the writings of Martin Dibelius, Karl Ludwig Schmidt, and Rudolph Bultmann. Its purpose was to get back to the preliterary phase of the Gospel development; to trace the evolution of the "forms" into which the contents of the Gospel were poured by the primitive community with the help of parallel usage in the oral traditions of other countries; to pass judgment, to one extent or another, on the historicity of the content of the materials with relation to the historical Jesus. But it did not work. Behind all the forms in which they found the words and deeds of Jesus preserved, they always seemed to find a portrait of Jesus "contaminated" by faith. It was almost as if this Jesus might have proclaimed himself from the very beginning as an object of faith! But the conclusion to the quest for the historical Jesus was now clear, the dilemma unavoidable: either the historical Jesus was lost forever behind the faith of the primitive community, or one had to admit the entire search had been wrong in its principles from the very beginning.

b) The Gospel Accepted As Metahistory

Two forces have combined to open a way out of this impasse. A different approach to history and a far better understanding of the true nature of the Gospel have once again rendered dialogue possible between historians and theologians.

Many modern historians think of history as more than the precise record of what happened, exactly as it happened, and this primarily on the external level. To stop at this would not really establish understanding of even the facts themselves. The historian must find a relation between himself and the past events whose personal protagonists he faces. Only within the historical ordeal and existential problems of his own time and place can he understand the dead past as a living reality and so appreciate it adequately. The past and present must meet within his awareness of common existential challenge. Accordingly even the strictly scientific historian who studies the Gospel texts as a scientific historian is in a far better position to understand them today and also to appreciate their historicity and sympathize with their intentions.

Theologians, on the other hand, have today a much better understanding of the type of writing contained in the Gospel. The writers of the Old Testament did not compose pure history in the "scientific" understanding of that term. Furthermore, they were quite well aware that they were not doing so. The Deuteronomic school wrote a theological interpretation of historical events in the magnificent synthesis of Deuteronomy — Joshua — Judges — Samuel — Kings and quite explicitly and repeatedly warned its readers that if they wished to read about the events themselves, devoid of this theological framework, they should go elsewhere. Recall the standard refrain which ends their theological judgment on each monarch, for example, in 1 Kings 11:41:

Now the rest of the acts of Solomon, and all that he did, and his wisdom, are they not written in the book of the acts of Solomon?

Furthermore, one could read history, if so inclined, in the "Book of the Chronicles of the Kings," either of Judah (cf. 1 Kgs 14:29) or of Israel (cf. 1 Kgs 14:19); and one could find another theological investigation thereof in the work of the Chronicler (1 and 2 Chrn, Ezr, Neh). Events are unique but interpretations may change and develop, and so also can theological understanding. The Deuteronomist explored the sad events of the past in order to comprehend the present existence of God's people under judgment, but the Chronicler viewed the same history to find in it the seeds of restoration and the hope of a future.[2] The presence of God to his people forged new and ongoing understanding of their history as occasion demanded, and his people saw no contradiction in this process. Furthermore, minor details of time and place, of personage and position, were quite often deliberately changed, rearranged, added, or even omitted, but only in order to explain more clearly the divine meaning and finality behind the central event of the discussion.

This single example of the Old Testament view of history makes it obvious that we are dealing with a special category of national self-consciousness and its written description. We might term it metahistory, on the analogy of metaphysics, for it seems to plunge through the veneer of historical events to find within their depths the teleology willed by the Lord of creation and of history.

All four accounts of the Gospel are likewise metahistorical documents. Grounded in Jesus' own theological understanding of his mission and his destiny, the early community of his risen presence continually probed the meaning of his being for their own life. Their ongoing self-consciousness, their response of faith to their own historical situations, quite rightly colored their preaching and their teaching about Jesus' words and deeds. The various accounts, archetypal comments on Jesus as Lord of the

---

[2] For an analysis of the theological interpretation of the Deuteronomist cf. W. Harrington, "A Biblical View of History," *ITQ*, 29 (1962), 207–222; and for the Chronicler's cf. D. N. Freedman, "The Chronicler's Purpose," *CBQ*, 23 (1961), 436–442; R. North, "The Theology of the Chronicler," *JBL*, 82 (1963), 369–381.

community, show us their understanding at different times and in divergent places during that first generation's life. Moreover, it never occurred to them that they were deceiving anyone; they never claimed to be writing "ordinary" history; in fact they did not believe such a thing existed in any case. Mark, the earliest record, opens with, "This is how the Good News that Jesus is both Christ and Son of God all began" (1:1). John, the last analysis, closes in self-description with, "These are written that you may believe that Jesus is the Christ, the Son of God, and that believing you may have life in his name" (20:31). The Gospel writers were convinced that certain events which had happened in their time and in their space were climactically important and abidingly relevant as the fulfillment of the world's past and the beginning of the world's future. They had good news to proclaim, not just history to write.

2. The Gospel and Jesus

As the members of the first community were guided by the Spirit in their recall of Jesus' ministry, they divided it into his works and his words. In itself this is not exactly a profound intuition; these will normally be adequate categories to recall any human existence on this earth. But the fact that they have the habit of considering them precisely in that sequence, first works and then words, gives us pause for thought. Some examples may help to focus the problem.

The earliest preaching in Acts seldom goes beyond the event of the death and resurrection; when it does mention the public ministry, it insists on the works rather than on the words of Jesus. At Pentecost, Peter says in 2:22:

> "Men of Israel, hear these words: Jesus of Nazareth, a man attested to you by God with mighty works and wonders and signs which God did through him in your midst, as you yourselves know — "

Later in his conversion sermon to Cornelius in 10:38 he speaks of how:

> ". . . God anointed Jesus of Nazareth with the Holy Spirit and with power; how he went about doing good and healing all that were oppressed by the devil, for God was with him."

When Luke starts the second volume of his Gospel by recalling the content of the first book, he sums it up, in Acts 1:1:

> In the first book, O Theophilus, I have dealt with all that Jesus began to do and teach.

We can also find an example on a much larger scale. Many scholars argue that Matthew has structured the public ministry in 3–25 as a new Pentateuch bringing the old to its destined perfection. He has divided this section into five books (3–7; 8–10; 11–13:52; 13:53–18; 19–25) on the analogy of the Pentateuch. What is significant here is that in this theory each of the five sections is itself composed of a balance of works (3–4; 8–9; 11–12; 13:53–17; 19–23) followed by appropriate words (5–7; 10; 13:1–52; 18; 24–25). Matthew has tried to group actions and sermons of Jesus around five central themes, but for each of the themes events precede interpretative comments.

Our understanding of the relationship of works and words is somewhat obscured by a polemical insistence on the value of Jesus' miracles as apologetic argument to authenticate his mission. This is not to deny that they have any such apologetical value; as early as Mark 1:27–28 and as late as John 9 the community makes such use of the miracles. But is probative force actually the deepest and most important function of these actions, especially to the mind of Jesus himself? It would seem the answer must be negative, for the following reasons.

One of the temptations of Jesus was to perform startling miracles in order to win faith and acceptance. A challenge to do this is refused to Satan in Matthew 4:5–7, and to some of the authorities in Matthew 12:38–42. The disbelief of hometown Nazareth does not beget proofs from Jesus; and the strong statement in Mark 6:5, "He *could* do no mighty work there," is softened down in the parallel verse of Matthew 13:58 to, "And he *did* not do many mighty works there, because of their unbelief." Cures are given to Gentiles only twice, but each time after an awesome act of faith: to the Capernaum centurion in Matthew 8:5–10, and to the Syrophoenician woman in Mark 7:24–30. Finally, one recalls the constant refrain of Jesus demanding faith before he heals, and his repeated, "your faith has made you well," for example in Luke 18:42. None of this strikes one as the actions of a man who is performing miracles primarily to establish identity or to prove a mission. He acts only where faith is already present, not in order to create its advent. What then is Jesus' purpose in performing these actions? If it is not primarily, let alone exclusively, apologetic, what is it?

Any discussion of the acts of Jesus must extend beyond healings to include such events as, for example, the symbolic destruction of the temple (Mk 11:15–17), or the cursing of the fig tree (Mk 11:12–14, 20–21). These actions force our attention back to the prophetic heritage of Israel in which the seers of God's people proclaimed the divine message not only by words alone, but also in symbolic works which were immediately followed by interpretative words. Two examples will suffice. In Jeremiah 19:1–13 the prophet breaks an earthen vessel on the rubbish dump of Jerusalem and immediately (19:11) explains his action with:

> . . . "Thus says the Lord of hosts: So will I break this people and this city, as one breaks a potter's vessel, so that it can never be mended. . . ."

This prophecy of judgment and destruction is balanced by the prophecy of salvation and redemption in, for example, Jeremiah 32:1–15. The prophet buys land outside the city when Babylon stands at the very walls of Jerusalem and interprets his deed with:

> ". . . For thus says the Lord of hosts, the God of Israel: Houses and fields and vineyards shall again be bought in this land."

These prophetic works/words are no mere terrestrial symbol of some celestial reality, as the shamrock is a symbol of the Trinity. They are not just empty examples, they are divine promises. The line from promise to fulfillment is horizontal, not vertical. They represent God's down payments on judgment or salvation; they begin the very process itself. It is a vessel from the doomed city itself that is smashed — the firstfruits already of total destruction to follow; it is land in the hills of Judah that is redeemed — the firstfruits already of total restoration to follow.

So also with the activity of Jesus, be it for blessing or for cursing, for healing or for warning, for salvation or for judgment. Over against all the disorder of the world, its sin and its hate, its unconcern and its unlove, its hunger and thirst, pain and anguish and ignorance, Jesus places his acts of healing and love as divine down payments on the kingdom to be established around his risen presence. This kingdom recalls man to his ancient destiny:

to take dominion over evolution and mold its future out of love, concern, and commitment to his fellows (Gn 1:26–28).

We can now understand why John uses the term "signs" for all the actions of Jesus.[3] The incident at Cana is termed "the first of his signs" in 2:11, and he terminates the entire account with the statement in 20:30 that "Jesus did many other signs in the presence of the disciples, which are not written in this book." John traces the actions of Jesus, including the miracles of course, within the realm of prophetic "signs," in the Old Testament sense. These prophetic actions, from the forgiving of sins to the healing of pain, are Jesus' beginning of the kingdom's advent; and the acts of symbolic destruction are the reverse, Jesus' prophetic statement of what awaits the world in rejecting that kingdom. His actions were not to prove *that* God is but to show *what* God is. He cured, not to authenticate what he had to say, but to inaugurate what he had to bring.

3. The Gospel and Its Structure

The overall plan which John gave his Gospel flows immediately from his understanding of Jesus' ministry as one of "signs." The good news falls naturally into two parts: 1:19–12:50 and 13:1–20:

---

[3] For the bonds between history and such "signs" cf. H. Musurillo, "History and Symbol: A Study of Form in Early Christian Literature," *TS*, 18 (1957), 357–386; J. Leal, "History and Symbol in John's Gospel," *TD*, 11 (1963), 91–96. On the relationship between the "signs" of Jesus' ministry as recorded in John and the sacraments of the later Church cf. B. Vawter, "The Johannine Sacramentary," *TS*, 17 (1956), 151–166, and *TD*, 6 (1958), 11–16; R. E. Brown, "The Johannine Sacramentary Reconsidered," *TS*, 23 (1962), 183–206, or *New Testament Essays* (Milwaukee, 1965) pp. 51–76. On a wider level cf. also D. M. Stanley, "The Conception of Our Gospels as Salvation History," *TS*, 20 (1959), 561–589. We would insist here that the connection between these "signs" and the later sacraments cannot be taken as simply the relation of past material action (cure of blindness) and present spiritual reality (gift of faith). Jesus' earthly activity attacked all the evils of human existence, including both sin and sickness. The continuance of sickness is from human unconcern and Jesus identifies this unconcern with sin. Our historical inability to handle both penance (for sin) and unction (for sickness) may well indicate our failure to understand the duality of Jesus' actions and the concern of the early Church with both. That the "signs" reach consummation after the hour of glorification and retain power in the sacraments of the community is perfectly true, but the line between them is homogeneous and not a jump from the material level to the spiritual.

31.[4] The public ministry before the passion is a time of prophetic signs. In symbolic acts followed by interpretative discourses, John shows how Jesus' life is God's groundwork for the coming kingdom, it is the divine down payment on the gift of eternal life. After the overture in 1:1–18, the section in 1:19–12:50 is thus a promissory note from God on what the kingdom will offer all mankind. In order to handle these traditional data John constructs his first major section in seven sign complexes and in all cases there is a balance of works and words of Jesus; in all cases the works either precede the words or the two are intertwined. Moreover, John seems to have arranged the seven units of the public ministry in parallelism varied by reversal (a, b, c, d, c', b', a',) so that the central unit (d) is the climax which the others surround in chiastic form.

The second major division is the great moment of fulfillment when all these fragmentary and promissory signs pass into enduring reality. In John 13–17, however, the words must precede the works in John 18–20 so that the "discourse at the last supper" is the interpretation of the events of the passion, resurrection, ascension, and gift of the Spirit which immediately follow. It is only at this "hour" that the gift of eternal life, the light in which alone man grasps authentic existence, is finally given no longer in sign but in reality. In the community of faith around Jesus' risen and returned presence "those who have not seen but yet believe" (20:29) accept and acknowledge the consummation of all the images of the public ministry. Each of these works/words of Jesus were protosacraments, fragmented promises of the one great sacrament of the risen Lord who abides in the community of faith, which both communicates his gift of eternal life to its members and also witnesses his efficacy before unbelief through their commitment to assist the anguish of human existence. Each of the seven units of works and words in 1:19–12:50 is a microcosm of the great salvific event which climaxes the Gospel in 13:1–20: 31. The believer is not at any disadvantage compared with those

---

[4] The tendency to place the sections of the Gospel in a new order has been generally abandoned today since every critic who attempted to establish the proper order and original sequence invented a different one. Cf. A. Power, "The Original Order of St. John's Gospel," CBQ, 10 (1948), 399–405; C. H. Dodd, The Interpretation of the Fourth Gospel (Cambridge, 1953), pp. 289–290; C. K. Barrett, The Gospel According to St. John (London, 1955), pp. 18–21.

who saw and heard Jesus during his ministry. These men saw the signs and heard the promises; the fulfillment and reality is equally open to all men of all times and in all places.

Special note must be taken of the discourses of Jesus in John. We have seen that the overall plan is schematic and artificial rather than chronologically and historically sequential. This would be true, for example, of Matthew also. But the difference between the sermons of Jesus in John and in the Synoptics is very striking. An analogy from the Old Testament sapiential literature may help us understand the method of composition used by John in reconstructing these discourses of Jesus. The scribes of Israel often collected sayings and proverbs and merely juxtaposed them side by side without reference to subject matter. This can be seen in the earlier sections of the book of *Proverbs*. In later wisdom writing, such as *Sirach*, there is a tendency to group sayings around common themes even though the individual proverbs still retain their original form. Later still, in a work such as *Wisdom*, sapiential essays are constructed in which proverbs on a common subject are reworked into a smoothly flowing discussion on that theme. A similar process lies behind John's narration of the discourses of Jesus. One can imagine three stages in its construction. Jesus would have spoken, as any rabbi of his time and every prophet before him, in sermons of some length. The early community recalled these long discourses in terms of short, brief pronouncements which summed up the content of Jesus' teaching. Jesus himself might well have used such summarizing epigrams and this form rendered recall of the content much easier. As time progressed the early community started to regroup such isolated sayings, many of which had lost their time-space setting, and to connect them either around a common theme (for example, "riches" in Lk 16) or sometimes by mere word associations (for example, the sayings in Mk 9:33–50). John has gone a step further. Having chosen the main themes he wished to discuss, and knowing from personal experience and common tradition many of these sayings and pronouncements of Jesus, he carefully reworked and heavily rephrased these words so that the discourse flowed quite smoothly around its main theme using expressions often more universal than the form first used by Jesus (for example, his phrase "eternal life" instead of Jesus' "kingdom of heaven"). These sermons are thus artificial constructions recasting the teachings of Jesus into new unities and also into new vocabulary and expression. It brings to completion processes already at work in the construction of Jesus' discourses in Luke and Matthew, and establishes forever the absolute need of rephrasing the message of Jesus anew for every new generation. More than any of the others, John wrote his account for us, since it was a deliberate attempt to rephrase Jesus' thought in more universalist categories, in terms more relevant for a worldwide situation.

B. INTERPRETATION OF THE GOSPEL

We used the first letter of John as a prologue to a discussion of his Gospel. But the Gospel itself has actually its own prologue, its own overture in which the great Johannine themes are summarized and synthesized, and once again we meet the equally characteristic chiastic structure.[5]

1. *The Overture to the Gospel*

It should be remembered that an overture is not merely the opening or the beginning of a composition, but is rather a summary of all that is to follow. It is a miniature of the entire process which it precedes. It is with this in mind that John 1:1–18 is termed an overture.

a) Structure of the Overture

In discussing 1 John 1:1 we considered the meaning of the expression "Word of life" in the theology of John. The Word of God expresses all the divine causality and finality behind the onward thrust of evolution and this has reached its climax in the

---

[5] Besides the major works cited in the bibliography at the end of this book, the following are useful for the Gospel in general: A. Wikenhauser, *New Testament Introduction* (New York, 1958), pp. 277–320; L. Johnston, "The Making of the Fourth Gospel," *Scr*, 12 (1960), 1–13; P. Fannon, "The Four Gospels: 4. St. John's Message," *CIR*, 47 (1962), 597–609. For the problems of Jn 1:1–18 in particular cf. M.-E. Boismard, *St. John's Prologue*, tr. Carisbrooke Dominicans (London, 1957); J. A. T. Robinson, "The Relation of the Prologue to the Gospel of St. John," *NTS*, 9 (1963), 120–129; J. L. McKenzie, "The Word of God in the Old Testament," *TS*, 21 (1960), 183–206, or *Myths and Realities* (Milwaukee, 1963), pp. 37–58.

Word become flesh and in the community of his risen and returned presence. In 1:1–18, however, another Old Testament idea has been joined to that of the Word of God, namely, the wisdom of God.

In the books of *Proverbs, Sirach,* and *Wisdom* one can trace a gradually deepening fusion between the earlier ideas of the Word of Yahweh, which summed up the entire theme of his historical action, and the scribal interest in Wisdom, that is pithy aphorisms on the practical exercise of living. This was the first attempt at bringing together in dialogue the revealing word of God and the experimental and experiential philosophy of an alien culture. God's word became identified with divine wisdom as the "vertical" word of God was combined with the "horizontal" wisdom of man to become the divine wisdom of Yahweh as communicated to man. Thus the idea of the Word of Yahweh took on a more abiding presence as wisdom; the Word is wisdom. The ancient confession of faith whereby Israel proclaimed Yahweh's action behind the screen of historical events (in, for example, Dt 6:20–23; 26:5–9; Jos 24:1–13; Ps 105; Neh 9:6–31), has now become quite beautifully rephrased in terms of his gift of wisdom to the personal protagonists of the drama. Just as the Word of Yahweh had been at work in creation, in the covenant with Israel, and throughout her history, so now the wisdom of God was at work in creation (Prv 8:22–36; Sir 1:1–10; 24:1–7, Wis 9:1–18), and in the covenant (Sir 24:23–27; Wis 6:1–11), and in history (Sir 44:1–50:21; Wis 10–19). One can well imagine how such a new statement of the ancient faith would be more open to the international traditions of the sapiential movement and would gradually open Israel more and more to encounter God's work outside her national and intellectual boundaries. But the process of dialogue with an alien philosophy came to an agonized halt when Antiochus IV Epiphanes tried to enforce that alien philosophy in place of faith (cf. Dn; 1 and 2 Mc; Jdt). John takes up the dialogue once more and shows Jesus as the culmination of the Word and the wisdom of God, but while the former point is quite vocal and obvious, the latter is rather oblique and is seen in the form rather than in the content of the overture.

Within the sapiential books just mentioned there occur certain hymns to the wisdom of God. Three points repeat themselves in all these poems. Wisdom dwelt with God from all eternity (Prv

8:22–26; Sir 1:1–8; 24:1–4; Wis 9:9a). Wisdom played a special role at creation (Prv 8:27–30; Sir 1:9–10; 24:5–7; Wis 9:9b). Wisdom came down into human history with gifts from God to man (Prv 8:31–35; Sir 1:11–30; 24:8–34; Wis 9:10–18). The same sequence of three points is used by John for the Word of God in the overture, thereby identifying Jesus as both the Word and the wisdom of God. These three points, along with a special reference to the Baptist as the forerunner of the ultimate advent of the Word/wisdom of God in Jesus, give the basic structure of 1:1–18. But, as one might have expected, John also discusses these points in reversed parallelism so that the full, balanced construction of the overture appears:

a) Word with God (1–2)   a′) Son with Father (18)
b) Role in old creation (1:3a)   b′) Role in new creation (17)
c) With gifts to man (1:3b–5)   c′) With gifts to man (16)
d) The Baptist (1:6–8)   d′) The Baptist (15)
e) Incarnation (1:9–11)   e′) Incarnation (14)
INCARNATE WORD GIVES DIVINE SONSHIP TO MAN (12–13)

This sums up the entire Gospel to follow. The Word/wisdom of God came into the world at creation, and in the covenant with Israel, and throughout all her history, but was not received by many; finally, the Word/wisdom of God came into the world incarnate in Jesus of Nazareth and was again rejected by many, but gave a share in the divine life to those who accepted him.

b) The Meaning of the Overture

Since John 1:1–18 is synoptic of all that is to follow, we shall look at it in more detail than will be possible for other texts. The divisions are those outlined in the above structure.

1) *1:1–2.* The *Logos* or Word of God is eternal, is personal ("with God"), and is divine ("God"). The opening words recall those of Genesis 1:1.

2) *1:3a.* With many modern critics and also many early Fathers, it seems best to conclude this verse by punctuating as follows: "Without him was not anything made," in other words, "Without him nothing was made." In the eternal Word all things were created; for the incarnate Word all things were destined.

3) *1:3b–5.* In this punctuation, we read the verses as follows:

"What was made in him — was life . . ." In other words, all creation only reaches full, true, authentic life and being in this Word. He not only creates by initial action; his presence is thrusting evolution ever onward and upward toward true life. Once again we see the life-light tension. In this revealing Word man receives not only life but articulate self-consciousness about that life's presence, purpose, and meaning.

4) *1:6–8.* In all probability John is reworking and enlarging an ancient liturgical hymn to the *Logos.* The section on the Baptist appears on both sides of the parallelism, in 1:6–8 and 1:18, and breaks the continuity of the thought. There are three points made on the Baptist. He is not the light (1:8a); but he gives witness to the light (1:7a, 8b); that all may believe (1:7b). These same three points will appear again with regard to the Baptist in 1:19–28, 29–34, 35–39, and in 10:41–42, and the first two points will be repeated in 3:22–30. Obviously these three ideas sum up what John has to say of the Baptist and he constantly reverts to them. They also summarize the destiny of every Christian and also of the entire community of faith itself.

5) *1:9–11.* This verse continues the thought of 1:3b–5. Only in the Word can the world find light, find true understanding of its own finality, find full awareness of its inbuilt destiny. But from the moment man dwelt upon this earth the coming Word received refusal. Before man's advent, refusal was impossible; lower forms of evolution cannot choose and therefore cannot sin. Man, whose willing acceptance of stewardship for evolution was to be the crown of that process and to bring to perfection the community of love on earth, failed to acknowledge his election and the Word was initially refused. Finally, the Word came as man and the pattern of refusal reached its peak — but so also did that of acceptance.

6) *1:12–13.* In the structure suggested earlier these verses formed a climax. It is a description of the final advent of the Word but couched in functional rather than metaphysical terms; it describes what he came to do rather than simply what he came to be. The incarnate Word's function was to offer to mankind the gift of life as children of God, to share in God's life of love, but only on condition that they would "believe in his name." This is the Hebrew way of stating: Accept him for what he is, namely, the perfect revelation of the depths of God and so also the depths

of man. The wording in 1:13 with its reiterated negatives serves to combine the virginal birth of Jesus from Mary, her acceptance of the Word in faith, along with our baptismal rebirth from the community of God, our acceptance of the Word in faith. The description of baptism is unnecessarily negative here, compared for example with that in 3:3–5, and John's purpose was to show the birth of Jesus as archetypal model for our rebirth. Mary as archetype for the Church, model by her faith for all faith to follow, will appear as an important theme in the Gospel and so it is obliquely alluded to here in the overture — but at its very center.

7) *1:14.* This verse parallels 1:9–11 in its statement of the fact of the incarnation. The Word finally "became flesh," that is, man in all his weakness and frailty. The Word "dwelt" translates a verb which literally means "pitched his tent" and recalls the term for God's dwelling among his people in the tent of the covenant during their desert exodus from Egypt (cf. Ex 33). The permanent dwelling of God with his own was one of the promises of the prophets for the great age to come, for example, in Joel 3:17, 21. We are not dealing with some past and vanished presence of the Word among his people, we are talking about God's permanent dwelling with mankind. The statement of Ecclesiastes 5:2, "for God is in heaven, and you upon earth; therefore let your words be few," is here outdated. In its place we must read Apocalypse 21:3, "Behold, the dwelling of God is with man. He will dwell with them, and they shall be his people, and God himself will be with them." The term "grace and truth" is a quasi-technical term similar to "righteousness" as discussed earlier with regard to 1 John 2:28–4:6. It means God's gratuitous fidelity and unswerving mercy in fulfilling all his promises despite man's sin and infidelity. Despite all the world's past refusal of the Word, he came to men as man in the fulfillment of God's ancient promise. We have seen Jesus, consummation of God's merciful love.

8) *1:15.* This balances 1:6–8 and repeats the term "witness," which is another characteristic phrase from the Johannine theology. John 1:6–8 and 1:15 paraphrase the recurring theme of the Baptist in the rest of the Gospel. As witness to Christ, the Baptist already exemplified the destiny of the community of faith yet to come.

9) *1:16.* The gifts the Word/wisdom brought to this world

in *1:3b–5* (life and light) have been offered to all mankind in ever increasing abundance ("grace upon grace") since the incarnation of Christ.

10) *1:17.* This parallels 1:3a so that the action of the eternal Word in the ancient creation is balanced by his present activity in the new creation, the redemption of man's unconcern through commitment to love. God's first great redemptive moment was the gift of the law to Israel on Sinai as he began to reveal true human life to his people, making Israel the nation for all nations. Christ came to bring this form of revelation to its perfection and to open its challenge to all mankind.

11) *1:18.* The opening words in 1:1–2 showed the Word with God from all eternity. It is this same Word, the Son of God, who has revealed to the world the inner life of the divinity as a tension of dynamic interpersonal love and in that revelation showed also what the community of earth must become.

This overture talks only of the Word's constant approach and deepening immersion in the world until the final ultimate presence within the community in 1:12–13. The end of the overture is not a departed Christ but a Christ still vitally present in those reborn to true life in him.

2. The Challenge to Rebirth
Read John 1:19–4:42.

a) Structure and Theology

The first unit is 1:19–4:42 and it consists of two sections of works by Jesus: the new creation in 1:19–2:11, and the new temple in 2:12–25. These are then interpreted in two long discourses: one with Nicodemus in 3:1–36, and the second with the Samaritan woman in 4:1–42. Two sets of works precede two corresponding sets of words; action is interpreted by discourse. The entire construction is dominated by the theme of the new creation. Christ has unleashed into the world a force of love and concern which, if accepted, will immediately begin to change the individual believer, will gradually develop a community of such love and response to the needs of others, will finally acknowledge its full responsibility for the evolutionary process in which God has immersed it, so that it controls and directs it forward out of love for others.

This is the reality behind such phrases as "the new creation" or "the new heavens" and "the new earth." These phrases denote the evolution now depending upon man's acceptance of his God-given destiny as stated in Genesis 1:26–28 to forge its future in love for others.

As the Spirit brought creation from the waters of chaos at the beginning (cf. Gn 1:1–2), so the Spirit and the waters of baptism bring the new creation into existence out of the enduring chaos of unlove. The call of the first disciples, culminating with their consecration in faith at Cana (1:19–2:11), is the creation of the new being which is the community of Christ. This community has its focal point in the glorified humanity of Christ which will bring to perfection the temple in which God dwelt among his people of old (2:12–25). Into this new creation one enters by a rebirth in the Spirit and water (3:1–21), just as the Baptist had foretold the coming of the Spirit-baptizer (3:22–30). It is Christ alone who can effect this passage of man into new existence, which is the existence of God from whence he came (3:31–36). By this rebirth one receives an unfailing life-force within him whereby he can adore the Father in unity of spirit and not just of place (4:1–42).

b) The New Creation (1:19–2:11)

The account of the creation in Genesis 1 is divided into three days of preparation and division (Gn 1:1–13); then three days of population and decoration (Gn 1:14–31); and finally a seventh day of rest (2:1–4a). John seems deliberately to have followed this pattern in the structure of the sequence in 1:19–2:11: there are three days of preparation as the Baptist bears witness to Jesus and turns his own disciples over to him (1:19–39); and then three days of "population" as Jesus lays the basis of his own community or, more accurately, establishes it in miniature form (1:40–51); and finally there is the messianic banquet, the confirmation in faith at Cana (2:1–11).[6]

---

[6] For the structure of Gn 1 cf. C. Hauret, *Beginnings: Genesis and Modern Science* (Dubuque, 1955), pp. 35–74: B. Vawter, *A Path Through Genesis* (New York, 1955), pp. 37–49. On the similar construction of Jn 1:19–2:11, cf. M.-E. Boismard, *Du Baptême à Cana* ("Lectio Divina," 18; Paris, 1956); T. Barrosse, "The Seven Days of the New Creation in St. John's Gospel," *CBQ*, 21 (1959), 507–516.

Notice especially the "chronological" ligaments which constitute this structure:

1:29: "The next day" would be the second day.

1:35: "The next day" would be the third day.

1:41: "First," which appears as "in the morning" in certain manuscripts, would be the fourth day.

1:43: "The next day" would be the fifth day.

2:1: "On the third day" would be the seventh day.

John has made a deliberate effort to narrate the events in the artificial frame of a seven-day span. This does not mean that he has invented these happenings; rather he has so recorded the initial activity of Jesus' public ministry as to highlight its theological aspect as a new creation. In this schematic structure we have the following events and days:

The first day: The Baptist is Messianic herald and water-baptizer (1:19–28).

The second day: The Baptist is witness to Jesus as Spirit-baptizer (1:29–34).

The third day: The Baptist sends his own disciples to Jesus (1:35–39).

The fourth day: Jesus calls Simon as the rock (1:40–42).

The fifth day: Jesus calls Philip as the "typical" apostle (1:43–46).

The sixth day: Jesus calls Nathanael as the "typical" Israelite (1:47–51).

The seventh day: Jesus and Mary are at Cana — the consecration in faith (2:1–11).

1) The First Day (1:19–28). The three points which delineated the Baptist's function as witness to the light in 1:6–8 are fully developed on the first three days of the new creation, one point for each day. On the first day he witnesses that he is not himself the Messiah; he is not the one awaited by Israel as the protagonist of the ultimate manifestation of Yahweh in human history, the center figure of the coming "Day of the Lord" (1:19–28). On the second day he is witness to Jesus as the Messiah (1:29–34). On the third day this witness will beget faith for his own disciples (1:35–39). The Old Testament had spoken of the Messiah under various symbolic veils, and at times there was confusion as to whether there was one who would appear before him as his forerunner or not. The Baptist apparently understands

the Messiah himself to be intended under such titles as "the new Elijah" and "the new Moses" and so he declines to accept such titles for himself. The only function he will acknowledge is to stand as the fulfillment of the promise in Isaiah 40:3. The unknown prophet of the exile whose poetry is preserved in Isaiah 40–66 had spoken words of consolation to the people of God held captive in Babylon. He told them that a passage was being prepared in the desert between Babylon and Palestine so that God could bring his people home. The Baptist held a like mission. He was to prepare the path of reunion between God and his estranged people.

2) *The Second Day* (1:29–34). This is the positive witness of the Baptist to Jesus as the awaited Messiah. The term "lamb of God" would most likely have meant for the fiery mind of the Baptist the great, all-conquering, apocalyptic lamb of current Jewish writing. This lamb was to lead the flock of God's people to victory and security over their enemies. But two other Old Testament ideas would have been combined with this one in the mind of John by the time he came to record the words of the Baptist: that of the paschal *lamb*, the symbol of deliverance from the bondage of Egypt, and that of the servant of Yahweh, who was led like a *lamb* to the sacrifice.

On the night of their salvation from Egyptian doom, the children of Israel had sacrificed a lamb according to God's instruction:

> "In this manner you shall eat it: your loins girded, your sandals on your feet, and your staff in your hand; and you shall eat it in haste. It is the Lord's passover" (Ex 12:11).

Later, at the time of their deliverance from Babylonian exile, another prophet spoke of Israel's destiny as suffering witness to the nations, a destiny which reached its culmination in Jesus of Nazareth:

> He was oppressed, and he was afflicted,
>   yet he opened not his mouth;
> like a *lamb* that is led to the slaughter,
>   and like a sheep that before its shearers is dumb,
>   so he opened not his mouth.
>
>   (Is 53:7.)

Three biblical ideas are thus combined in the term "lamb of God": the lamb of paschal sacrifice from the book of *Exodus*, the lamb of silent suffering from the book of *Isaiah*, and the lamb of final victory from current Jewish writings at the time of the Baptist.[7] All three point to Jesus as God's gift of ultimate salvation for his waiting people. He will lead them to victory but in suffering and sacrifice, not in triumphant militarism.

In 1:33 another word is used which is important in the theological vocabulary of John: "sent." It is closely allied to "witness" but stresses the source of mission rather than the action itself. All of creation and of history is "sent" by God as a challenge to mankind freely to accept his place as its crown. The final perfection of evolution, our word for creation and history in the unity of their divinely willed finality, is the community of the risen Lord, and this is the "sent" par excellence. The Baptist is the end of the preparatory "sending," the one who would immediately prepare for Jesus, the *Sent* of the Father. The word thus includes the whole idea of created being within the overall thrust of its evolutionary process as the great sacrament of God's presence.

3) *The Third Day* (1:35–39). The result of the Baptist's witness is faith for his hearers. Only in reading John do we obtain an account which makes understandable how the first followers of Jesus offered their allegiance to him. There are good reasons to associate the Baptist with the movement of reform and preparation for the Day of Yahweh which we now know more fully since the discoveries of the Dead Sea Scrolls and the excavations of the monastery at Qumran. His use of Isaiah, his polemic with the Jerusalem authorities, his apocalyptic message, his priestly background, his connections with the desert close to the Dead Sea, all show close similarities with the community at Qumran.[8] When he went forth to bear his witness he gathered around him his own following, his own students. It is these he now turns over to Jesus as men already schooled in his own fervent expectations.

---

[7] For the details of modern research on this title cf. S. Virgulin, "Recent Discussion of the Title 'Lamb of God,'" *Scr*, 13 (1961), 74–80; E. K. Taylor, "'The Lamb of God,'" *CIR*, 48 (1963), 285–292.

[8] Besides the general works on Qumran cited on p. 4, cf. R. E. Murphy, *The Dead Sea Scrolls and the Bible* (Westminster, 1956), pp. 58–63; R. E. Brown, "Three Quotations from John the Baptist in the Gospel of John," *CBQ*, 22 (1960), 292–298, or *New Testament Essays* (Milwaukee, 1965), pp. 132–140; J. A. T. Robinson, "The Baptism of John and the Qumran Community," *Twelve New Testament Studies* ("Studies in Biblical Theology," 34; Naperville, Ill., 1962), pp. 11–27; "Elijah, John and Jesus," *ibid.*, pp. 28–52.

In the Synoptic accounts, Peter, Andrew, James, and John form an inner four within the Twelve. We noted this earlier when discussing the authorship of the Johannine literature, but we can now understand the reason for this special favor. It is not that they are singled out from among the Twelve by Jesus, but rather that the Twelve are built up later with these as the core. These disciples of John from beside the Jordan are the firstfruits of the kingdom. We have here the actual account of the vocation of Peter (1:41–42), and Andrew (1:37–40). Most likely the unnamed companion of Andrew in 1:37–40 is John, but he never names himself in the pages of his Gospel. Likewise James, his brother, may well have joined Jesus by the Jordan although he is never mentioned in the Gospel of John. The beginnings of the Twelve, and some others as well, came directly to Jesus from the Baptist.

The narrative in Mark 1:16–20 which is drastically stylized for catechetical purposes is not the first vocation of these four but rather their invitation to start the first preaching tour with Jesus (Mark 1:29, 36–38). But the purpose of Mark is exactly that of John — to show this vocation and response as the ideal pattern for all human reaction to Jesus. This can be seen in the pregnant theological vocabulary of the encounter between the disciples of the Baptist and Jesus. When we read 1:36–39 very carefully we find the following archetypal structure. The witness *looks* and *speaks*. The inquirer *hears* and *follows*. He dialogues with Jesus as to *what* and *where*. He *goes* in order to answer the *where*, and he *sees* to answer the *what*. He *stays*. It is obvious that in this first meeting with Jesus John has wished to draw an ideal encounter between the believer and him to whom he is to commit his life. There is a deliberate parallel in the sequence: the Baptist to Andrew, and Andrew to Peter (1:35–42); then, Jesus to Philip, and Philip to Nathanael (1:43–51). Obviously the pattern of the Christian witness is forming; when one believes, one must proclaim.

4) *The Fourth Day* (1:40–42). The work of the Baptist is now completed and Jesus himself takes over. It would seem that at the end of the third day the two disciples of 1:37–39 stay the night at the dwelling of Jesus. The tiny detail, "for it was about the tenth hour" (about four in the afternoon), is a discreet signature by John and an indication that he was the unnamed dis-

ciple, the companion of Andrew. There is a textual difficulty in
1:41 which is of some importance for the structure of the seven
days. The reading, "He first found," is not very meaningful. There
is manuscript evidence which warrants the reading, "Early in the
morning he met his brother," and this makes more sense. It is
not that Peter just happened to be the first he met; he went to
find him first thing in the morning.

The first act in the symbolic establishment of the kingdom is
the promise of a new title, a new being to Simon. Jesus himself
fell heir to the Old Testament prophecy about the rock of security which God would establish for his people in the age to
come. Matthew 21:42; Acts 4:11; and 1 Peter 2:7 all allude to
Jesus as the fulfillment of the statement in Psalms 118:22;

> The stone which the builders rejected
> has become the head of the corner.

Romans 9:33; 10:11, Ephesians 2:20, and 1 Peter 2:6, also refer
to Jesus as the fulfillment of the citation in Isaiah 28:16:

> "Behold, I am laying in Zion for a foundation
> a stone, a tested stone,
> a precious cornerstone, of a sure foundation:
> 'He who believes will not be in haste.' . . ."

Just as, later, Simon-Peter will receive (21:15–19) the shepherd
function of Jesus (10:11–18), so now he is promised the rock or
stone-mission of Jesus. Peter is not the Twelve, nor is he the entire community, but he is the stone on which both are founded,
the efficacious symbol of the unity of all. In the light of the ideal
or pattern nature of the narrative on the establishment of the
community in 1:35–51, one may well ask how did this element
find its continuance thereafter. If the seven-day structure is accepted as indicative of a new creation, then Peter's role, designated
on a separate day, and indeed on the first day of the actual "population" of the kingdom, must find an abiding place within that
kingdom's continuity.

5) *The Fifth Day* (1:43–46). The vocation of Philip is portrayed as that of the ideal apostle: he immediately goes out and
brings others to Jesus. Nathanael is quite possibly the Bartholo-
mew mentioned after Philip in the apostolic lists in Mark 3:16–
19; Matthew 10:2–4; and Luke 6:14–16; cf. also Acts 1:13. The
statement in 1:46 repeats the "come and see" of 1:39. This is the

paradox of Christian commitment: only when it has been made ("come"), does one understand its meaning ("see").

6) *The Sixth Day* (1:47–51). Once again we have an ideal picture. Nathanael-Bartholomew is the ideal Israelite, the perfect believer in Jesus. He confesses Jesus immediately as the awaited Messiah, using the messianic titles of "Son of God" and "King of Israel." The believer is not somebody over against Israel and he is not converted *out of* Israel. Rather he belongs to the community in which Israel reaches its perfection and fulfills its destiny. Only in this community can Israel consummate its purpose, and only with Israel can this community attain its end. The final words of Jesus in 1:51 are addressed to "you" in the plural, to all believers. They will yet see in Jesus an even more magnificent vision. They will see in him the eschatological or perfect presence of Yahweh foreshadowed in the vision of Jacob in Genesis 28:10–17. The ladder which Jacob saw in his vision was but a shadow of Jesus, the living bond between God and man in whom and through whom Yahweh will henceforth live forever with his people.

The three days of "preparation" saw the Baptist turn his disciples over to Jesus. The three days of "population" saw Jesus structuring this miniature of his kingdom in functional pattern: the rock, the apostles, and the believers. There remains only the seventh day in which the new creation will receive its consecration as the old creation had obtained its blessing by God's resting on the seventh day and establishing it forever as the reminder that both creation and time were his.

7) *The Seventh Day* (2:1–11). The story of the wedding feast at Cana has evoked much discussion in recent years.[9] Any explanation, however, must keep two factors in mind. The exegete must explain the schematic structure of 1:19–2:11 in which the

---

[9] The following works give some indication of the debate: C. P. Ceroke, "Jesus and Mary at Cana: separation or association?" *TS*, 17 (1956), 1–38; D. M. Stanley, "Cana as Epiphany," *Worship*, 32 (1958), 83–89; C. P. Ceroke, "The Problem of Ambiguity in John 2, 4," *CBQ*, 21 (1959), 316–340; S. Hartdegen, "The Marian Significance of Cana," *Mar Stud*, 11 (1960), 85–103; R. J. Dillon, "Wisdom Tradition and Sacramental Retrospect in the Cana Account," *CBQ*, 24 (1962), 268–296; J. D. M. Derrett, "Water into Wine," *BZ*, 7 (1963), 80–97. For the understanding of faith in this Gospel cf. T. Barrosse, "The Relationship of Love to Faith in St. John," *TS*, 18 (1957), 538–559; J. Gaffney, "Believing and Knowing in the Fourth Gospel," *TS*, 26 (1965), 215–241.

Cana incident represents the seventh and culminating day of the new creation. Secondly, this "first of his signs" (2:11) must be understood in view of the Johannine "signs" mentioned earlier. These signs usually involve a physical action which is followed by an interpretative discourse, but in some cases, as we shall see, the discourse is completely intertwined with the narrative of the action (for example, in Jn 7:1–8:59 and 11:1–54). The narrative in 2:1–11 is another example of this combination of action/discourse where the former exemplifies the latter and the latter interprets the former. The meaning of the physical miracle at Cana depends on the dialogue in 2:4–5. We shall have to consider the reply of Jesus to Mary in some detail.

i) "*Oh, woman.*" Jesus does not address Mary as "Mother" but as "woman." This latter term is of course quite polite, but the problem is why did Jesus not use "Mother" rather than "woman," whether "woman" is a polite address or not. When we recall the hint of future separation already given in Luke 2:41–50, we suspect that it is precisely this relationship of mother and son that Jesus wishes to "deny" for the moment. During the public life Mary will no longer stand to Jesus as his mother, with all the rights and privileges inherent in such a relationship. Instead there is a new relationship, or better, a deepening understanding of the older relationship, already implicit in the title "woman." Her full destiny is to be the "woman" of Genesis 3:15 (cf. also Ap 12), but the moment for that completion has not yet arrived.

ii) "*What have you to do with me?*" This translates a Semitic idiom which reads literally: "what to me and to you?" As an idiom it must be interpreted against our general knowledge of the language; it is to be understood in parallel with the use of the phrase in both Old and New Testament. All the Old Testament usages (for example, Jgs 11:12; 2 Sm 16:10; 19:22; 1 Kgs 17:18; 2 Kgs 3:13; 2 Chrn 35:21), and also the New Testament places (for example, Mt 8:29; Mk 1:24; 5:7; Lk 4:34; 8:28), have the basic meaning of a denial of relationship, and in each case the negated relationship is to be determined from the context. In general the denied relationship is either that of hostility or of unity. Thus, the speaker in all cases wishes to assure the one to whom he addresses the idiom that there is not between them a relationship which this person has presumed to exist. At Cana, then, by the logic of the idiomatic expression, "what to me and to you?" Jesus is denying to Mary a presumed relationship of unity between them. This completes what we have seen already in his use of "woman" rather than "Mother" as the form of address.

iii) *"My hour has not yet come."* These final words actually specify the strict denial implicit in the opening part of the sentence. What is there denied is so done because this enigmatic "hour" has not yet arrived. Presumably, then, when it arrives this relationship will be renewed in some manner. The term "my hour" must be interpreted according to the special usage of this expression in John. The term "hour" is often accompanied either by the definite article or the possessive pronoun; and up to a certain point in the Gospel it has not yet arrived; but thereafter it is said to have come. This can be seen in 2:4; 7:30; 8:20; 12:23, 27; 13:1; 17:1 (and cf. also 7:6, where "time" is used instead of "hour"). In context it is clear that this "hour of Jesus" is that of the passion, for 12:1 is the turning point in which "has not come" turns into "has come." This is also the hour of glorification, that is, public manifestation, wherein the passion shows openly and forever that God is "love." To see in "my hour has not yet come" at Cana any other meaning than the statement that the moment of the passion or glorification has not yet arrived would be against all the rules of contextual interpretation. Thus, Jesus is denying to Mary during the public life their relationship of mother and son, whereby she has every right to ask favors, miracles, etc. of him. Instead, he is promising her a new role, that of the Woman, at the future moment when the cross manifests completely the divine love for men. It is at this hour that Jesus will again call Mary "woman" in 19:25–27 and fulfill the promise made at Cana. The point is not really whether Jesus will perform the miracle or not. There is no question but that he will. But the miracle must become a "sign" of what is to happen in the full arrival of God's presence to mankind at the cross. The miracle is the change of the water into wine at the request of Mary which gives birth to the faith of the disciples. This symbolizes the future change of the community of the Sinai covenant into the community of the Golgotha covenant. At the moment of this renewed covenant Mary will represent the Church which is to bring faith to all mankind. Her role as mother of Jesus must be deepened into that of the Woman, archetype of the Church which begets all mankind in faith. The seven days of the new creation represent the steps in which Jesus establishes in ideal pattern the renewed community of love which will be his Church. The consummation of the entire work is the way in which the faith of the disciples is mediated to them through the joint action of Jesus and Mary, which is a symbol of how faith will be born in all men of all times and all places through the presence of the risen Lord in the Church, of which Mary is here declared to be the archetype. This "first of his signs" in 2:11 serves as a frame for the entire work along with the expression in 20:30, "many other signs." All that Jesus will do must be signs, divine down payments of what will happen later in the Church, the community of his risen and abiding presence.

c) The New Temple (2:12–25)

The transitional statement in 2:12 is a Johannine relic of the tradition that Jesus used Capernaum as his base of operations for the Galilean ministry. This appears in Mark 1:21; Matthew 4:13, and Luke 4:31; but John merely mentions it in passing, possibly as an indication of what he is omitting.

At the center of creation was the temple at Jerusalem, the symbolic representation of God's dwelling among his people as Lord of both creation and history. At the center of renewed creation Jesus places the event of his death and resurrection whereby God can tent forever in the camp of mankind (1:14), and erect an abiding ladder between heaven and earth (1:50–51). The sign given by Jesus in 2:12–25 fortells this perfective replacement, just as the Old Testament prophets had long ago warned of such consummation. Throughout the discussion it must be remembered that we are dealing with a symbolic action in the line of such prophetic warnings. We should not envisage any wild stampede. God makes his point when a prophet overturns even a single table.

The event takes place during the final week in the Synoptic tradition (Mk 11:15–17; Mt 21:12–13; Lk 19:45–46). But in all three cases the following discussions with the authorities are not directly connected with this action; there is no *immediate* argument with them such as that found in John's account. In other words the connection of the event with the other happenings narrated in the Synoptics is not very rigid and it may well be that the event is simply placed during that last week because this is the only time that Jesus is at Jerusalem in the Synoptic accounts. It is possible to argue, of course, that John has placed this temple sign at the head of his record for compositional reasons, as Luke had done with the Nazareth rejection (Lk 4:16–30). But it seems better to consider John's location as being the correct one from a historical point of view and the Synoptic position as the compositional one. Indeed the only vestige of the row between the authorities and Jesus which ensued from his action, and which is preserved in the Synoptics, is found in the trial accusation of Mark 14:57–58 and Matthew 26:60–61 and in the Golgotha taunts of Mark 15:29–30 and Matthew 27:39–40. But these vestiges are important indications that the debate in John 2:18–20 is no mere Johannine creation; its mysterious meaning rendered it very difficult as a basis for even an accusation, and it is in John alone that the full sign-value of the entire incident becomes clear.

The people of God were warned by the prophet Jeremiah that their continued refusal to preserve covenant fidelity with regard to human concern and social commitment could not be excused by mere liturgical participations, mere annual pilgrimages to the temple of Jerusalem. The prophetic polemic against liturgy as refuge from, rather than consecration to, the needs of others flowed without break from Amos 5:23–24 and Hosea 6:6, through Isaiah 1:10–17 and Micah 6:6–8, and reached its still unheeded climax in Jeremiah 7:13–15:

> "And now, because you have done all these things," says the Lord, "and when I spoke to you persistently you did not listen, and when I called you, you did not answer, therefore I will do to the house which is called by my name, and in which you trust, and to the place which I gave to you and to your fathers, as I did to Shiloh. And I will cast you out of my sight, as I cast out all your kinsmen, all the offspring of Ephraim."

Sacramental worship without social justice was not only useless, it was an insult to the God who considered the defenseless his own special possession. Jesus continued and indeed consummated this polemic against externalism by himself citing Hosea 6:6, "for I desire steadfast love and not sacrifice," in Matthew 9:13 and 12:7. James 1:27 is speaking in the same tradition when he says, "Religion that is pure and undefiled before God and the Father is this: to visit orphans and widows in their affliction, and to keep oneself unstained in the world."

In the Synoptic tradition Jesus symbolically destroys the temple by "overturning" the economic and fiscal necessities on which its life was quite legitimately based, and which took place equally legitimately in the parts of the outer courts reserved for such activities. The problem was not commercialism but formalism. Jesus' action is performed with a quotation from Jeremiah 7:11 on his lips. To act unjustly and then hurry to meaningless liturgy turns God's sanctuary into a refuge, a hiding place, a "den of thieves." God will destroy his own sanctuary if that continues, was the message of Jeremiah, and Jesus repeated it in the prophet's own words. But let one point be very clear. This action does not represent an attack on Judaism, neither for Jeremiah nor for Jesus, but an attack on liturgical formalism as a refuge from concerned life. The moral: look homeward.

As John reviews this prophetic action of Jesus he is not satisfied with the Synoptic presentation, for the understanding there is primarily negative. He does not wish merely to talk of the temple's destruction as the end of the ancient prophetic warnings, but rather of what is thereafter the sacramental center of the renewed people of God — the risen and glorified presence of Christ to the community. Accordingly, in John 2:16, Jesus does not cite Jeremiah 7:11 but rather alludes more generally to Zechariah 14:21 where there is a prophecy that on the great Day of Yahweh all creation will be sacred and sacramental and there will no longer be any need for special traders to sell the ritually pure beasts in the courts of God's house. The use of Psalms 69:9 in John 2:17 refers to the fact that it was precisely this talk of the temple's destruction that was produced much later as accusation of blasphemy at the Sanhedrin trial of Jesus. Such statements would cost Jesus his life, as previously they had almost cost Jeremiah his (Jer 7 = Jer 26).

At the center of the renewed creation (1:19–2:11) is a renewed cultic presence (2:13–22), that of God in the risen glory of Jesus, and when, despite the sacramentality of that presence, we become unconcerned for human beings, we can read again and apply again to ourselves this prophetic warning of what will happen to our temples.

d) Into the New Creation (3:1–36)

After the two narratives of 1:19–2:11 and 2:12–25, there follow two discourses. When all four sections are taken together they form a sign-complex in which the discourses and narratives are mutually illustrative and interpretative. The structure of 3:1–36 which refers more specifically to the renewed creation of 1:9–2: 11 is composed of 3:1–21, which begins in a dialogue with Nicodemus and then gradually and smoothly passes into a monologue into which John has gathered teachings of Jesus from elsewhere relative to this same theme. Then follows an interlude in 3:22–30 which compares the baptism of John the Baptist and of Jesus; this is linked to the proceeding section by the common theme of baptism. Finally, in 3:31–36, some concluding remarks are added in which John sums up the message of the entire preceding section of 1:19–3:30.

In discussing the theme of love in 1 John we saw that Jesus had launched a pointed attack, not only on hate, but most especially on unconcern for the needs of others and indifference to the pain of human existence. Man's primeval sin was his refusal to accept responsibility for the future of God's evolution, a vocation to which he had been solemnly called as co-worker with the Creator in Genesis 1:26–28. This original refusal created on earth a community of alienation, estranged from its God, from itself, and from the very depths of its being. This is the community of Genesis 4–11, the archetypal image of meaningless humanity. It is a community in which hate appears as Cain's murder of Abel, and this finds its seedbed in the classic statement of unconcern in Genesis 4:9: "Am I my brother's keeper?" Thereafter children are born into an alienated world. Were this earth still a community of love, as God had destined it to be, their birth would have been into such a society immediately, and from their infancy they would have been trained into concern and love. But such is not this world and human birth immediately, even though through no personal fault of their own, makes them partakers of a world long alienated from its Lord. They must break out of this state either by an adult acceptance of Christ in the sacramental sign of baptism/confirmation (for example, Acts 8:4–25), or else by being sacramentally accepted within the community of concern by infant baptism and then personally ratifying this inclusion through adult confirmation. Such an understanding of human existence is presumed as background to this section of John. We can now study 3:1–36 in more detail.

1) 3:1–21. This section is very carefully structured as dialogue
(3:1–13) moving without interruption into monologue (3:14–21).
The opening dialogue in 3:1–13 consists of three interchanges
between Nicodemus and Jesus in which the words of the former
are gradually shortened while those of Jesus are gradually lengthened: the master of Israel must cede place to thé Master from
God. These are the three main steps of the conversation: (a)
Nicodemus to Jesus (3:1–2): he admits that Jesus is a teacher
with divine authority; (b) Jesus to Nicodemus (3:3): Jesus says
this admission is not enough. A rebirth is required. The word
translated by "anew" can also mean "from above" and John
may possibly intend both meanings. (c) Nicodemus to Jesus
(3:4): The master in Israel has to ask "how?" is this to happen;
(d) Jesus to Nicodemus (3:5–8): The answer is that birth even
into the chosen people is not sufficient any longer. The rebirth
in the Spirit and water, that is, in the sacramental water through
which the Spirit moves, is now necessary. (e) Nicodemus to
Jesus (3:9): he is finally reduced to a brief repetition of his
preceding question; (f) Jesus to Nicodemus (3:10–13): The
master in Israel must now give way to Jesus. His double "how
can this be?" (3:4, 9) serves to highlight the serene and solemn
assurance of the thrice repeated, "Truly, truly, I say to you"
(3:3, 5, 11), with which Jesus each time opens his part of the
dialogue. In truth the "teacher of Israel" (3:10) is no match
for the one whom he has confessed as "a teacher come from God"
(3:2). His words become fewer as those of Jesus gradually in-
crease in number.

In turning to the theology of 3:1–21, the following may be
noted. The expression "Kingdom of God" appears in John only
in 3:3 and 3:5. Instead of this term John uses "eternal life" or
some equivalent which he deemed more congenial to the minds
of those not attuned to such a Palestinian expression as the
"Kingdom of God." It is interesting that he should preserve it
only here in a dialogue situation and in a context which has
close Synoptic parallels. This would certainly make one hesitate
to accept too easily the idea that the dialogue framework so
common in John is a purely literary creation to suit the customs
of the Greek milieu in which John was written and in which such
dialogues were a common artificial framework and setting for
philosophical and religious discussion.

The insistence of John that to see (3:3) and to enter (3:5) this ultimate kingdom demand a new birth makes one wonder if baptismal rebirth is not really the idea behind the Synoptic sayings about "becoming like a little child." Possibly this is the full depth of Jesus' demand that only children enter his kingdom, that is, that only the reborn can do so.

In 3:14–21 John tells us when this rebirth will be possible for man, and here he uses "eternal life" (3:15, 16) and no longer refers to the kingdom. But these expressions both mean the same thing. In the risen Lord the final presence of God as a community of love, as a Trinity, has definitively manifested itself in human history, and demands a response for or against this presence as love. Acceptance is to participate in the very life of God, in eternal life, in love. This manifestation of the presence of love at the heart of human existence demands a decision. Man either accepts love and moves beyond judgment or condemnation into eternal life here and now, or he refuses it and lives in death and darkness instead, also here and now. Judgment and salvation are now, here on earth. We look in faith to the present, we have hope for that which is beyond the grave. But here and now we stand in the valley of decision.

In Numbers 21:9 God punished the Israelites by serpents, and Moses set up a brazen serpent on a pole so that those who looked at it would be healed by God. In Wisdom 16, in the course of a long meditation on the plagues of Egypt (11:7–18:19), the author discusses how God punished Egypt by means of animals, and even Israel herself was sometimes punished in this same manner (16:1–4). Then he mentions the bronze serpent and insists that those who looked on it were not saved by its sight but by their faith in God's power (16:6–12). In the same way Jesus will be "lifted up" on the cross in order to give eternal life to all who "look" upon him in faith.

2) 3:22–30. The insertion of this passage into the present sequence is similar to the insertions about the Baptist which we saw already in the prologue, in 1:6–8 and 1:15. The Baptist had baptized in water. He had foretold Jesus as the baptizer in the Spirit. But Jesus actually brought a baptism in both water and the Spirit, far greater than that of John. Possibly the presence of disciples of the Baptist at Ephesus (Acts 18:24–19:7) would make such a statement as this necessary.

3) *3:31–36.* These concluding words summarize for all time the message of the discourse with Nicodemus, and what preceded it. Jesus came from above as the ultimate manifestation of the God who is love, and this is his testimony. Man is then faced with a choice: faith in God manifested in Jesus which begets eternal life here and now in the believer, or disbelief which lets that man live, but a life that is not really life, in abiding wrath. Notice the word "sent" in 3:34. In Jesus the external manifestation of God's inner being and therefore of man's inalienable destiny, here and hereafter, has reached its climax. He is *the* Sent of God. It is by faith and acceptance of this challenge that man enters the new creation and begins to return evolution toward its divinely given goal in total concern and universal love for others.

e) In the New Temple (4:1–45)

Within the overall unity and balance of the works and words in 1:19–4:42, this second discourse looks back more directly to the second narrative, that of the new temple in 2:12–25, and interprets this event by the words of Jesus. The structure of the discourse is an introduction (4:1–6); Jesus and the woman (4:7–26); Jesus and the disciples (4:27–38); Jesus and the Samaritans (4:39–42). Notice especially the fine filigree work of the dialogue in 4:7–26. Jesus opens and closes the conversation (4:7, 26). He speaks to the woman seven times in all (4:7, 10, 13–14, 16, 17b–18, 21–24, 26). The woman answers Jesus six times (4:9, 11–12, 15, 17a, 19–20, 25), and her seventh and final word is uttered in 4:29. Once again structure indicates theology. The seventh statement of Jesus is seen in 4:26: "I who speak to you am he." The seventh statement of the woman appears in 4:29: "Come see a man who told me all that I ever did. Can this be the Christ?" In other words the climax of Jesus' part of the dialogue is the revelation that he is the awaited Christ; and the climax of the woman's part of the dialogue is her confession to the villagers concerning Jesus. As always for John, to know Christ means necessarily to proclaim him.

1) *4:1–6.* The setting for the discussion is quite important as it looks back into the earliest moments of Israel's destiny, with Abraham (Gn 12:6), with Jacob (Gn 33:18–20), and with

Joshua's renewal of the covenant (Jos 24). Near Sychar, close to ancient Shechem, Jesus has gone out of his way, it would seem, to choose the most strikingly unlikely person to receive his first formal statement of mission. He is speaking to a Samaritan, whose people the Jews considered apostates since the conquering Assyrians had planted settlers in that region (2 Kgs 17:24-34). He is speaking to a woman, and rabbis usually avoided such conversations in public. He is speaking to a sinner.

When we mention water, we often think immediately of washing, of cleansing. For the Hebrew, schooled to the harsh exigencies of a dry land and a desert heritage, water meant life. Naturally, then, water is a biblical symbol for life, for the gift of authentic human existence here on earth. This is why the theme of water dominates the entire section in 1:19-4:42. For example, water is mentioned seventeen times in these chapters and only six times elsewhere in John. Water symbolizes life and this section discusses the new life which is opening to mankind and to all creation in Christ.[10]

2) 4:7-26. Instead of the water which must be drawn laboriously from the deep crossroads well, Jesus promises the gift of the Spirit which is the source of eternal life. The Spirit denotes God's dwelling among mankind as the dynamic force for life based on total love and complete openness to and concern for the needs of others. A phrase occurs in 4:21 and is repeated in fuller form in 4:23; it also appears in 5:25, 28; 16:2, 25, 32. The statement that an "hour is coming, and now is" connects again with Israel's prophetic expectation. The first half of this statement, "an hour comes," would be the Greek equivalent of the prophetic expression for the great final era to come in the distant future: their "days are coming." The second part of the expression, "and now is," would be the announcement that this promised final era is now present, that the works and the words of Jesus are already the divine firstfruits of that era. In the course of this dialogue, then, Jesus announces the arrival of the end era (4:21, 23), and that he is the Messiah (4:26) whose mission it is to usher in the final period of human history. The divine

---

10 J. Bligh, "Jesus in Samaria," HeythJ, 3 (1962), 329-346; F. J. McCool, "Living Water in John," The Bible in Current Catholic Thought, ed. J. L. McKenzie ("Gruenthaner Memorial"; New York, 1962), pp. 226-233. On the theme of the temple cf. D. M. Stanley, "The Christian Mystery and the New Temple," Worship, 32 (1958), 233-239.

rhythm of evolution has gone through all the preparatory stages and the moment for the opening of the last and final era of the world is now at hand. Environment had previously molded beings to further change, but now mankind must take control over his own environment and form it out of love for others. He lives in the divine milieu, the environment of love and concern. Failure to conform to that God-given environment can only bring both personal and cosmic disaster. The longest statement of Jesus is in 4:21–24, which links directly with the sign of the temple. In this coming era the relation of believers with the Father will no longer be in unity of place but in community of spirit. God's "place" is the entire world and the responsibility of the believer extends that far as well.

3) 4:27–38. The words in 4:36–38 would be especially applicable if this event took place on the first return from the Jordan to Galilee with the new disciples. The Baptist had toiled and they are now to reap the fruits of his labors. But before and beyond the Baptist stands the long history of Israel's fidelity to her mission. Prophets might have castigated her failures, but without Israel Jesus would be unthinkable and inexplicable.

4) 4:39–42. There is surely a symbolic meaning in the record of the rather human snub given by the people to the woman in 4:42. One comes to Jesus because of the testimony, the witness, the word of another; but one stays with him because one then comes to know the power of the saving presence of Jesus in personal experience.

This, then, is the challenge to rebirth. Mankind is confronted with the revelation that the era foretold by all of Israel's destiny is arriving in Jesus of Nazareth. To accept him is to receive authentic life and to mold the new creation out of love for others; to refuse him is to receive judgment and to walk thereafter in the dark frustration of meaningless existence.

3. The Victory Over Death

Read John 4:43–5:47.

This sign-complex consists of two narratives and a discourse: the story of the healing of the official's son (4:43–54), and of the paralytic in Jerusalem (5:1–9), and the discourse which fol-

lows (5:10–47).[11] The mutual relationship of works and words
is, of course, the same as usual. The eternal life which stems from
rebirth in water and Spirit (1:19–4:42), is given to man only
in Jesus. Jesus gives life to the dead (4:46–54) and to the alive-
in-death (5:1–9), and then in the following explanatory conversation he shows that he has received from the Father the latter's
power to give divine life here and now on earth (5:10–47). The
section moves beyond the preceding one in that it shows the
alternative to rebirth is not some other form of life but a living
death, a groping in darkness and insecurity. The rebirth is thus
a victory over its alternative which is life-in-death. The alternatives to a life based on concern and to a world grounded in love
are all the forms of personal, social, and cosmic unlife which
we know too well today.

a) Life Against Death (4:43–54)

Like 2:12 previously, 4:43–45 is a transitional phrase. John
quite possibly intends a symbolism behind his "After the two
days . . . he came again to Cana" (4:43, 46). Both miracles at
Cana would thus have taken place on a "third day" (2:1) and
would represent foreshadowings of the great miracle of the
resurrection to be consummated likewise "on the third day." The
words about the Galileans reflect in summary the situation more
fully told in the Synoptic tradition of Mark 6:1–6; Matthew
13:53–58; and Luke 4:16–30. The brief notice of differing opinions
in 4:44–45 represents the similar tension found in Luke 4:16–30
and one wonders, in the light of John, if the rejection by
Nazareth was that of the people in general or of some of their
religious authorities.

The healing of the official's son is the same miracle as that in
Matthew 8:5–13 and Luke 7:1–10, but details were changed as
the different accounts were handed down in the oral period. For

---

[11] J. Bligh, "Jesus in Jerusalem," Heyth J, 4 (1963), 115–134, argues that
this entire chapter is a Christian apologetic composed by the Jerusalem
Church after the resurrection. This would indicate the way in which such large
units were gradually assembled before their final redaction and present
position. Cf. also D. M. Stanley, "The Mission of the Son," Worship, 33
(1958), 27–34; J. Howton, " 'Son of God' in the Fourth Gospel," NTS, 10
(1964), 227–237; J. L. McKenzie, "The Judge of all the Earth," The Way,
2 (1962), 209–218.

example, it is his "son" who is sick in John, but his "servant" in Matthew and Luke. Since the original Aramaic narrative would have used *talya*, which means either child or servant, this discrepancy is easily accounted for and it was most probably his son who was actually sick. The gratuitous statement of Jesus in 4:48, "Unless you see signs and wonders you will not believe," also receives its explanation from the Synoptic parallels. In Luke 7:1–10 the official did not come directly to Jesus himself but sent some of the spiritual authorities of Capernaum to plead for him. We know that these men were not exactly friends of Jesus (Mk 1:21–22). In the actual happening, John 4:48 may well be addressed not to the official himself but to these authorities. This is all the more likely in that "you see" and "you believe," supposedly addressed to the official, are in the plural in Greek. Other differences in the three accounts are not such as militate against a common event behind all three stories but rather such as might be expected by the vagaries of oral tradition and catechetical usage.

It is significant that the only two miracles performed by Jesus for Gentiles, those involving the son of the Capernaum official and the daughter of the Syrophoenician woman (Mk 7:24–30; Mt 15:21–28), are not performed for the askers but for loved ones sick at home. No doubt the early community saw in this fact a prophetic promise of the conversion of the Gentiles *far away*. We can take another important point from it as well. Two "pagans" find faith in Jesus in their concern for the pain and anguish of others. "Pagans" still find God in such concern; believers have often lost him because of their unconcern.

The triple assertion that the boy "lives" in 4:50–51, 53 makes the point clear. Jesus brings life for those who are dying. At the conclusion this miracle is directly connected with the previous Cana miracle (4:54) as a "second sign that Jesus did when he had come from Judea to Galilee." They both looked forward to the final definitive moment of the risen Lord's presence to his own, "on the third day" and "coming from Judea to Galilee" (Jn 21:1). So far, Jesus' prophetic signs have given faith to his disciples (2:11), and to his own people (2:23), and now to the Gentiles (4:53). These actions are all promissory actions of the coming of the kingdom and the demand for faith in the totality of its advent.

b) Life Against Paralysis (5:1–9)

The second incident is joined to the preceding one for the same purpose. The Gentiles can only receive true life from Jesus as the final revelation of the depths of human existence (4:43–54). But the Jews can likewise find their own completion and the full meaning of their divinely given destiny only in Jesus of Nazareth. The law of Sinai has not been revoked by Jesus nor has a single utterance of the prophets been lost by his arrival. "Think not that I have come to abolish the law and the prophets; I have come not to abolish them, but to fulfil them" (Mt 5:17). Human life (Gentiles) or divine Torah (Jews) never could or ever shall find fulfillment save in him, in the Son of man, in the anointed of Israel.

The pool of 5:2 has been identified with an area excavated beneath the church of St. Anne to the northeast of the old city, close to the fortress Antonia. Originally, it was presumed that "the five porticoes" was an example of creative masonry on the part of John, created for symbolic reasons. Now that the pool has been discovered, with four porticoes on its four sides and a fifth in the center separating an upper from a lower pool, one is inclined to discount the symbolism entirely. But the mind of John does not choose history or symbolism, but rather seeks the symbolism in the historical events of Jesus' life. The pool has five porticoes because the builder gave it such. But this minor fact is mentioned in John only because of the symbolism, and not from any pedantic preoccupation with architectural exactitudes. What then would be the symbolism seen by John in this detail?

In the discourse section (5:10–47), Jesus is the giver of eternal life (5:21, 24–26, 40). The Torah was not enough to establish the kingdom of God upon the entire earth. It had never been intended to do so, but rather was to prepare the way for the coming of the Messiah as the opening of the last era of the world's life and the establishment of the kingdom of concern and understanding, of mercy, peace, and love. This warning appears clearly in the words of Jesus in 5:39 and 46–47. The five porticoes would turn the mind of the reader trained in the Old Testament to the five books of the law of Moses. Just as the pool with its five porticoes had failed to give ultimate life to the cripple, so that Torah with its five books could not give ultimate life to Israel. There is another step in the symbolism; one may possibly deny it any cogency, but in dealing with a theologian such as John, it is necessary to tread very carefully. The paralytic had been afflicted for thirty-eight years, had been unable to find full life for that period. This is the same period of time in which the people of Israel who had received the law on Sinai languished in the desert until the entire generation was gone:

> "And the time from our leaving Kadesh-barnea until we crossed the brook Zered was thirty-eight years, until the entire genera-tion, that is, the men of war, had perished from the camp, as the Lord had sworn to them" (Dt 2:14).

John intends these minor details to highlight the fact that the law could not bring all mankind to the climax of their destiny, but was rather supposed to prepare the way for that culmination. This is actually a development of the statement seen already in 1:17 that "the law was given through Moses; grace and truth came through Jesus Christ." The law was absolutely necessary, good, and holy, and brought Israel to Jesus and Jesus to Israel. But now that he had come, the law had to face him. This is the meaning of Jesus' question to the man in 5:6. It is quite obvious that the man was there because he wished to be made healthy, but Jesus wished to stress that even though the man himself desired life, he was unable to obtain it for himself with the means at hand. He needed another to bring him to the water.

The combined point of the two signs is now clear and it is the same as that of Romans 1–2. The Gentiles are dying and Israel is paralyzed with regard to its ultimate human destiny — until Jesus' proclamation of the kingdom.

c) The Source of Life (5:10–47)

Once again, the discussion section analyzes and emphasizes the meaning of the preceding narratives. The discourse begins in dialogue (5:10–18) and concludes with monologue (5:19–47). This is the characteristic feature of Jesus' discourses as artificially reassembled by John around his main themes. The discourse has three parts: the triple dialogue (5:10–18); the monologue in chiastic balance (5:19–30); and a concluding statement on Jesus' witnesses (5:31–47).

1) 5:10–18. The dialogue moves through three steps: The Jews and the paralytic (5:10–13); the paralytic and Jesus (5:14–15); Jesus and the Jews (5:16–18). The term "the Jews" in all these controversial or inimical contexts in John means those among the authorities opposed to Jesus. For example, the opposition of "the Jews" in 5:10, 15, 16, 18 only means those authorities with power to seek the death penalty. In the Synoptic tradition, the clash over Sabbath healings is always with the authorities. For example, in Mark 3:2–6 the authorities in Galilee put up a test case in the very synagogue itself on the Sabbath and thereafter they determine to put Jesus to death.

Jesus did not accept the naïve notion that personal sickness is an immediate result of personal sin. Job's ancient repudiation of that too simple thesis was echoed on his lips in 9:1–3. But neither is it true that there is no connection between sickness and sin, between the disorders of the universe and the evil heart of man. It is true that man's personal acts of hate and violence have often left disease and disaster behind them. But, on a far wider level, it is man's unconcern that allows these ills to remain in our world without their being destroyed by the onslaught on them to which man was called by God in Genesis 1:26–28, and to which he was urged in love by Jesus. Man's primordial sin did not bring physical disorder into the universe. This, we now know, was always in the world as the necessary back-wash of the evolutionary process. There was no physical "Golden Age" in the distant past. But man's vocation was to take control of these forces in obedience to his Creator and in love for that Creator's universe and to mold them into order, harmony, and safety. When his own selfishness made him rebel and ever continues to do so, the continuing disorders of the world become then the results of his unconcern, the symbol of his sin. Unconcern is at the heart of the world's evil and Jesus brackets unconcern with sin. When we use the awesome forces of the cosmos to destroy one another, or even when we fail to use these same forces to control our environment out of love for one another, we fail both our God and our destiny. Sin is far worse than sickness, but both are a blight on the face of God's world, and the activity of Jesus attacks at once all that destroys man: sin, sickness, disease, and death. To talk about "mere physical evils" or "simple temporal problems" renders meaningless the amount of time Jesus spends healing human pain and answering human needs. The believer, like Jesus before him, is one who accepts his election to destroy the evil of the universe, both sin and unconcern, and all the disease, disorder, and disaster which are their festering results.

2) 5:19–30. The structure of this section is in reversed parallelism (chiastic construction) like that seen already in 1:1–18. We can outline it as follows:

a) 5:19–20:   The Son acts only from the Father.
b) 5:21–23:   The Son gives life or judgment like the Father.
c) 5:24:   Life and judgment are now.
b′) 5:25–29: The Son gives life or judgment like the Father.
a′) 5:30:   "I" act only from "the one who sent me."

This structure warns us immediately that the key verse is 5:24. The prophets of Israel always talked of the great "Day of Yahweh" as a day of both judgment (death) and salvation (life). The majestic poetry of Amos described the judgment aspect:

It is darkness, and not light;
    as if a man fled from a lion,
    and a bear met him;
or went into the house and leaned with his hand against the wall,
    and a serpent bit him.

But this dark side in 5:19–20 finds its later correlative of hope in the image of plentiful harvest in 9:13:

"Behold, the days are coming," says the Lord,
    "when the plowman shall overtake the reaper
    and the treader of grapes him who sows the seed;
the mountains shall drip sweet wine,
    and all the hills shall flow with it."

Now, Jesus tells his audience, is the Day of the Lord, and judgment or salvation rests solely in his own hands. To accept Jesus as the ultimate revelation of human existence is to move immediately into eternal life, then and there, now and forever. To refuse him is to take judgment and condemnation upon one's self and to move thereafter in eternal meaninglessness. This happens here and now on earth at the moment of decision as the hearer confronts the challenge of God on the lips of Christ. Israel had expected the resurrection of the dead on the Day of the Lord. But mankind is already living in death unless he accepts Jesus. When he does accept him, the eternal life may then begin; it cannot be interrupted by death, but continues with God forever. By the same token, those who live in deliberate estrangement from the meaning of their being here on earth will have that choice ratified for all eternity by God. The decision is now and the decision is forever. Once again we see clearly the difference between theoretical humanism and theoretical Christianity. The former offers the good life, and latter offers the only life.

3) 5:31–47. After such a claim, John naturally adds a statement with regard to "testimony" concerning Jesus. We have seen already how frequently he discusses those who "witness" to Jesus, not those who prove him, for he is beyond proof, but those whose lives make explicit and obvious the awesome reality of his challenge. Jesus says he has a witness in the Baptist (5:31–35), as we saw earlier in 1:6–8, 15, 19–37; 3:22–30. There is also a far greater witness than this. He has the Father, who bears him double witness: through the work he is now performing (5:36), and the fulfillment of the word of God concerning the future in Scripture (5:37–47). The great kingdom of mercy and love awaited by all of Israel's past and shining through every page of her sacred writings is now breaking into human history in the "works" of Jesus of Nazareth, works of assistance and kindness to be consummated by the cross. This section reflects the bitter polemic between Jesus and those forces in spiritual authority who oppose him in the name of the same God. The Father is testimony to Jesus for it is the divinely given rhythm of evolution that he is opening to man's gaze. The statement of 5:40, "You refuse to come to me that you may have life," sums up this discourse as explanation of the two preceding miracles. Only in Jesus as the culmination of Israel's preparation can man find, not a better life, but the only life. It is in his (notice the order) "works" (5:36) and "words" (5:47) that God brings his work to completion.

4. The Promise of Life

Read John 6:1–71.

Man must accept the exigency of a rebirth in order to obtain the fullness of his divinely willed existence here and hereafter. This rebirth is commitment to concern for the future of evolu-

tion out of love for others. Man enters it as obtaining *life* for
himself and becoming *light* for others, and by joining the visible
community of all those who so live. Hence, the baptismal symbolism of water, denoting new life in the Spirit of love (1:19–
4:42). The alternative to this rebirth is not some other way of
life, but rather a living death, walking in judgment and condemnation, meaningless groping in the darkness of alienation
(4:43–5:47). In the third major section, 6:1–71, the main thought
is taken a step further by concentrating primarily on Jesus as this
new life for mankind. It is not as if totally new ideas are introduced as we go from one of these seven units to the next, but
rather one theme, latent or secondary in a previous section,
becomes later the central thrust of another section. One must
think of musical rather than logical composition.

We have the usual balance of work and word, but in a somewhat different arrangement. The narrative has three parts: the
multiplication of the loaves and fishes (6:1–13); the reaction of
the multitudes (6:14–15); and the true revelation to the disciples (6:16–21). This is followed by a discourse with three
corresponding sections as well: Jesus is the true bread (6:22–59);
the reaction of the crowds (6:60–66); the acceptance by the
Twelve (6:67–71).[12]

It would be possible to draw up in parallel columns two sets
of sayings of Jesus, one sacramental and one human, and both
with the same absolute imperatives. For example, sacramental demands appear without any qualifications in Mark 16:15–16:

---

[12] There is hardly a chapter in John whose content and composition has
excited more debate than the present one. The structure argued here is
basically that of C. H. Dodd, *The Interpretation of the Fourth Gospel*
(Cambridge, 1953), p. 334; cf. also *Historical Tradition in the Fourth
Gospel* (Cambridge, 1963), pp. 213–217. The following works indicate the
process of recent research: P. J. Temple, "The Eucharist in St. John 6,"
CBQ, 9 (1947), 442–452; J. L. Lilly, "The Eucharistic Discourse of Jn
6," *CBQ*, 12 (1950), 48–51; D. M. Stanley, "The Bread of Life," *Worship*,
32 (1958), 477–488; E. J. Kilmartin, "Liturgical Influence on John 6," *CBQ*,
22 (1960), 183–191; "The Formation of the Bread of Life Discourse," *Scr*,
12 (1960), 75–78; E. D. Johnston, "The Johannine Version of the Feeding
of the Five Thousand — an Independent Tradition," *NTS*, 8 (1962), 151–
154; H. Montefiore, "Revolt in the Desert?" *NTS*, 8 (1962), 135–141;
G. H. C. MacGregor, "The Eucharist in the Fourth Gospel," *NTS*, 9
(1963), 111–119; T. Worden, "The Holy Eucharist in St. John," *Scr*, 15
(1963), 97–103; 16 (1964), 5–16; R. E. Brown, "The Eucharist and
Baptism in John," *The New Testament Essays* (Milwaukee, 1965), pp.
77–95.

And he said to them, "Go into all the world and preach the gospel to the whole creation. He who believes and is baptized will be saved, but he who does not believe will be condemned,"

or here in John 6:53–54:

So Jesus said to them, "Truly, truly, I say to you, unless you eat the flesh of the Son of Man and drink his blood, you have no life in you; he who eats my flesh and drinks my blood has eternal life, and I will raise him up at the last day."

On the other hand, and equally without any qualification, stand the human imperatives, which we saw already with regard to the parable of the good Samaritan (Lk 10:30–37) and of the great judgment (Mt 25:31–46). We must live in the sacramental community; we must be concerned with all the anguish of our human situation. Is it a case of either/or, or of both/and? What is the relationship between liturgy and life in the mind of Jesus? In his own works, Jesus deliberately went out of his way to cure on the Sabbath, thereby breaking the liturgical law as far as the Pharisees were concerned. Quite legitimately, they asked him if he could not perform his cures on another day than the Sabbath, thereby obtaining both respect for the Sabbath day and assistance for the sick man (Lk 13:10–17). His point, made in work, not word, was that liturgy is for love and not vice versa. The same point appears when he declares the Sabbath, the heart of the liturgical worship, "was made for man, not man for the Sabbath" (Mk 2:23–28). To the mind of Jesus, as in the teachings of the Old Testament prophets before him, the liturgy is the sacramental dynamism for an ongoing life of love, and when this latter is not present, the former is sacrilege. Both imperatives stand, but the sacramental is for the human, and together they point creation toward its God. We are human and we live by sign and greet one another in symbol. We are human and we find perfection only in community. God meets us also in sign. In the sacramental liturgy, as climactic moment of the one great sign which is the divine evolution, God drives us onward to live more and more perfectly in community. Those others who have never known or understood, never heard or even envisaged sacramental liturgy, may still find God, or rather be found by him, in the human imperatives of Jesus, the absolute demands of mutual love. One day there will be no more liturgy, but there will always be a community of perfect love as sacrament of God. In reading this chapter, we must never forget the tension between sacramental and human in which Jesus worked and taught.

a) The Multiplication of Bread (6:1–13)

The incident of the multiplication of loaves and fishes was extremely popular in the early Church. Two accounts of the same event, differing only in minor statistical data, appear in Mark 6:30–44 and 8:1–10 and also in Matthew 14:13–21 and 15:32–39. Luke seems to have suspected that the second narrative was not another event, but merely a different account of the same miracle, and so he has only the former story (Lk 9:10–17). The reason for this popularity is also quite clear. The four key words describing Jesus' miracle: *took, blessed, broke, gave,* appear again in the institution of the Eucharist at the paschal meal. Compare, for example, Mark 6:41 = 8:6; Matthew 14:19 = 15:36; Luke 9:16, with Mark 14:22; Matthew 26:26; Luke 22:19. Obviously, then, it is because of its foreshadowing of the Eucharist that this miracle was held in such esteem. John makes the same point in a more profound manner. Since he has no account of the institution of the Eucharist, he cannot depend on the vocabulary contact to draw his readers' attention to the promissory nature of the miracle. Instead, he allows the discourse in 6:22–59 to draw out quite fully all the sacramental depths of the preceding miracle. The two reactions to the miracle, the division among his disciples in 6:14–15 and 6:16–21, will likewise be more fully explicated in the discourse sections of 6:60–66 and 6:67–71 respectively.

It is worth noting that in the Synoptic tradition the miracle is performed by Jesus as an act of kindness and consideration for those who have come to a desert place to listen to him, who have stayed with him for some time, and for whose strength he fears if they must return to their homes without any food. However much sacramental symbolism we may quite correctly see in this miracle, it can never be forgotten that it was performed originally as a loving response to ordinary human need. John does not mention this fact, but the Synoptics recall to us that the Eucharist was intended by Christ as a ritual act, efficaciously creating in the participants the determination to live totally in response to the needs of the world, for whose want human hunger is the abiding symbol. It is not just hunger that cries to God, but hunger in a world of plenty. It is that hunger which accuses the over-plenty of others, that signifies their unconcern and renders their religion spurious. When men take the Eucharist seriously, they will know they have committed themselves to cure the hunger of others. They will not think that man can live by his own bread alone, but they will know that he can live by bread alone, if that bread be given to others in love.

b) The Reaction of Misunderstanding (6:14–15)

The action of Jesus and the desert setting of the miracle aroused the patriotic hopes of the multitude. Had not Moses fed them manna in the desert and then led them toward the conquest of their promised land? Was this the great prophet who would inaugurate the Day of Yahweh by ridding Israel of the pagan Roman with the power of the sword? This was not a temptation to mere material conquest, but a nostalgic recall of the days of the Maccabees and of the judges. The miracle, then, begets misunderstanding among the multitudes.

c) The Gift of Understanding (6:16–21)

The confession of Simon-Peter that Jesus is the awaited Messiah of Israel took place at Caesarea Philippi in the Synoptic traditions (Mk 8:27–30; Mt 16:13–20; Lk 9:18–21). In the account of Matthew, Jesus replies that Peter's faith is a gift from his Father (16:17). It is most likely this same event which lies behind John 6:67–71 and John uses the walking on the waters in 6:17–21 as the revelation from God which prepares the apostles for their communal confession through Peter. The misunderstanding of some of the people (6:14–15) leads to their walking no longer with Jesus (6:60–66), but the revelation of God to his own (6:16–21) results in their acceptance of Jesus (6:67–71). This theme of decision and division will become the central consideration of the next complex in 7:1–8:59.

The point of the story is the "It is I" of 6:20. On the surface this is merely an assertion of identity but one wonders why such was really necessary. Most likely John intends in it a reference to the fact that the Greek phrase of which this is a translation, *egō eimi*, sometimes translates the Hebrew "name" of God in the Old Testament, *'ani hu'*, "I [am] He." For example, in Isaiah 48:12 God speaks:

> "Hearken to me, O Jacob,
> and Israel, whom I called!
> I am He, I am the first,
> and I am the last."

The Hebrew phrase for "I am He" is here put into Greek as *egō eimi*. When John cites Jesus' "It is I," for which a much better translation would be, "I am He," it is an oblique but obvious statement that Jesus is the revelation of the depths of God, that in him man sees God, and so also sees most clearly himself. The Hebrew mind had always seen the ceaseless thrust of the sea against the land, ever threatening yet never prevailing, as an indication of the power and mercy of the Creator. For example, in Job 38:11, it is the power of God alone which says to the sea:

> ". . . 'Thus far shall you come, and no farther,
> and here shall your proud waves be stayed' . . ."

Jesus' walking upon the sea and his accompanying statement of divine being would have been a majestic combination to such a mentality.

d) The Meaning of the Bread (6:22–59)

We saw earlier how John's penchant for symbolic numbers, and probably also for catechetical mnemonics, led him to structure the dialogue between Jesus and the Samaritan woman so that each participant made seven statements (4:7–29). The same artificial arrangement prevails in the dialogue between Jesus and the people in 6:24–66. The people speak seven times: 6:25, 28, 30–31, 34, 41–42, 52, 60. Jesus also speaks seven times; 6:26–27, 29, 32–33, 35–40, 43–51, 53–58, 61–65. Once again the tension of the debate can be summarized in the seventh statement of each side: the disbelieving, "This is a hard saying; who can listen to it?" (6:60); and Jesus' "This is why I told you that no one can come to me unless it is granted him by the Father" (6:65).

In line with the special Johannine use of "the Jews" to denote those among the authorities who oppose Jesus from the first, it is interesting to note how the participants change in name after the debate becomes embittered. In 6:22–34, the only ones in contact with Jesus are the ordinary people; it is simply "the people" who are mentioned, for example, in 6:22, 24. But at precisely the moment when the hearers begin to murmur against him, these are described as "the Jews" (6:35–52). As the mood changes from respectful questioning in 6:22–34 to severe criticism in 6:35–59, John no longer talks of "the people," but of "the Jews." As in all inimical situations in John these terms are never synonymous.

We must now consider 6:22–59, the discourse explanation of the "sign" (6:14) of the bread in 6:1–13. The structure of 6:22–58 falls into three parts. The introduction in 6:22–34 is followed by two sections in perfect mutual symmetry in 6:35–47 and 6:48–59.

1) 6:22–34. This question and answer structure (sevenfold) may well reflect the Christian passover liturgy. At the Jewish paschal liturgy four questions were posed to the father of the family on the meaning of the ritual they were performing. Here the people address Jesus four times. Three times they question him: "when?" in 6:25; "what must we do?" in 6:28; "what do you do?" in 6:30. Finally, they request, "Lord, give us this bread always," in 6:34. The three replies of Jesus (6:26–27, 29, 32–33) take them gently from their thoughts of material bread for themselves (6:26–27), through the absolute necessity of faith to know what he is doing (6:29), and into an awareness of the "true bread" (6:32–33). They ask for a "sign" and Jesus' words will show them the sign-value of what he has already done for them. By referring to the manna in the desert (Ex 16), Jesus turns their minds to the meaning of the multiplication. It is a sign of the true bread "for the life of the world," the bread which is love and concern for the universe.

2) 6:35–47. In rabbinical circles the metaphor of the Torah as divine bread given by God to Israel for her life was well-known. So there would be some readiness for the idea of divine bread as something to be believed in. The section develops in three steps: the claims of Jesus (6:35–40), the reaction of the audience (6:41–42), and Jesus' reiteration of his claims (6:43–47).

To come to Jesus, that is, to believe in him, is to accept the divine bread for life. This life is eternal life, accepted here and now but enduring forever. Death cannot vanquish this life, for the believer lives on forever with God. The protest made by "the Jews" in 6:41–42 recalls that hinted at earlier in 4:43–45. Jesus offers no arguments and no proofs, but simply repeats his previous statements. Only those who have been already touched by God, through the very depths of reality, can find him in Jesus of Nazareth. But those who do, here and now, on this earth "have eternal life." It is not that they will receive it sometime in the distant future. They have it already, and the future can never despoil them of it. To walk in love is to walk with God and to have eternal life here and now.

3) 6:48–59.   Certain scholars have long questioned whether this section could have been offered to the ordinary people of Galilee at this time. Be that as it may, the artificial similarity in form and content between 6:35–47 and 6:48–59 renders it quite likely that John has combined later material, possibly from the paschal supper, in which Jesus appears as eucharistic bread, with an earlier discourse after the multiplication miracle in which Jesus is metaphorical bread to be eaten, that is, to be accepted by faith. Thus, the finished product of 6:35–59 would insist that the eucharistic bread is eaten only in faith. One approaches Jesus in faith before receiving him as Eucharist. The artificial nature of the balanced sections in 6:35–47 and 6:48–59 appears clearly from the following parallels:

i) *General Parallels.*   The tripartite structure is identical for each section: the claims of Jesus (6:35–40 and 48–51); the reaction of the audience (6:41–42 and 52); and Jesus' repetition of his claims (6:43–47 and 53–59).

ii) *Specific Parallels.*   Both sections open with the same statement: "I am the bread of life" in 6:35 and 6:48. Second, the characteristic vocabulary of 6:35–47 is "to come to Jesus" (6:35, 37, 44, 45) which is a Johannine equivalent for "to believe in Jesus" (6:35, 36, 40, 47); but the typical vocabulary of 6:48–59 is "to eat" (*esthiō* in 6:49, 51, 52, 53; *trōgō* in 6:54, 56, 57, 58) and "to drink" (6:53, 54, 56). Third, both pericopes predict the same result: "have eternal life; and I will raise him up at the last day," in 6:40 and 6:54, for the one "who sees the Son and believes in him" (6:40) and for the one "who eats my flesh and drinks my blood" (6:54). Finally, both pieces close with the same expression, just as they opened with the same one: "He who believes has eternal life" in 6:47, and, "he who eats this bread will live forever" in 6:58.

Obviously, then, 6:35–47 and 6:48–59 are similar both in form and in content. For eternal life, it is necessary that one approach the eucharistic Jesus in faith, and this is the total message of the parallel sections. Most likely, the original discourse, which took place after the refusal of Jesus to allow himself to be forced into political messianic revolution, was that contained in 6:35–47. The full implication of these assertions is brought out by John's addition of 6:48–59, whose original context might well stem from the Last Supper where the action of Jesus must have entailed some explanation to the disciples. Notice especially throughout this section the balance of eternal life and resurrection in such texts as 6:40, 44, 54. The believer receives eternal life here and now and resurrection is its climactic fulfillment. But the believer enters into eternal life not at the moment he is confronted with death but at the moment he is confronted with love. The one who does not believe enters into eternal alienation, not at the moment he is confronted with death, but at the moment he knowingly chooses unlove.

e) The Result of Misunderstanding (6:60–66)

If one accepts the above hypothesis on the composition of John 6 as a Christian liturgical composition from different historical locations in the life of Jesus, the events of 6:60–66 and 6:67–71 would most likely be taken as the culmination of the discourse given in 6:35–47. "The Jews" had already grumbled at this section of the talk in 6:41–42 and their point was the claim of Jesus to have had a divine origin. The final complaint in 6:60, which elicits the response of 6:61–65, is presumably on this same point. The answer of Jesus is that they will only understand his divine origin when they witness the end of his life. Jesus speaks in the realm of the Spirit and offers life; many of his hearers cannot accept it for they judge merely on the level of the external and the physical. In its present position, 6:61–65 would refer not only to the discourse in 6:35–47 (Capernaum) but also to 6:48–58 (from the Last Supper?) and would be a warning to the early Christian readers, as in 1 Corinthians 11:17–34.

What may lie behind this section is the fact that the crowd has been severely disappointed with the failure of Jesus to assume a politico-messianic role after the multiplication of the loaves which seemed an excellent introduction to revolt. The discourse (6:35–47) does little to reassure them, and many of those who looked to Jesus for revolution left him at this point (6:66). But we should note that there is no word of attack on Jesus or any such violent reaction. Some of the disciples simply beat their mental swords back into plowshares and went forth to their fields again.

f) The Reply of Understanding (6:67–71)

This is the same historical event as the confession of Peter at Caesarea Philippi in the Synoptic traditions. It also follows the multiplication there, most closely in Luke. John would have combined it here for the same liturgical didactic purpose as was behind the creation of the entire unity of John 6. Peter speaks for the Twelve (6:68) and his confession is messianic as in the Synoptic traditions. The gift of understanding given to them (6:16–21) demands and produces this open proclamation of the true being of Jesus.

The three sections of narrative receive their complete elucidation in the three portions of the corresponding discourse. Jesus offers himself in the Eucharist to be accepted in faith as the dynamic and liturgical center for a life of love and response to others. Some, however, do not understand this symbolic reality and turn from it in disappointed hope, while others accept it as the gift of authentic existence.

5. The Crisis of Decision

Read John 7:1–8:59.

In ordinary human decisions, we usually envisage three possibilities: for, against, and undecided or neutral. In the Old Testament, Israel is never offered three choices with regard to Yahweh. She must always choose between the living God, who alone works upon creation and history, or gods who are made by hands. This absolute challenge appears in all the prophetic writings. The categories are judgment and salvation, life and death; there is no middle ground. The reason for this is that they spoke of the ultimate meaning and purpose of human existence and we cannot take leave of absence from life in order to decide how to live it. We are thrust into the world and every moment of our being moves us toward or away from our deepest fulfillment. This dichotomy is rooted in our human freedom, the fact that we must say "yes" or "no" to the reality which we are. There is no way to say "maybe" or "later" to existence. This is why so many of Jesus' parables have their imagery divided into two classes, and why one can say without qualification, without any discussion of the gray, the neutral, or the yet undecided. "For he that is not against us is for us," in Mark 9:40, and also, "He who is not with me is against me," in Luke 11:23. There is no middle ground left between those two statements.

This is also the constant teaching of John for he also insists that now during our life here on earth is the crisis of decision. When we confront the revelation in Jesus that God is a community of love and therefore mankind can only find authentic existence here on earth within the community of love refracting this divine reality, we face an ultimate decision. The prophet Joel (3:14) had looked forward to the oncoming Day of the Lord with this vision:

> Multitudes, multitudes,
> in the valley of decision!
> For the Day of the Lord is near
> in the valley of decision.

But the decision is not some distant reality. Jesus claims we are all born into that lonesome valley and we must decide to walk it either in love for others or in unconcern and hate.

Of the seven units of John's composition in 1:19–12:50, the present one is the central and pivotal section. It brings the preceeding sections to their climax. The rebirth in water and Spirit (1:19–4:42), whose alternative is living death (4:43–5:47), and whose continuance is a life of communal love in the eucharistic Lord (6:1–71), is man's deepest decision, man's ultimate crisis of choice (7:1–8:59).

The structure of this complex is different from that of the preceding ones. The duality of narrative and explanatory discourse, of work and of word, does not appear here in consecutive sections. Instead, the narrative runs throughout the two chapters and the discourse is supplied by a constant dialogue between Jesus and his listeners. The narrative section is thus the background to the discourse rather than its introduction. This narrative background comprises three main points. First, there is the liturgical framework of the events. The temple at Jerusalem during the feast of Tabernacles is the setting (7:14, 37; 8:59). Second, there is the constant discussion among the people with regard to Jesus (7:20, 25–27, 31, 40, 43). Third, the gathering hostility of a section of the authorities appears quite clearly. As usual, these are simply referred to as "the Jews." Notice, for example, the term "Jews" in 7:15; 8:48, 52–53, 57–59 but "Pharisees" in 7:32, 44–52; 8:13. Once again, our attention is drawn to the fact that there is no support in the Gospel for the idea that the majority of the people of Israel, or even of Jerusalem, were against Jesus, let alone engineered his death. Here also in John 7–8 a cursory reading in which one takes "the Jews" at face value might confuse the historical perspective. However, one must notice the evidence of such statements as 7:11–12:

> The Jews were looking for him at the feast, and saying, "Where is he?" And there was much muttering about him among the people. While some said, "He is a good man," others said ,"No, he is leading the people astray." Yet *for fear of the Jews*, no one spoke openly of him.

The phrase "the Jews" gives reason for pause. Since everyone involved is a Jew, this "fear of the Jews" can only refer to the inimical segment of the authorities and not to all the people. This appears clearly in 7:25–26:

> Some of the people of Jerusalem therefore said, "Is not this the man whom *they* seek to kill? And here he is, speaking openly, and *they* say nothing to him! Can it be that *the authorities* really know that this is the Christ?"

This sentence makes a distinction between the "people of Jerusalem" and "the authorities" who were seeking to kill Christ. So throughout this section, the term "the Jews" refers to this hostile group in power.

The discourse, which is here intertwined with the narrative rather than consecutive to it, is composed of an introduction (7: 1–13) followed by seven main dialogues (7:14–24, 25–36, 37–44, 45–52; 8:12–20, 21–30, 31–59).[13] We shall treat of 8:1–11 as an appendix to this entire section.

a) The Setting for the Dialogues (7:1–13)

This introduction establishes the main narrative themes of John 7–8. The liturgical setting for the crisis of decision, the choice for or against Jesus, the constant discussion and debates on him among the people as well as the growing danger from certain of the authorities are all sketched briefly in this opening paragraph. There seems also to be a deliberate symbolism in the secret arrival of Jesus at the temple for the feast, his activity there during the feast, and his departure thereafter. The sequence of secret arrival (7:14), the witness which demands ultimate choice of those who hear it, and the mysterious departure (8:59) show in the narrative realm the mystery of Jesus' secret arrival from the Father, his challenge to the world, and his return to the Father from whence he came. John is warning his Christian audience that it is in liturgical confrontation with their God that they make a commitment for or against the vision of love which has appeared in Jesus of Nazareth.

b) The Seven Dialogues (7:14–8:59)

This is another example of John's preference for the symbolic number seven and his tendency to arrange his material schematically in units thereof. It is also another example of his use of the literary device of reversed parallelism. The seven dialogues

---

[13] For general Jewish background to this complex cf. C. W. F. Smith, "Tabernacles in the Fourth Gospel and Mark," NTS, 9 (1963), 130–146; G. F. Moore, Judaism in the First Centuries of the Christian Era, Vol. II (Cambridge, 1927), pp. 43–49; R. de Vaux, Ancient Israel. Its Life and Institutions (New York, 1961), pp. 495–502. On the theology cf. D. Mollat, "St. John's Conception of Christ's Divinity," Son and Saviour (London, 1960), pp. 113–151. Further discussion of the difficult section in 7:37–39 can be seen in K. H. Kuhn, "St. John vii, 37–38," NTS, 4 (1957), 63–65; J. Blenkinsopp, "John vii, 37–39; Another Note on a Notorious Crux," NTS, 6 (1959), 95–98; S. H. Hooke, " 'The Spirit was not yet,' " NTS, 9 (1963), 372–380.

are mutually related in that 1 and 7, 2 and 6, 3 and 5, relate to one another, and the central dialogue in 4 is a summation of the entire section.

1) *Moses and Jesus* (7:14–24). The theme of the death of Jesus was already announced in the introduction in 7:1. It forms an inclusion between the phrase, "Why do you seek to kill me?" in 7:19, from the first dialogue, and the phrase, "You seek to kill me," in 8:37 and 8:40, from the seventh dialogue. In between these "frames" threatening death to Jesus, there is a constant theme of "arrest" in 7:30, 32, 44, 45; 8:20.

The initial puzzlement is quite harmless. The rabbinical authorities wonder where Jesus studied as they know he had not done so at the schools in Jerusalem. Jesus answers that his knowledge comes from God. The words in 7:21–23 might well connect these discourses with the cure of the cripple in 5:1–9 which happened at an unnamed feast (5:1). Possibly John wanted to separate a single incident and its attendant dispute for purposes of literary construction. It is possible then that John 5 and John 7–8 are based on the same historical occasion. Notice that the crowd (7:20) does not know of the intention of the authorities to kill Jesus and that these authorities are simply referred to as "the Jews" throughout this section. Circumcision was of value because of its symbolic import. Jesus now declares that his cure is far more important than circumcision because of its far more important symbolic value.

2) *The Decision Is Now* (7:25–36). Both the authorities ("the Jews" in 7:15) and "the crowd" (7:20) are present as Jesus teaches. As the crowd ("the people of Jerusalem" in 7:25) begins to wonder if Jesus might be the Messiah, and Jesus as usual refers attention from himself to the One who has sent him, "they," presumably the authorities present, wish to arrest him (7:30); but many of the crowd think he is the Messiah (7:31). These murmurs in the crowd provoke the authorities to send guards to arrest Jesus (7:32), but they are unable to do so, as we shall see later in 7:45–52. Meanwhile Jesus gives them a solemn warning. Very soon he is returning from where he came and they will be unable to find him or to join him (7:33). At this very moment these people confront their ultimate decision, to accept as the center of existence Yahweh revealed in Jesus as a community of love and to structure their lives accordingly, or now to refuse

him and live thereafter having lost the moment of grace. John is telling his own readers that in the moment of their own liturgical confrontation with the risen Lord in the new temple of the new covenant they will face a like decision of similar urgency. Just as the first and seventh dialogues made common mention of those among the authorities who sought to kill Jesus (7:19 = 8:37, 40), so the second and sixth dialogues have the common theme of Jesus' imminent departure and the inability of those who have refused him credence to find him thereafter (7:34 = 8:21). Also, they both contain the statement that "many believed in him." (7:31 = 8:30).

3) *The Offer of Life* (7:37–44). The background to the word of Jesus in 7:37–38 would be the liturgical ritual at the feast of Tabernacles. In this rite libations of water were poured out as a ritual prayer for the gift of rain from God. The background to this rite is in the agricultural origin of the feast in Canaan. The commemoration of the miracle in the desert in Exodus 17:1–7; Numbers 20:8 (cf. Is 48:21; Ps 105:41) was later connected with this ritual as well.

John 7:37–38 is a very important statement that presents three problems: (i) the punctuation of the verses; (ii) the quotation from the Old Testament; (iii) the exact meaning of the words.

i) *The Punctuation of the Verses.* It seems most likely that "he who believes in me" should be punctuated (in the Greek) with the preceding verse and not in its present position. We would thus have a clear case of Semitic parallelism only slightly obscured by the Greek translation. The verses would then read, in parallelism, as follows:

> "If one thirsts, let him come to me,
> and let him drink who believes in me."

When one punctuates after the "in me" one has a typical Johannine parallelism of "come" // "believe" and "thirsts" // "drink." With regard to style, a better expression of this parallelism can be seen in 6:35:

> "He who comes to me shall not hunger,
> and he who believes in me shall never thirst."

There were similar problems with regard to the punctuation of 1:3–4 and 1:9 earlier. This resembles the way in which the parallelism in Matthew 19:29 was not understood as it was handed down and therefore changed in Mark 10:30 and Luke 18:30.

ii) *The Quotation From the Old Testament.* The citation in 7:38b does not appear anywhere in the Bible. If this is not a direct quotation from an extrabiblical book or from one of the Aramaic translations of the Bible, it may simply refer to the spiritual renewal of the temple as envisaged in the prophets, for example, in such texts as Ezekiel 47:1–12, or Zechariah 13:1:

> "On that day there shall be a fountain opened for the house of David and the inhabitants of Jerusalem to cleanse them from sin and uncleanness."

The prophets foresaw this purification and revitalization, symbolized by water, which would be accomplished for God's people on the great future Day of Yahweh, that day now announced as present in Jesus. For the Hebrew, always close to the desert, water denoted life and so became a symbol thereof. New life, revitalization and renewal, consummation and fulfillment, were all aptly expressed by the image of streams of pure water. Jesus would thus be referring the words to himself and saying that he is the purification of the temple, the source of the waters which symbolized the outpouring of God's Spirit.

iii) *The Exact Meaning of the Words.* In 7:37–38, as explained above, Jesus states that the awaited revitalization of God's people has been accomplished by himself. But now it was happening only in promise and symbol, in the divine beginning and initiation. This is the meaning of the comment in 7:39. Only after death consummated his life's witness and the resurrection made him abidingly present to all future history would the total renewal be accomplished. The presence of the Spirit means the force of God's presence now fully revealed and efficaciously confronting mankind forever through the risen Christ. The term "glorification" denotes external manifestation. John terms the death of Christ his glorification because it manifests externally what he is. He is the perfect sign of God's love, the man of total love and absolute commitment to the needs of others. At the end of the third dialogue the crowd is divided with regard to Jesus (7:43). It would seem that 7:44 refers to the guards of the Pharisees sent to arrest Jesus and waiting in the crowd for the chance to do so (7:32, 45–46). It can hardly be that some of the

crowd themselves want to do the arresting. The third dialogue
has as its liturgical background the water ritual of the feast of
Tabernacles. Instead of the natural water which begets life,
Jesus promises the Spirit which gives eternal life. The offer of life
in the third dialogue (7:37–44) is, of course, completed by the
offer of light in the fifth dialogue (8:12–20). Ever since the inaugural announcement in 1:4 the themes of life and light go
always hand in hand for John. To have life may be sufficient for
the individual, but to have it in articulate self-conscious understanding of the gift of God (life) is to be able to witness God's
being to others (light). It means knowing that and how and
why one receives life: that to live means dwelling in a community of love here on earth since God is from all eternity and for
all eternity a community of love.

4) *Division Among the Authorities* (7:45–52). Throughout
John 7–8 the focus has been on the element of decision. The
people argue and discuss, agree and disagree, debate and conclude — and many believe in him. "The Jews" represent the
forces in authority which are against Jesus and which he himself
bitingly reproaches. But in the central dialogue John indicates
that even among the authorities there was a division with regard
to Jesus (cf. 12:42–43). It is Nicodemus, whom we met in the
first sign-complex (3:1–13) and whom we shall meet again, at
least in symbolic promise, in the seventh (12:3, 7, and 19:39),
who speaks out against the intentions of those in authority who
oppose Jesus. The central dialogue thus sums up the tension of
the debate — even the authorities themselves are divided about
Jesus.

5) *The Offer of Light* (8:12–20). Recall that the ritual of
water (= life) at the feast of Tabernacles was the backdrop to
the third dialogue (7:37–44). Here again the ritual of lighting
great golden lamps (= light) in the court of the temple during
the same feast would form the liturgical background to Jesus'
offer in the fifth dialogue. Both rituals, and indeed the very
temple itself (2:13–22; 4:19–26), reach their destined fulfillment
in Jesus as the perfect presence of God. In the community which
would grow around his risen existence, God would dwell with
mankind forever, neither in one place alone nor in one symbol
only, but signed and externally symbolized by that community's
love for all mankind.

The symbol of light had become associated with the great future moment of eschatological or messianic salvation since it recalled the pillar of fire which had led the Israelites through the desert toward the promised land (Ex 13:21; Wis 18:3–4; cf. Is 9:1–2; 42:6; 49:6). The Pharisees try to catch him on a legal quibble. They object that he is bearing witness to himself (8:13). Jesus replies that, in any case, there is no possibility of a second human witness corroborating his statements. He comes from God and there is no human check on what he says or does. But even with regard to the legal prescription of Deuteronomy 19:15 which demanded two witnesses, he acts according to the law. The Father is his second witness and he corroborates both the words and deeds of Jesus. After the central episode in 7:45–52 the crowd is no longer on the other side of the dialogue with Jesus. Now those among the authorities who oppose him are in dispute with Jesus (8:13, 22, 48, 52, 57). As mentioned before, the meaning of "the Jews" which is so clear in John 7–8 must always be remembered when reading this Gospel.

It was suggested earlier that the unnamed feast of 5:1 might well be the same as the feast of Tabernacles in 7:2. Besides the contact of 7:23 with 5:1–9, there is another connection between 8:12–20 and 5:31–47. It is possible that John has divided between Chapter 5 and Chapters 7 and 8 events of one feast at Jerusalem. It would seem that Jesus was willing to accept the testimony of the Baptist in 5:31–47 because it was to the Messiah. But here he and the Father alone can testify since the testimony is to the ultimate presence of God in Jesus, to the divinity of the Word.

6) *The Decision Is Now* (8:21–30). As previously in the corresponding second dialogue (7:25–36), Jesus again emphasizes the short time left for his generation to make its decision. He is soon to depart, neither by travel (7:35–36) nor by suicide (8:22), but to God, and by being "lifted up" upon the cross. The term "lifted up" is of some interest. The Greek verb *hypsoō* is usually used for "to exalt" as distinct from "to humble" (cf. Mt 11:23). In the New Testament it is sometimes used in a more theological sense to mean the ascension, the glorification of the risen Lord (Acts 2:33; 5:31; Phil 2:9). But in John this same word is used of the passion itself. Jesus is elevated, enthroned on the cross (3:14; 8:28; 12:32, 34). For John the cross is glory

because it reveals most fully what God is, and it is then the crucified One who remains ever before the world in risen splendor (cf. 20:24–29; Ap 5:6). This mention of the cross moves the sixth dialogue beyond the second, but apart from this the main points are the same in each case. Jesus has come from the Father (7:29; 8:23–26). Jesus now returns to the Father from whom he came (7:33; 8:21). Those who do not believe will not now, nor ever, join him there; cf. 13:33; 14:3 (7:34; 8:21, 24).

7) *Abraham and Jesus* (8:31–59). John has used special care in constructing this last of the seven dialogues. Jesus speaks seven times: in 8:31–32, 34–38, 39b–41a, 42–47, 49–51, 54–56, 58. The forces among the authorities who are opposing him also speak seven times. They reply to him in 8:33, 39a, 41b, 48, 52–53, 57, and their seventh and last reply appears in 8:59: "So they took up stones to throw at him; but Jesus hid himself, and went out of the Temple."

In the opening dialogue Jesus compared himself with Moses, and in the final one he compares himself with Abraham. He announces himself as the real fulfillment of the joy which Abraham felt at the birth of Isaac in Genesis 17:17; 21:6. This was only a symbol of the great future joy to come in the arrival of the true heir to the promises made to Abraham (Gn 12:1–3). By the end of the discourse the authorities quite correctly discern that Jesus is making divine claims and they are going to stone him according to the law (Lv 24:16).

c) Appendix: The Woman Taken in Adultery (8:1–11)

This narrative is not found in its present position in the most ancient Greek manuscripts or in a large number of the ancient translations. In other manuscripts it appears marked with an asterisk. In still others it appears after Luke 21:38, or at the end of the Gospel of John, or after John 7:36 or 7:44. Most of the Greek Fathers do not know of its existence. It is also clear that this section breaks the carefully constructed unity of John 7–8 as outlined above. Accordingly, it seems certain that it did not pertain originally to its present position in John. The story fits well against the background of the last week in Jerusalem when Jesus went back outside the city for safety each night and only returned there in the morning (cf. 8:1 and Mark 11:11–12,

19–20, 27; 13:1–3). The narrative is part of the inspired record of the Gospel and it most likely originally belonged to Luke. The manuscripts clearly show that they know it belongs somewhere but are uncertain of its exact location.

The action of Jesus in 8:6, 8 is difficult to understand. It has been taken to mean that he is not concerned with the case; that he intends to doodle his disinterest on the ground. This is not, however, Jesus' usual way of handling these trick questions which are so calculated that no matter what decision is given somebody will be annoyed or displeased with him, as for example in Mark 12:13–17 or Matthew 19:3–9. It may be that we have here an allusion to the statement in Jeremiah 17:13 that those who turn away from God have their names written in the earth: that is, they shall not last, their names shall be obliterated like writing on sand. This would mean that Jesus accuses the accusers of being such as have turned away from God.

6. The Promise of Light

Read John 9:1–10:42

In the structure of reversed parallelism in which John has constructed his Gospel this fifth sign-complex (9:1–10:39) corresponds in position to the third one, seen earlier (6:1–71). In that earlier unit Jesus had promised mankind the gift of eternal life and found those who accepted his offer and also those who turned away in misunderstanding. In the present section Jesus offers his people light, and again the same tension ensues, but the polemical edge is now much more pronounced. The authorities who are opposing Jesus are seriously indicted for leading the people astray. They are not only culpably blind themselves but seek to take the light from others. In the overall development of the Gospel, this episode adds to what has gone before: a solemn warning to those who would mislead the flock of God's people. It concerns itself not only with the crisis of decision before the *life* and the *light* offered to the world in Jesus, but most especially with the responsibility of those in authority who would misdirect others in their own decision.

The complex consists of the customary illustrative narrative (9:1–38) followed by interpretative discourse (9:38–10:39). The narrative tells of the cure of the man born blind (9:1–7), to whom Jesus gives light, and of the immediate attack of the authorities opposing Jesus against the cured man (9:8–38). It is almost an attempt to undo and negate Jesus' work. The discourse opens in 9:39–41 as Jesus separates clearly those of the Pharisees who oppose him from those of the crowd who are accepting him. The discourse continues through three originally independent sections related by the common imagery of the flock of God's people, and here placed together in one long discourse (10:1–10, 11–21, 22–39). The imagery changes, but the original theme of light still persists (10:21). The main point, however, is what Jesus will do for the flock of God as opposed to what certain of the authorities are doing to it. Since these men do not work through him (10:1–10), they can only destroy where he would save (10:11–21), and they do this because they are actually themselves no longer belonging to God's flock (10:22–39). One must abandon such false leaders (10:40–42).

a) Healing and Judgment (9:1–38)

The narrative extends from the healing itself (9:1–7), through the dialogue of the cured man with his neighbors (9:8–12), with the authorities (9:13–34), and finally, with Jesus himself (9:35–38). It begins with the gift of sight (9:7) and is consummated in the gift of faith (9:38a). It is this human being, restored to full humanity and complete being, who then worships God in Jesus (9:38b).

1) 9:1–7. Jesus, like Job (42:7) long before him, repudiated the simple assumption that personal sickness meant personal sin; or, since this would hardly explain congenital disease, that sickness came from parental sin. There is a relationship between disease and all the disasters and disorders of God's world on the one hand, and man's sin on the other; but it is not quite so simple as this. As man refuses to accept his God-given place in evolution, and refuses to subdue the earth by taking dominion over its evolutionary thrust out of love for his fellows (Gn 1:26–28), this lack of concern for the pain and anguish of others renders him guilty for its continuance. Judgment is passed on mankind in Matthew 25 according to the criteria of love (31–40) and unconcern (41–46), not merely love and hate. So blindness, for example, stands in our world as a challenge to our con-

cern and love for others, that, by destroying it from God's world, we show forth the kingdom Jesus inaugurated. He did it in his way, and we do it in our way — when and if we care enough about it. This is not to say that sight is more important than faith, but that the kingdom comes in both, when both are the gifts of love.

There is obvious baptismal symbolism in the cure as narrated in the early Church. Jesus' power as "the Sent" of God is communicated to the waters of baptism here symbolized by the pool in Jerusalem whose Hebrew name means "sent."

2) 9:8–12. The neighbors of the cured man are shown to be as blind as he is. They do not even recognize him for certain (9:8). The blind man himself does not as yet know where Jesus is (9:12), just as the paralytic in 5:12–13 did not know who Jesus was. The neighbors realize their blindness, they question and ask; their guilt is thus less than that of the authorities, as will be made evident in 9:41.

3) 9:13–34. This ironic satire on the the attempts of the Pharisees is itself structured in three sections: the authorities and the cured man (9:13–17); the authorities and his parents (9:18–23); and the authorities with the cured man again (9:24–34). In both cases the man insists that Jesus must be from God (9:17–33). The final interrogation has a sevenfold dialogue between the Pharisees (9:24, 26, 28–29, 34) and the cured man (9:25, 27, 30–33). Notice how the text changes back and forth between "the Pharisees" (9:13, 15, 16) and "the Jews" (9:18, 22). Once again "the Jews" denote only those among the authorities opposing Jesus. After mentioning a division among "the Pharisees" concerning Jesus in 9:16 (cf. 7:45–52; 12:42–43), those who continued the attack are thereafter termed simply "the Jews." In 9:40 Jesus will sternly warn "the Pharisees" about what they are attempting to do.

In the mind of John there is probably a developing climax of confession from, "He is a prophet" in 9:17, to the "Christ" of 9:22, to the "from God" of 9:33. Jesus is not just a prophet, and not just the Messiah, but in him God is irrevocably present to mankind.

4) 9:35–38. The term "Son of God" was originally a term for any member of the people of God as a component of that people which was itself the chosen child of Yahweh. As such,

but with special emphasis, it was used for the Davidic monarch as the repository of God's promises in 2 Samuel 7:14. But most especially and preeminently was it the title of the Messiah, and as such it is often used of Jesus in the Gospel. By the time this phrase was recorded in the writing of John the term meant much more — Jesus was the ultimate presence of God, the final revelation of the divinity to mankind. Through the gift of sight (9:7) as an act of merciful concern and gracious love for another's human need, Jesus has opened to the man the revelation of God as total concern and absolute love. The man can now make an act of faith for he knows what God is and recognizes in Jesus the One sent from God.

b) The Meaning of Judgment (9:39–10:42)

In the narrative section (9:1–38) the man who received sight and faith was caught between two contending forces. He became a battleground between the kindness of Jesus and the opposition of a certain segment of the authorities. The discourse (9:39–10:42) intends to bring out clearly the implications of this for all God's people.

1) 9:39–41. The key verse to the artificially composed discourse in 9:39–10:42 is in 9:39–41. But at this point it is necessary to review certain of the statements Jesus has made with regard to "judgment."

> For God sent the Son into the world, not to judge the world, but that the world might be saved through him (3:17).

> The Father judges no one, but has given all judgment to the Son (5:22).

> ". . . I judge no one. Yet even if I do judge, my judgment is true, for it is not I alone that judge, but I and he who sent me" (8:15–16).

> "For judgment I came into this world, that those who do not see may see, and that those who see may become blind" (9:39).

These are obviously existential statements. Jesus was sent to save, not to judge, i.e., to condemn, the world (3:17). But insofar as judgment is necessary, it now resides in his person alone (5:22). Jesus himself does not judge anyone, even though he could do so

(8:16); it is they who judge themselves by their refusal of love (cf. 3:16–21). To those who resolutely oppose him, and thereby lose the revelation that God is a community of love, and negate the call to a life in union with God by living on earth in a sacramental community of love, Jesus has, in fact, through their own fault, come as judgment (9:39).

The Synoptics had often spoken of "the last being first and the first last." In 9:39, John rephrases this statement in his own typical language. The ordinary people, often dismissed as mere sinners by some among the Pharisees because of their inability to obey all the traditional interpretations of the law (7:49; 9:34), are entering the kingdom, while the spiritual authorities, who should be the first to enter, are frequently failing to do so (cf. Lk 7:29–30). But it is worse than this. Because of their position of spiritual authority over God's people, they are frequently able to hinder others from finding faith in Jesus and from seeing in him the fulfillment and the consummation of Israel's ancient destiny. It is those who say, "we see," that bear a terrible burden of responsibility. In the continuing discourse Jesus compares the people of God to a flock, a traditional Old Testament image, and discusses his relationship to this flock of God in comparison with that of the spiritual authorities who are opposing him and preventing many of God's people from finding faith in him.[14]

2) *10:1–10.* In the first sheep-image Jesus represents himself as "the door" (10:7) through whom and through whom alone the true shepherds can approach God's flock. He represents the Pharisees who are opposing him, and who have attacked the man to whom he gave salvation, as "thieves and robbers" (10:1,8) who can but destroy the flock of God's people because their understanding of salvation is false. This image is wider than the following one in 10:11–18 in that it envisages others who can lead God's flock in the name of Christ. Possibly the apostles were intended by this (cf. 21:15–17).

3) *10:11–21.* In this second sheep-image Jesus is the "true

---

[14] J. Quasten, "The Parable of the Good Shepherd: Jn 10, 1–21," CBQ, 10 (1948), 1–12, 151–169; F. Gryglewicz, "Breaking of the Contract of Work as mentioned in the Gospels," Scr, 7 (1955), 109–112; D. M. Stanley " 'I am the Good Shepherd,' " Worship, 35 (1961), 287–293; J. E. Bruns, "The Discourse on the Good Shepherd and the Rite of Ordination," AER, 149 (1963), 386–391. On the feast in 10:22 cf. R. de Vaux, Ancient Israel. Its Life and Institutions (New York, 1961), pp. 510–514.

shepherd" and those opposing him among the spiritual authorities of Israel are false shepherds. The background to the parable appears in Ezekiel 34. This prophetic indictment attacked the leaders of Israel for having ruined God's flock:

> "The weak you have not strengthened, the sick you have not healed, the crippled you have not bound up, the strayed you have not brought back, the lost you have not sought, and with force and harshness you have ruled them. So they were scattered, because there was no shepherd; and they became food for all the wild beasts" (34:4–5).

Because of their infidelity Yahweh himself would become the shepherd of his flock (34:11, 15; cf. Is 40:11; Jer 31:10), and the restored and purified Davidic dynasty would work God's will for his people (34:23). Jesus now declares himself to be the fulfillment of this prophetic promise. In him God returns to gather his scattered flock. Jesus is both the restored throne of David and the ultimate, or eschatological, salvific presence of God.

The concluding statement in 10:19–21, which links directly back to the cure of the blind man (10:21), involves an accusation by "many" of "the Jews" that Jesus was possessed. This attack came from among the spiritual authorities in the Synoptic tradition of Mark 3:22 and Matthew 12:24, although Luke 11:15 simply uses "the crowds" and deletes the specific designation to the authorities. This happens frequently in Luke since his Gentile audience would not have understood the more precise names such as Scribes, Pharisees, Sadducees. Compare, for example, Matthew 3:7–10 with Luke 3:7–9; or Mark 8:11–12; Matthew 12:38–40 and 16:1b, 4 with Luke 11:29–30; or again Matthew 16:1a, 2–3 with Luke 12:54–56. Like the use of "the Jews" in John, this use of "the crowds" in Luke can become very dangerous for the modern reader who may easily misinterpret these phrases to mean that all the people, or even the majority of the people, were against Jesus.

4) 10:22–42. This third section has been appended here because of the common sheep-image in 10:26–28. The debate with the hostile members of the authorities continues. These are "the Jews" (10:24, 31, 33) who appear here in the usual inimical Johannine sense. But again, of course, John notes that many of the people believed in him (10:41–42). The liturgical setting

for the debate is the feast of the Dedication of the Purified Temple by Judas Maccabee (1 Mc 4:36–59; 2 Mc 1:1–2:18; 10:1–8). This was closely modelled on the feast of Tabernacles and centered on illumination, hence it was also called the feast of Lights. The association with the preceding feast is clear; on both occasions Jesus uses the liturgy of the festival to explain his own challenge: he is the true light of the world, and he is the one who will guide his own sheep to life.

The authorities open the debate with the demand that Jesus tell them if he claims to be the Messiah (10:24). Instead of answering in the affirmative, Jesus tells them that they are not of his sheep (10:26), and that, far above messiahship, he and the Father are one (10:30). Since he is talking to theologians they must realize immediately the implications of his claim (10:31). Jesus however tries to explain his words to them in terms they can understand; he thus cites Psalm 82:6 in 10:34.

The text of Psalm 82 would no doubt have been applied to Israel's rulers who betrayed their trust by lack of concern for the needy and defenseless (82:2–4). They will therefore be punished by God even though, because of their special mission, he could address them, "you are gods." But just as Jesus fulfilled the role of the true shepherd replacing the evil shepherds of Ezekiel 34 in 10:11–21, so now he is the true "Son of God" replacing the evil "gods" of Psalm 82. His truth appears not only in his words but more formally in the works of concern and love, of mercy and forgiveness, of compassion and response for the needy and the poor. His actions are diametrically opposed to those of the bad "shepherds" in Ezekiel 34:4–6 as seen already, and to those of the bad "gods" of Psalm 82:2–4:

> "How long will you judge unjustly
> and show partiality to the wicked?
> Give justice to the weak and the fatherless;
> maintain the right of the afflicted and the destitute.
> Rescue the weak and the needy;
> deliver them from the hand of the wicked."

Jesus' acts of loving kindness are precisely those acts of Yahweh promised by the prophets to God's people on the great future Day of the Lord. Therefore, Jesus challenges them in 10:37–38:

> "If I am not doing the works of my Father, then do not believe me; but if I do them, even though you do not believe me, be-

lieve the works, that you may know and understand that the
Father is in me and I am in the Father."

Jesus does not argue that he is of God and therefore can perform
miracles. He argues that he is of the God who is love and concern, and therefore all his actions are acts of love and concern
for others. The Christian may only speak in similar challenge
before unbelief; if we perform the works of love, believe us;
if we do not, ignore us. Words are easy both to speak and to
dismiss; but the kingdom of God and the gift of eternal life
come in works of love for others and remain abidingly in such.

7. The Victory Over Death

Read John 11:1-54.

Within the total construction of the Gospel this sign-complex
(11:1-54) corresponds in content and position to the second one
(4:43-5:47). In both, the emphasis is on the victory of life
over death in and through Jesus the Lord. In the former complex
Jesus gives life to the ruler's son and to the paralytic (4:43-5:9),
and then explains that all life, and all death likewise, is in his
hands alone (5:10-47). The same point is made here but with
some further development. First of all, the polemical overtones
are more explicit, and the danger of death for Jesus is much
more proximate. Jesus comes from "outside" (11:1-16), and at
the risk of his own life, and indeed at the cost of it (11:46-53),
gives eternal life to the dead; he then returns to "outside"
(11:54-57). Second, the message of 5:24-30 is summed up even
more succinctly in 11:25, where Jesus declares that the man who
has believed in him here on earth, "though he die, yet shall he
live," for death cannot break the bonds between the person (the
"he") and God. There is thus a greater note of urgency, of
heightened tension and expectancy throughout this episode, as in
all the narratives after the central crisis of John 7-8.

The general structure of 11:1-54 is similar to that of John 7-8
in that there is not a successive distinction of narrative and discourse but the two are inextricably intertwined. Their relative
function is the same as is all the other sign-complexes in John:
the narrative exemplifies what the discourse explains. There is,
however, another and more detailed similarity between these two

complexes, but with regard to form not content. John 7–8 was composed of an introduction (7:1–13) followed by seven dialogues (7:14–8:59). John 11 has a similar structure of introduction (11:1–4) and seven dialogues (11:5–44), and then an epilogue (11:45–57). The full outline of the structure is as follows:

Prologue: (11:1–4).
Dialogue 1: Jesus and Disciples (11:5–16) .
Dialogue 2: Jesus and Martha (11:17–27).
Dialogue 3: Jesus and Mary (11:28–32).
Dialogue 4: Jesus and the Jews (11:33–37).
Dialogue 5: Jesus and Martha (11:38–41a).
Dialogue 6: Jesus and the Father (11:41b–42).
Dialogue 7: Jesus and Lazarus (11:43–44).
Epilogue: 11:45–57.

a) Prologue (11:1–4)

The symbolic depths of the incident are indicated in the phrasing of this prologue. The one whom Jesus loves does not really die (11:3). Indeed, Jesus prefers to describe the death of such a believer as "sleep" (11:11), and only the lack of understanding on the part of his disciples reluctantly forces him to use the term "dead" (11:14). But even death, indeed death more than all else, challenges man to faith and compels him to face the ultimate questions of human existence and cosmic destiny (11:4, 15).

b) The Seven Dialogues (11:5–44)

The seven dialogues proceed in ever shortening length from the first long interchange between Jesus and his disciples in 11:5–16 to the terse command of Jesus to the dead Lazarus in 11:43–44.

1) 11:5–16. In the first dialogue, in characteristic Johannine fashion, there is a sevenfold interchange of words between Jesus and his disciples. This is a deliberate stylistic device to open the seven dialogues in a more solemn fashion. It is not mere coincidence as can be seen from the fact that John is forced to use the awkward 11:11a: "Thus he spoke, and then he said to them," in order to make up the full number seven. Jesus speaks four times, in 11:7, 9–10, 11, 14–15; the disciples three times, in 11:8, 12, 16. Their last and final statement is that of Thomas offering to die with Jesus. The symbolism of "he stayed two days" (11:6) is also clear especially since the same note was struck already in 4:43 (and cf. 2:1) in the second sign-complex which paralleled the present one. Mankind, like Lazarus, receives power from Jesus only on the third day, only through his own resurrectional efficacy. Only after the resurrection releases the salvific power of God upon the world can that world find eternal life and complete resurrection of all that constitutes the "I" confronting forever the "Thou" of God. It is also only after this resurrection that the apostles are able and ready to go forth with Jesus in witness to his life by their life and to his death by their own. Our attention is drawn to this Johannine symbolism in 11:6, 17 by the statement that Jesus loved the sick man and yet deliberately waited two days so that his response would come on the third day (11:5).

2) *11:17–27.* The statement of Martha in 11:21, reiterated by Mary in 11:32, is also of symbolic import. Where Jesus is, there is no death; who is with Jesus does not die. These two assertions serve as a frame for Jesus' own claim in 11:25. Martha confesses her faith in the resurrection at the end of the world. Jesus' own statement must certainly go beyond this point of Jewish faith, and it is quite unclear if we have as yet plumbed its depths. He declares that he himself is the resurrection and that whoever believes in him cannot be touched by what is ordinarily termed physical death; he lives on with God.

3) *11:28–32.* Mary repeats the faith of Martha but in the presence of others. Notice the difference between "the Jews" in 11:19, 31, 33, 44, which is the ordinary meaning of the word, as compared with the special Johannine usage in 11:8, 54.

4) *11:33–37.* The question of 11:37 is the beginning of the faith of 11:45. Jesus can both open the eyes of blindness and also, as a result of that, assure the man eternal life.

5) *11:38–41a.* Lazarus had been dead for four days since he would have been buried on the day of death (11:17; cf. Acts 5:6, 10). The death probably occurred even as the sisters were seeking Jesus' aid (11:3).

6) *11:41b–42.* The actions of Jesus, works of mercy and love,

are the gifts of the Father and show forth the inner nature of God. This is constantly stressed, in 5:19, 30, 36; 9:3; 10:32, 37–38; 14:10.

7) *11:43–44.* The final dialogue is very brief. Jesus commands Lazarus to come forth, and the dead man comes forth.

c) Epilogue (11:45–57)

Tension between Jesus and the authorities now reaches breaking point, mainly because of the preceding event so close to Jersualem itself (11:18). At a meeting of the Sanhedrin it is decided that Jesus must die lest he inaugurate a messianic revolt and bring destruction on temple and people alike. We know this verdict was not unanimous from 12:42–43; 19:38–39, and especially Luke 23:50–51. But as one approaches the pinnacle of any power structure, numbers become increasingly unnecessary to obtain results. After this decision Jesus has to remain away from their power and reach, no longer among "the Jews," although of course he is still among the Jewish people.

8. The Challenge to Rebirth

Read John 12:1–36.

In the first sign-complex in 1:19–4:42 the emphasis was on the necessity for man to accept in Jesus his place in the new creation centered on a new temple. This was illustrated and explained as new life, as rebirth from life which was really death, from that unlife which was lived unconcern and continued unlove. In the final sign-complex in 12:1–36, this theme is again repeated but with almost total emphasis on Jesus alone. Jesus must now himself, and must now first, and must now alone break through death into full and perfect resurrected triumph. Only through his risen rebirth is ours made possible. For the world could have seen his life as works of concern and love, of total and absolute response to the plea of human need and personal pain and still ask one damning question — what if he had to do all this at the price of his own life? The challenge of Jesus' life could find only one consummation — in death freely accepted as ultimate witness. Thereafter the resurrection, the return of Jesus to confront the world in the power of God's Spirit, would hold forever this life and death, these works crowned by the last work, these words crowned by forgiveness for one's murderers, before mankind not just as a life but as the only possible life, the only salvation, the only authentic human existence. Only after this is there any harvest (12:24), any hope for others (12:36).

The complex is composed of narrative succeeded by interpretative discourse. The narrative is composed of three events whose juxtaposition in sequence establishes the point. The anointing at Bethany brings up the subject of Jesus' death (12:1–11). This is followed by a vision of acclaim and glory as Jesus enters Jerusalem (12:12–16). Finally, the narrative notes how both Jews (12:17–18) and Greeks (12:20–22) are listening to him, and the Pharisees make the central comment which brings out the point: "the world has gone after him" (12:19). Then follows the discourse section which explains the meeting of this sequence of death, glory, cosmic faith (12:23–36). This is structured in typical Johannine fashion with seven speakers: Jesus (23–28a), the Voice (28b), the crowd (29a), others (29b), Jesus (30–32), the crowd (34), Jesus (35–36a).

a) The Advent of Death (Jn 12:1–11)

Both Mark 14:3–9 and Matthew 26:6–13 speak of an anointing of Jesus at Bethany, but upon the head. This would seem more appropriate at a banquet situation where the sweet-smelling ointment would perfume the long hair and beard of the person involved. In Luke 7:36–50 there is a similar incident concerning Jesus and a woman at a banquet. The repentant sinner falls at his feet and, having shed tears of gratitude upon them, wipes them dry with her loosened hair. She then anoints them. The incident in John 12:1–11 speaks of Mary of Bethany (11:1–2) who anointed his feet (not his head) and wiped off the ointment (not her tears) with her hair. This latter action seems somewhat incredible both with regard to propriety and to hygiene. It is more likely that there has been some confusion of details between the Lucan and Johannine traditions of two quite separate but similar events: an unnamed sinner wipes with her loosened hair tears of repentant gratitude from Jesus' feet in Galilee, and Mary graciously anoints his head at Bethany. The anointing with perfume in Luke really belongs only to the incident in Mark, Matthew, and John. The wiping with hair belongs only to Luke and not to John. Thus John agrees with Mark and Matthew but names the woman (12:3) and also the disciple who objected to the act, Judas (12:4).[15] Mary's ointment and Judas' money are alike warnings of impending doom. The value of the action, besides the graciousness of its hospitality, was in its prophetic down payment on the enbalming of Jesus' body after death, all too soon to follow (19:39-40). There is a similar prophetic sign in Acts 21:10-11.

The words in 12:9-11 are transitional but connect with 12:17-18. Notice the reversed statement: they come to Jesus to see Lazarus (12:9) — and they come to Lazarus to believe in Jesus (12:11). This highlights the impossibility of killing Jesus, for in order to do so it is necessary to kill every Lazarus as well, that is, every believer, every man who commits himself to total love (12:10).

b) The Promise of Glory (12:12-16)

In 12:1-11 the anointing at the banquet was explicitly connected to the anointing of death (12:7). So also here, the moment of glory at the entry into Jerusalem is explicitly associated with the great glorification to follow (12:16). The citation in 12:14-15 refers to the prophetic vision of the Messiah as a humble king in Zechariah 9:9. The glory of Jesus is that of the king of peace.

c) The Faith of the World (12:17-22)

After the promise of death and glory comes the vision of the harvest of both Jews (12:17-18) and Gentiles (12:20-22). Despite all the opposition of those in authority, they must themselves admit: "the world has gone after him" (12:19). With his usual

---

[15] The relationship between the Synoptic and Johannine accounts are discussed in R. C. Fuller, "The Anointing of Christ in Luke vii." *Scr*, 4 (1949), 90-91; A. Legault, "An Application of the Form-Critique Method to the Anointing in Galilee and Bethany," *CBQ*, 16 (1954), 131-145; J. J. Donohue, "The Penitent Woman and the Pharisee: Luke 7, 36-50," *AER*, 142 (1960), 414-421.

symbolical subtlety John now brings the narrative full cycle. At the heart of the new creation in 1:35–42, Andrew and another disciple had accepted Jesus and brought to him Simon-Peter who would later sum up Israel's faith by his credal statement in 6:68–69. Now, as the writing looks to "the other sheep, that are not of this fold" (10:16), it is again Andrew, together now with Philip, who brings the Gentiles to meet Jesus. The "seeing" of 1:38–39 has broadened out in promise to the entire universe in 12:21.

d) The Price of Victory (12:23–36)

Throughout this dialogue Jesus moves three times from a consideration of his own impending consummation to what it will obtain for all mankind (12:23–26, 27–33, 34–36). Jesus had to lose his own life in order to refind it in glory, and so must all mankind. They can only attain full human existence in complete dedication to love even when that costs bodily destruction (12:23–26). The Father will now "glorify his name," that is, reveal his own inner being as love and concern for mankind through Jesus' own love and concern even unto death. At the "lifting up" Jesus will draw all men into true and eternal life (12:27–33). Using another favorite image, Jesus gives man light, gives him clear, explicit, articulate knowledge and power for life's realization in total love. His own generation must accept this light while it confronts them and becomes themselves a light for the insecurity and uncertainty and anxiety of others. They must do so while time still waits for them, as we must while it stands still for our decision (12:33–36a). Afterwards, Jesus is hidden from them and from us and it may be too late (12:36b).

9. Summary and Sorrow

Read John 12:37–50.

These verses serve as an epilogue to the entire preceding section in 1:19–12:36 by summing up in sorrow their dominant themes. John cites a favorite text from the early Church's understanding of itself. Isaiah's prophetic vocation had been given him even though Israel would not accept his witness (Is 6:9–10). So also many did not accept Jesus. John is very fair in his summary.

"Even" among the authorities many believed in him but were afraid to be cast out of the synagogue — no mean threat for an honest Israelite. As one finishes these verses one wonders when the real break came between Judaism and Christianity. The ordinary people and many of their leaders were on the side of Jesus, not only before his death (Mk 11:18; 12:12, 37; 14:1–2), but even after it (Acts 2:41, 46, 47; 3:11; 4:4, 33; 5:13–14; 8:12; 9:31; 21:20), although some highly placed authorities opposed him from start (Mk 2:1–3:6) to finish (Jn 11:47–53) and even afterwards (Acts 4:1–22; 5:17, 26, 28; 6:8–8:3; 12:1–24). When did the final break occur, and if this took place *within* the people of God, did not both Judaism and Christianity suffer therefrom, then and now?[16]

In 12:44–50 John has Jesus utter a last desperate cry to his own generation, the archetypal community of both acceptance and refusal. In Jesus, God opens to mankind light in which to know fully and completely the meaning of his destiny here and hereafter (12:44–47). This vision was given for man's salvation, but, since it confronts him in his own freedom, he can either accept it and receive salvation, or reject it and receive judgment (12:48–49). In this acceptance of the light, man finds, and finds there alone, eternal life, true and authentic human existence here and hereafter, that is, life within a community of concern and love which climactically externalizes the being of God as community of concern and love.

10. The Consummation of the Gift

In the seven sign-complexes of 1:19–12:36, the works always preceded the words, or were concomitant with them; they never followed them. But now the last great work approaches and if there are to be words to explain it they must precede it, for afterwards Jesus will speak to believers only in the Spirit. Therefore, in the structure of the final eschatological sign-complex of

---

[16] R. Kugelman, "Hebrew, Israelite, Jew in the New Testament," *The Bridge*, ed. J. M. Oesterreicher, Vol. I ("A Yearbook of Judaeo-Christian Studies"; New York, 1955), pp. 204–224; G. Baum, *The Jews and the Gospel* (Westminster, 1961); J. Isaac, *The Teaching of Contempt: Christian Roots of Anti-Semitism* (New York, 1964); D. M. Crossan, "Anti-Semitism and the Gospel," *TS*, 26 (1965), 189–214, and the critical comments on this, *ibid.*, pp. 663–671.

John 13–20, the paschal supper discourse of Jesus (13–17), precedes the narrative (18–20). The function of this discourse is to
assemble together into one place all the words which explain the
passion, the resurrection, the gift of the Spirit, and the future of
the community, which he recounts in the succeding narrative.
Like Jacob in Genesis 49, or Moses in Deuteronomy 33, Jesus,
before his consummation, looks through and beyond that event
in a long and ultimate dialogue with human history. He begins in
discussion with Peter and Judas primarily (13:1–35), then talks
to the apostles in general (13:36–16:33), and concludes in solemn
dialogue with his Father (17:1–26). After this explanatory discourse the narrative recounts the consummation of Jesus' destiny
and Jesus' witness to mankind in the passion (18:1–19:42), the
resurrection (20:1–10), the ascension (20:11–18), the gift of the
Spirit (20:19–23), and the closing vision of the community's
ongoing faith (20:24–31).

a) The Words of Consummation

Read John 13:1–17, 26.

The characteristic Johannine movement from dialogue into
monologue appears again in the artificial structure of 13–17. In
this instance, however, the ultimate monologue will no longer
take place between Jesus and mankind but between Jesus and
his Father; and the subject will be the future of history.

The opening verse in 13:1 requires special attention. It is not
merely a preface to 13:2–35, which has its own preface in 13:2–3,
but rather the key statement for all of John 13–20. The passion
is the last great act of Jesus' love, the act which consummates
beyond discussion or argument his life of total and absolute
response to human pain, and to the destruction of evil in all its
manifestations. This act completes God's attempt to force the
beachhead of the kingdom onto the reluctant sands of human
time. This is love "to the end." Never again can anyone ask how
far must one go in response to another's need. The answer has
already been given, the challenge already declared. Once there
was upon our earth a man who was wholly God, and whom we
therefore saw as infinite love, mankind could never be the same
again — either for judgment or for salvation. On all previous

levels of God's evolutionary process, beings could fail to adjust to their environment and so cease to take part in the onward thrust of its movement. Mankind, as free consciousness, can not only fail but even refuse to accept the divine milieu of love in which he alone has a future, can refuse this environment made radiantly clear to him in Jesus, but he can do so only at the price of personal destruction here and hereafter. In John's symbolic theology the seven sign-complexes of 1:19–12:36, which were down payments on man's future, reached their climax in the last and eighth sign-complex of John 13–20. Thereafter God rests his case.

There is a very significant change in terminology between John 1–12 and 13–20. Terms such as "life; to live; to give life" appear fifty times in 1–12 but only six times in 13–20; and "light; to light" appear twenty-four times in 1–12 but not at all in 13–20. On the other hand, the words "love; to love" are used six times in 1–12 but thirty-one times in 13–20. The change in basic terms makes an important point clear to us even from the vocabulary. The gift of life, authentic human existence here and hereafter, and of light, articulate and self-conscious understanding thereof, alike flow to us as modalities of the God who is love. He offers his being to us in Jesus' presence, especially as consummated on the cross and ever after efficacious in the resurrectional gift of the Spirit. To abide in love is to have life and light together, to exist fully and to know how and why we do so.

1) *Dialogue With Betrayal* (13:1–35). The explanatory discourse opens in a dark mood. Jesus performs two signs, two prophetic actions, one focusing on Simon-Peter but applying also to the other apostles (13:4–20), and the other for Judas alone (13:21–30). The meaning is explained by the accompanying words within the action and then stressed again together in the concluding phrases (13:31–35). But the two actions are closely connected by the joint preface of 13:2–3, and by the constant mention of the names of Peter (13:6, 8, 9, 24) and Judas (13:2, 27, 29).

i) *13:2–3.* Jesus is deeply aware that the time is at hand and that soon his mission and his presence in this world will depend no longer on his own works and words but on their continuation in the men who now surround him. Two terrible possibilities of betrayal confront him, one in Judas, immediate, proximate, and already decided upon (13:2). But there is also another possibility, less immediate, less proximate, but nonetheless deadly: will those who thereafter speak and act in his name, speak and act as he would have them do (13:4–20)? The betrayal by Judas is more obvious, but the second possibility of betrayal, by those to whom he has given authority over his flock (cf. 10:1–10, 11–18), is also present. Having mentioned the treachery of Judas (13:2), Jesus turns immediately to offset the second possibility.

ii) *13:4–20.* After a solemn overture which warns us of the importance of the action (13:3), Jesus performs a prophetic sign or work (13:4–11) which he immediately explains by words (13:12–20). The washing of the feet is a manifestation of utter humility on the part of Jesus. It was an act that was not supposed to be performed toward a Jew by his Jewish slave if a non-Jewish one was available. But like any sign it is the words which determine the precise meaning of the action. Peter refuses the action and Jesus explains that this is the last but absolutely necessary act in their preparation; it brings to completion the long training he had given them. In our terminology, it is their ordination to rule the people of God, and it also shows clearly the paradoxical manner of their rule. It is a rule of humble service; it is vocation and election to wash the feet of the people of God. The words usually explained as those constituting the apostles shepherds of God's flock in Luke 22:19 and 1 Corinthians 11:24–25 find their Johannine equivalent here in 13:15. They must feed the flock of God with sacrament and word, but they must do so as a humble service best symbolized as washing the feet of God's people. The explanatory words in 13:12–20 make all this very clear. Jesus does not for a second deny who or what he is (13:13). Indeed, the whole point is that it is as their "Teacher and Lord," twice repeated (13:13–14), that he demonstrates such a being as humble service (13:15). He is going to send them out, and others may call them similar titles in the future, but they will then know how they are to act as such, in humble service (13:16–17). The service of Jesus and, therefore, the service of those sent in his name, humble service though it is, can be refused only at the expense of alienation from God and from one's inmost being (13:8 and 13:20). Like the doctor who offers diagnosis and remedy, it is a matter of life and death. He need not command, because his most imperative force stems

from the patient's own desire to live. The service of the apostles
opens to mankind the word and the sacrament, the gifts of God,
which both diagnose the malaise of human existence and with
that analysis offer both cure and redemption.

The same point is made in Luke 22:25–27:

> And he said to them, "The kings of the Gentiles exercise lord-
> ship over them; and those in authority over them are called
> benefactors. But not so with you; rather let the greatest among
> you become as the youngest, and the leader as one who serves.
> For which is the greater, one who sits at table, or one who
> serves? Is it not the one who sits at table? But I am among
> you as one who serves."

How well Peter learned the lesson of these words may be seen
from 1 Peter 5:1–4:

> So I exhort the elders among you, as a fellow elder and a witness
> of the sufferings of Christ as well as a partaker in the glory that
> is to be revealed. Tend the flock of God that is your charge, not
> by constraint but willingly, not for shameful gain but eagerly,
> not as domineering over those in your charge but being examples
> to the flock. And when the chief Shepherd is manifested you
> will obtain the unfading crown of glory.

iii) 13:21–30. The dark atmosphere of betrayal announced in
13:2 pervades the entire section. Even when discussing the possibility of betrayal by abuse of future apostolic authority in
13:4–20, there is twice reference to the more immediate betrayal
of apostolic responsibility on the part of Judas in 13:10–11 and
18–19. Now the scene focuses completely on Judas. Matthew
saw Judas as the embodiment of the false Ahithophel who
had betrayed David (cf. Mt 27:5 and 2 Sm 17:23). Luke saw
him as the evil one who mocked the death of the just man (cf.
Acts 1:18 and Wis 4:18–19). John sees him as the one who
departs from the safety and sanctity of the paschal community
and goes out into "the night" where the avenging angel of God
can strike him in judgment (cf. 13:30 and Ex 12:12–13; Wis
18:14–16).

The early writers all insisted that the death of Jesus was freely
accepted out of love for mankind and obedience to his own
divinely given destiny. This was indicated not only by the
incident in the garden (Mk 14:36; Mt 26:39; Lk 22:42; cf. Jn
12:27), but even earlier at the supper. There seems to be a

deliberate play on the Greek words for "hand over" (*paradidōmi*) and "give" (*didōmi*): while Judas "hands over" Jesus to his death, Jesus himself actually "gives" himself for the salvation of the world. This explains the close association of betrayal and Eucharist as early as 1 Corinthians 11:23. It also explains why the passion is told in Mark as three stages of "handing over" (*paradidōmi*): Judas to the inimical Jewish authorities (14:10–11); these authorities to Pilate (15:1); and Pilate to death (15:15). But before this, Jesus already "gave" himself (*didōmi*) in Mark 14:22–23. Here in John, the same point was foreshadowed already in 6:64 and 70–71 in a eucharistic setting; repeated in 13:2, 10–11, 18–19 at the paschal meal; and finally symbolized by the action and instruction of 13:27. Judas acts only *after* Jesus offers himself to God the Father.[17]

iv) *13:31–35*. These words bring together in reversed order the lesson of the two actions, the washing of the feet and the giving of the morsel to Judas. In 13:31–33, recapitulating 13:21–30, it is clear that Jesus knows and accepts what is to happen. Only by so crowning his life can both God and himself be glorified, that is, be manifested fully to the world as they really are. For those of his own generation who rejected him he is gone forever (8:21), but for those who accepted him the separation is but temporary (14:2–3, and cf. also 14:18–19, 28; 16:16–22). Then, in 13:34–35, summing up 13:4–20, Jesus declares that their love and that of the community would be the perfect sign, external symbol, and sacrament of their discipleship and of God's presence among them.

2) *Dialogue With the Apostles* (13:36–16:33). In the liturgical celebration of the paschal meal, four questions were posed to the father of the family with regard to the meaning of the ritual (Ex 13:8, 14–15). This next section is a long dialogue, or better a monologue interrupted by questions, between Jesus and

---

[17] On the institution of the Eucharist in the other Gospels cf. J. Jeremias, *The Eucharistic Words of Jesus* (London, 1955); P. Benoit, "The Holy Eucharist," *Scr*, 8 (1956), 97–108; 9 (1957), 1–14; C. Vollert, "The Eucharist: Quests for Insights from Scripture," *TS*, 21 (1960), 404–443; B. Cooke, "Synoptic Presentation of the Eucharist as Covenant Sacrifice," *TS*, 21 (1960), 1–44; B. Ahern, "Gathering the Fragments: The Lord's Supper," *Worship*, 35 (1961), 424–429; J. H. O'Rourke, "The Passover in the Old Testament," *The Bible Today*, 5 (1963), 302–309; G. Wood, "The Eucharist — The New Passover Meal," *ibid.*, 310–317; W. E. Lynch, "The Eucharist — A Covenant Meal," *ibid.*, 318–323.

his disciples. Its present formation may well owe something to a composition for the Christian celebration of the paschal meal. There may be a remnant of this in the fact that four apostles are mentioned by name as questioning Jesus. The structure of the section is as follows: (i) Peter and Jesus (13:36–14:4); (ii) Thomas and Jesus (14:5–7); (iii) Philip and Jesus (14:8–21); (iv) Judas (not the Iscariot) and Jesus (14:22–16:15); (v) the apostles and Jesus (16:16–28); (vi) the apostles and Jesus (16:29–33). Thus, the questioning by the four individual disciples leads up to the final clarification of 16:16–28 and this in turn to the great act of faith in 16:29–33.

i) *13:36–14:4.* Peter alone of the four questions Jesus twice. The announcement of Peter's denial leads to an invitation to faith and hope which deserves some close consideration. At first glance Jesus seems to be saying that he is leaving this world, that they cannot leave now, but that soon he will return and they can leave it with him. One would presume that Jesus refers only to death. But this seems to contradict the main drive of the rest of the discussion in John 14–17. There Jesus insists that he himself is returning to them in resurrectional triumph (14:18–19, 28; 16:16–22), or, in other words, the Spirit of the risen Lord will dwell with them forever (14:16–17, 25–26; 16:7–15), or, in still fuller words, the Trinity will hereafter pour out its power upon them through his own permanent risen efficacy (14:23). But this will happen to the disciples (17:6–19) and to the community (17:20–23) in this world here below. Jesus, the Spirit, and the Father do not work to take mankind out of the world but to preserve them from evil in this world (17:15) so that they may live in love forever. From the moment of 1:14 when God pitched his tent in the camp of his people, to the great vision of Apocalypse 21:1–4, the good news is that "God's dwelling place is among men." We do not live in this world forever. But only here can we meet God. If we meet him here, we meet him forever; if we lose him here, we lose him forever. Upon this earth is the critical moment of eternal destiny. The meaning of 14:14 must be seen against this background. Jesus is opening for mankind the way of authentic life, and opening it to its perfection. When this has been done by the cross, he returns to the earth to confront all future generations with this challenge. The believer who accepts God in Jesus can never lose him either here on earth or for all eternity. Jesus will return to dwell with him upon the earth, to lead him at death to that life's eternal continuance. "Let not your hearts be troubled."

ii) *14:5-7.* After Peter, Thomas takes up the questioning of Jesus. In answer to him Jesus declares that he is the way in which man meets God; he is moreover the only way of such encounter; finally, this encounter is full human life. In him man sees the authentic (*truth*) vision (*way*) of existence (*life*). To exist within a community of love is man's only possible fulfillment, for the God who made him is irrevocably such, a Trinity, a community of love. To say that they "saw" God in Jesus means that only in absolute, total, and universal love presently incarnated in response to the needs of the one who confronts you do you "see" God. Such love is the ultimate sacrament of his presence; it is thus the summit of the entire evolution which continually "signs" his being to mankind.

iii) *14:8-21.* Philip now picks up the dialogue. The reply of Jesus repeats an earlier discussion from 10:37-38. The works of Jesus, all of them acts of love and concern but revealing thereby the absolute necessity of such a mode of living, manifest the Father, the depths of the Godhead, to them. They can believe the words or the works for they both say the very same thing.

The statement in 14:12-14 causes one to pause. If Jesus' love and concern showed themselves in a frontal attack on all that caused human suffering, on both sin and sickness, on both ignorance and fear, on pain and anxiety and insecurity, what would happen within a world-community of concern and love? What would happen to the flood and the tornado, to alcoholism and drug addiction, to hatred and violence and war, if we incarnated his vision upon our planet? Do medication and hospitalization, research and diagnosis, education and communication belong to God or not? We were called at creation to take dominion over evolution (Gn 1:26-28), or in the more poetic imagery of Genesis 2:15, "to till [the garden] and to keep it." Yet instead of concern and love for one another, we have used evolution as a bludgeon of hate and we now sleep in fear of what we have created. Ultimately, the world fights on the side of God, not of evil. In unconcern, we shall be destroyed eventually; in hate, just a little more swiftly. Yet to assume control and responsibility for evolution out of love for others and in response to the call of Jesus is to do "greater works" than he himself has done. But it will be to do it as a continuing manifestation of his own archetypal concern for human anguish.

The balance of 14:15–17 and 14:18–21 is quite significant. The section begins and ends with the same expression, but in reversed parallelism: "If you love me, you will keep my commandments" (14:15), and: "He who has my commandments and keeps them, he it is who loves me; and he who loves me will be loved by my Father, and I will love him and manifest myself to him" (14:21). We already know from 13:35: "By this all men will know that you are my disciples, if you have love for one another." Later we shall read in 15:12: "This is my commandment, that you love one another as I have loved you" (cf. 15:17). Here then in 14:15 and 14:21 Jesus says that our love for one another on this earth would be the manifestation of his own risen presence among us and thereby of God's dwelling with us. Communal love is the sacrament of the divine encounter (cf. 1 Jn 3:16–18; 4:7–21). Within these frames of 14:15 and 14:21 three ideas are expressed in parallelism. The Spirit is coming to the community as counselor (14:16); but the world (i.e., the forces of evil) will neither see him nor know him (14:17a); while the community of faith will both see him and know him for they will recognize his manifestation (their own mutual love) in themselves (14:17b). These three ideas are then repeated again in 14:18, 19a, 19b–20 and in this parallelism a very important point emerges. To say that the Spirit is to come from God to the community (14:16) is exactly the same as to say that Jesus is coming back to his own (14:18). During the earthly ministry, God worked in Jesus of Nazareth (Acts 2:22; 10:38), but after that unique period God confronts the world in the risen presence of that same Jesus, in the abiding efficacy of that life and death. To say that the Spirit comes, or to say that Jesus returns, is to state this fact in different words. During the rest of this dialogue we shall find a constant movement between these two expressions: (a) I go to send the Spirit; (b) I myself shall return. Either statement denotes the indwelling of the Trinity within the community of love whose communal concern sacraments that existence to the world.

iv) 14:22–16:15. The question of Judas (14:22) starts a long monologue by Jesus. The two poles of the discussion are already given in the question: "Lord, how is it that you will manifest yourself *to us*, and not *to the world?*" The question is answered in principle in 14:23–24 and the same division appears: 14:23 refers to "us" and 14:24 refers to "the world." In other words, why is there a community of acceptance and another of refusal? The full answer which follows has to concentrate first on the former group ("us") in 14:25–15:17, and then on the latter ("the world") in 15:18–16:15.

The basic reply of 14:23–24 is that Jesus has not decided to reveal himself to some and not to others. When his own generation was confronted with his works and words, they either accepted his message on the necessity of loving others and entered into vital contact with God or they rejected Jesus' witness and refused the kingdom of love and so lost the presence of God. But they, not he, made the choice.

In 14:25–15:17, Jesus turns his attention to the community of faith, to the "us" of Judas' question. In 14:25–31 we have the two ways of phrasing their future relationship with God: the coming of the Spirit (14:26) or the return of Jesus in risen glory (14:28). This future relationship will actually represent a far more powerful presence of God to the community than that of even the earthly ministry of Jesus.

In 15:1–8 Jesus uses a favorite Old Testament symbolism for the people of God, that of the vine (Ho 10:1–2; Is 5:1–7; 27:2–5; Jer 2:21–22; 12:10–11; Ez 15:1–8; 17:1–10; 19:10–14; Ps 80). The point is that the life of God flows to the branches only through Jesus as the vinestock; God is love and through Jesus' life and death he has offered to mankind the possibility of salvation through life in communal love as an external symbol of his presence and internal contact with himself.

In 15:9–17 there is a commentary on this image of the vine. Two ways of expressing the same reality are used. One is more juridical and external, the other more personal and internal. We must obey Jesus as he obeyed God; or, we must love one another just as Jesus loved us, even to death, and so manifested God as love. We may state it in legal terms: God commanded Jesus to love us; he did so, and also commanded us to love each other. Or we can set it in metaphysical language: God is a community of love; he has shown forth his being externally and physically in the life and death of Jesus; to be fully human we must also live such a life and become thereby the external sign of God's presence before the unbelieving world. Jesus explains his death with: "Greater love has no man than this, that a man lay down his life for his friends" (15:13). But indeed as Paul points out in Romans 5:6–8:

> While we were yet helpless, at the right time Christ died for the ungodly. Why, one will hardly die for a righteous man — though perhaps for a good man one will dare even to die. But God shows his love for us in that while we were yet sinners Christ died for us.

There is, in fact, a greater proof of love than dying for one's friends, and that is dying for one's enemies. But this is precisely what Jesus did. The only way Jesus could manifest God as love was by total love at whatever cost. This was perfect response to what God needed of him. The only way we can make a perfect response to God's need of us is to love one another and so bring his evolution to perfection and consummation. To love is still response to another's need. To love Jesus is to respond to his own need — which is that we love one another and complete his work. To love God is the same. On this earth we love another person by responding totally to his need. On this earth we love God by responding totally to the need of all mankind.

In 15:18–16:15 the other side of Judas' question is approached. After the vision of the community of acceptance in 14:25–15:17 comes that of the community of refusal. It must always be remembered that "the world" in such Johannine contexts as this is a synonym for hate and unlove, for all the forces opposed to God. It does not mean the world as we use the term. Opposition to the apostles is also to Jesus and so to God; who opposes love, fights against God. But in this struggle they are not alone.

At this point it is necessary to look more closely at the special term used of the Spirit already in 14:16, 26 and here again in 15:26 and 16:5–11: he is "the Counselor." In Deuteronomy 18:15–22 Israel is promised an ongoing prophetic witness. But immediately the problem is also faced:

> "And if you say in your heart, 'How may we know the word which the Lord has not spoken?' — when a prophet speaks in the name of the Lord, if the word does not come to pass or

come true, that is a word which the Lord has not spoken; the
prophet has spoken it presumptuously, you need not be afraid
of him" (18:21–22).

This statement is very surprising. One would have expected the
criterion of true prophecy to have been given as personal sanctity
or the power to work miracles. Yet the only guarantee or test
offered is — experience. However, the force of this becomes clear
when we consider that the prophet dealt only in life and death,
be it for Jerusalem or for all of God's people. Experience would
prove them right far too late for those to whom their warning
had been given in vain. Jeremiah, for example, was proved correct as he sat amid the ruins of Jerusalem; but that was scant
consolation for anyone concerned. Jesus appeals to the same
criteria — experience or history. God's continuing work in this
world through his risen presence or, in other words, the advent
of the Spirit, would have a special function as counselor or
vindicator. Time would tell whether Jesus' "love or perish" was
false prophecy or ultimate word from the depths of being.

God's work through the risen Lord will confront human history not only within the community of faith but also outside of
it. This is the meaning of 15:26–27. The community which lives
by concern and love for others vindicates by the holiness and
humanity of its existence that Jesus was correct (15:27). But all
the forces of psychology, sociology, history, etc., that show what
becomes of individual, social, and cosmic man when he lives
outside the milieu of love are also vindications for the same
witness of Jesus. They need never mention the names of either
God or Jesus, maybe even deny them any validity, yet still the
counselor vindicates Jesus, for his presence is at the very heart of
being and speaks at times with a terrible silence (15:26).

After the death of Jesus, and amid the persecution of those
who first attempt to live out his mandate, God's presence must
vindicate his continuing efficacy in this world on three counts
(16:8–11). The world will become convinced of sin, that is,
that those who opposed Jesus were wrong (16:9). It must, as a
correlative to this, become convinced that the vision of Jesus
was correct, was in fact the only authentic possibility of true
human life, and that Jesus abides forever with God (16:10).
Third, it will come to see, not only these two facts, but that
at the very moment when evil seemed to have conquered and

love seemed to have been vanquished the reverse became irrevocably accomplished — the cross was victory (16:11).

v) 16:16–28. The dialogue approaches its conclusion. The
four, Peter, Thomas, Philip, and Judas, have questioned Jesus
and now the disciples in general speak with him (16:16–28)
and, finally, confess their faith (16:29–33). One of the longest
sections of the Gospel which appears in similar sequence in all
four accounts is that of the passion. Scholars usually conclude
from this fact that a basic passion-narrative must have been
fixed with relative security in oral or written form at a fairly
early stage in the development of the tradition. But the second
longest section is; the discourse on the future in Mark 13 =
Matthew 24 = Luke 21. This must, then, have been deemed of
great significance in the early community; yet none of it appears
in John. This requires some explanation. It would seem that in
giving his message Jesus addressed himself with desperate urgency
to his own generation, that archetypal generation whose acceptance or rejection of him would be basic in causality and ex-
emplarity for all that was to follow. He warned them constantly
that to refuse him as the Messiah, as the ultimate revelation
from God, the perfect witness to God as community of love,
would end in destruction for their own generation. To accept
him would bring to fulfillment all of the ancient prophecies
when the Son of Man gathered in the elect of Israel around
his royal throne. All of this was originally couched in prophetic
and apocalyptic imagery. John finds little of this conducive to
understanding for his own particular audience. So he ignores
quite frequently the particularity of that first audience and lets
the message speak openly to all mankind *in its own generation.*
The end of that first archetypal generation was portrayed in
Mark 13 etc., as the climax of Jesus' presence in the world, the
coming of the Son of Man to execute judgment and salvation on
themselves. In 16:16–22, John abstracts this and insists that the
return of Jesus to his community took place at the resurrection
and was sealed by the gift of the Spirit, which meant God's
continuing pressure on the world through the risen Lord. In
16:16–22 he mentions the term "a little while" *seven* times.
There is only "a little while" between supper and passion; there
is likewise a similar "little while" between passion and resurrection or return. Their present sorrow is as passing as that of a

woman in labor; Jesus will return to live in the community forever and their joy cannot be taken from them thereafter. Such
terms as "second coming" or "return" of Jesus in the future are
highly questionable after that first archetypal generation had
passed away. Jesus has returned in the Spirit and together with
him we now work toward the ultimate victory of his presence
and not toward the ultimate return of an absent one. Notice
how obviously John pounds on the meaning of "little while" in
this section. The "little while" of absence is over, but the
future is long before us. Each of us in our own generation
faces the same awful choice of judgment or salvation as confronted that first generation; like them, we decide for ourselves,
and like them, we find judgment or salvation incarnated in
ruined cities, torn families, and estranged existence, or else in
eternal life begun already here below within a community of
love on earth (3:14–21; 5:19–29). Accordingly, one would not
consider that this is a description of the lot of the Church
in the world until some day in the future when Christ will
return. This subject was considered in 14:22–16:15. Instead, this
section details the sufferings of the apostles at the death of
Christ and their joy at his return to them in the Spirit; this
joy cannot be taken from them. Notice also the phrase "her
hour has come" in 16:21. This expression for the hour of birth
pangs recalls the usual Johannine expression, "his hour," for
the death of Jesus.

There is a constant refrain concerning petition "in the name"
of Jesus in 14:13–14; 15:16; 16:23–24. This means life and action
in the very being of the risen Lord. The life lived in love opens
the awesome power of God upon that person and unleashes the
possibility of the new creation. Life within the community of
love immediately starts to reshape our entire evolutionary future.
This is the same point as announced in Mark 11:23 and Matthew
21:21 on the power of faith and prayer. It can do the impossible
— hurl a mountain into the depths of the sea. In other words,
faith and prayer open the believer at that moment to the greatest
power conceivable, that of God, but even this can only touch
him when he allows his free consciousness to respond to it. It
will never force him against his will. When this opening occurs,
the man at prayer is changed to immerse his life in concern and
love, and nothing in his world is the same again. To move

mountains is relatively easy today; to change a free human will to ultimate concern still takes the power of the divinity. To pray in Jesus' name is to live in full awareness of one's destiny within a community of love and in articulate acceptance of that life. At that moment and for that person, a challenge to subdue the earth out of love for others has been accepted and a new creation has begun around him.

vi) *16:29–33*. The interchange concludes with the profession of faith by the apostles: "by this we believe that you came from God" (16:30). Jesus' reply is the theme which will be developed later in the Apocalypse itself: "I have overcome the world." In Jesus' life and death love has established its possibility and its presence; the rest is only a matter of time.

3) *Dialogue With God* (17:1–26). This prayer is still part of the explanatory discourse in which the events of John 18–20 are elucidated. It is more than a prayer; it is rather the solemn promise of Jesus that the community which will remain behind to receive his return in the Spirit will be what God wishes it to be, both now and forever. It is a vision of the future community. The prophetic vision is divided into three sections: Jesus and the Father (17:1–5); Jesus and the apostles (17:6–19); Jesus and the future community (17:20–26).

i) *17:1–5*. The moment of complete manifestation has come. In his passion, as the ultimate witness to love (12:27; 13:1; 15:13), Jesus has manifested God to the world. In biblical and Johannine language, he has "glorified" him and thereby opened to man the possibility of authentic existence, eternal life in vital contact ("to know") with the God who reveals himself as love in Jesus. He is the final manifestation to the world of what God was before it ever existed (1:1).

ii) *17:6–19*. Jesus now speaks of the apostles, the small band on whom the future depends. He repeats that they are *in the world*, and this is how it must be (17:11, 15). But his prayer is that they may be, even while in the world, a community of love just as the Trinity is a community of love (17:11). Only thus can they become "the Sent" of Jesus just as he was himself "the Sent" of God (17:18).

iii) *17:20–26*. The future community of faith is described in three points, twice stated (17:21 and 22–23). This community is, first of all, to be united in one *as* the Trinity is united; that is, it must be a community of love (21a). Second, it must be one not only as the Trinity is one, but, even more profoundly, in the Trinity (21b). The unity of their love is to be the external sign, the visible and tangible effect, the abiding sacrament of the presence of that Trinity itself within them. Third, it is through the community that the world sees God and is challenged by him for only then does it get sufficient vision of what God really is to make faith possible (21c). These three points are then solemnly repeated in 22–23. This community takes over "the glory," that is, the role of external manifestation of God as love, which first belonged to Jesus — one in love as the Trinity is (22), in the Trinity (23a), that the world may believe God is love (23b). United with the risen Lord and with the Trinity in such community here on earth, we shall find that union present for all eternity (17:24–26).

b) The Works of Consummation

Read John 18:1–20:31.

The words of explanation are now ended and the works of consummation begin: passion (18:1–19:42),[18] resurrection (20:1–10), ascension (20:11–18), gift of the Spirit (20:19–23), and vision of the future community in the Spirit (20:24–31).

1) *The Passion of Jesus* (18:1–19:42). The intricacy of structure in which John composes his work has by now been well established in these pages. We have already seen seven major units in 1:19–12:36. Second, each of these seven sections has

---

[18] On the relations between the account of the passion in this Gospel and that in the other three cf. P. Borgen, "John and the Synoptics in the Passion Narrative," NTS, 5 (1959), 246–259; I. Buse, "St. John and the Marcan Passion Narrative," NTS, 4 (1958), 215–219; "St. John and the Passion Narratives of St. Matthew and St. Luke," NTS, 7 (1960), 65–76; C. H. Dodd, *Historical Tradition in the Fourth Gospel* (Cambridge, 1963), pp. 21–151. For the structure of John's account of the passion cf. A. Janssens de Verebeke, "La structure des scènes du récit de la Passion en Joh., XVIII–XIX," ETL, 38 (1962), 504–522 for which an abstract appears in NTA, 7 (1962–1963) 327–328; and for its theology cf. D. M. Stanley, "The Passion according to St. John," *Worship* 33 (1959) 210–230; I. de la Potterie, "Jesus, King and Judge according to John 19:13," Scr 13 (1961) 97–111 and TD 11 (1963) 21–26. Two important points of historical background are discussed in P. Gaechter, "The Hatred of the House of Annas," TS 8 (1947) 3–34; J. J. Twomey, " 'Barabbas was a Robber,' " Scr 8 (1956) 115–119.

within itself another example of such sevenfold construction: 1:19–2:11; 4:7–29; 6:25–65; 7:14–8:59; 9:24–33; 11:5–16; 12:23–36. Third, the central unit (7:1–8:59) not only has seven dialogues within it (7:14–8:59), but the final dialogue itself has a sevenfold structure (8:31–59). Nowhere, however, does this work seem to be as detailed and delicate as in the narrative of the passion itself. Once again it is noted here not merely to admire form, but to elucidate content, not only to appreciate art, but to understand the theological viewpoint of the author. Although the narrative has the same basic sequence as the three Synoptic accounts, it is, most probably, an independent tradition and not based on any of them. All four probably go back in substratum to a very early and fairly general written schema of the passion. But John 18–19 as it presently stands is completely Johannine in both form and content.

The structure is a drama in three acts with each act divided into seven scenes, as follows:

Act I (18:1–27):   arrest, Jesus before Annas; denial by Peter.
  Scene 1 (18:1):   the setting in the garden of Gethsemane.
  Scene 2 (18:2–3):   Judas and the band from the authorities.
  Scene 3 (18:4–11):   dialogue of Jesus and capturers ("I am he").
  Scene 4 (18:12–14):   transition of place and focus.
  Scene 5 (18:15–18):   Peter denies Jesus once.
  Scene 6 (18:19–24):   dialogue of Jesus and Annas.
  Scene 7 (18:25–27):   Peter denies Jesus twice more.

Act II (18:28–19:16):   Jesus before Pilate.
  Scene 1 (18:28–32)   OUTSIDE: authorities demand death.
  Scene 2 (18:33–38a)   INSIDE: Pilate questions and Jesus answers.
  Scene 3 (18:38b–40)   OUTSIDE: Jesus declared innocent.
  Scene 4 (19:1–3)   INSIDE: Jesus is crowned as king.
  Scene 5 (19:4–8)   OUTSIDE: Jesus is declared innocent.
  Scene 6 (19:9–12)   INSIDE: Pilate questions and Jesus answers.
  Scene 7 (19:13–16)   OUTSIDE: authorities obtain death.

Act III (19:17–42):   crucifixion; anointing; burial.
  Scene 1 (19:17–22):   the crucifixion of Jesus.

Scene 2 (19:23–24): the robe without seam.
Scene 3 (19:25–27): Mary and John.
Scene 4 (19:28–30): the death of Jesus.
Scene 5 (19:31–37): the thrust of the lance.
Scene 6 (19:38–40): the anointing of Jesus.
Scene 7 (19:41–42): the burial of Jesus.

It is clear that the central Act II (18:28–19:16) is the most care-fully structured of the three acts. The interplay of OUTSIDE and INSIDE the praetorium of Pilate; the exact balance of the seven elements in reversed parallelism; and the central importance of the crowning of Jesus as king in 19:1–3 all indicate careful artistry. The structure of Acts I (18:1–27) and III (19:17–42), while also in seven scenes, presumably from the influence of the central Act II, does not seem to demonstrate any reversed parallel-ism. But even in these cases the fourth scene of each act seems again to be central to the structure: 18:12–14 forms a transition from Judas to Peter; and 19:28–30 is the death of Jesus himself. But even though there is no reversed parallelism or chiastic con-struction within Acts I and III in themselves, John has de-veloped the two acts as far as possible in such parallelism with regard to each other; thus Act I, Scene 1 looks to Act III, Scene 7 and so on, as follows:

I, 1 (18:1): in a garden.

III, 7 (19:41–42): in a garden.

I, 2 (18:2–3): infidelity of Judas.

III, 6 (19:38–40): fidelity of others.

I, 3 (18:4–11): double witness.

III, 5 (19:31–37): double witness.

I, 4 (18:12–14): "one must die."

III, 4 (19:28–30): one dies.

I, 5 (18:15–18): Peter denies.

III, 3 (19:25–27): Mary affirms.

I, 6 (18:19–24): Jesus is struck.

III, 2 (19:23–24): Jesus is stripped.

I, 7 (18:25–27): Peter denies twice.

III, 1 (19:17–22): Pilate affirms twice.

Thus the overall structure balances Acts I and III in reversed parallelism around the central nucleus of Act II whose core is

19:1–3. It is clear that the crowning of Jesus as king, the mocking indignity of the thorns borne out of love for mankind, is the key to the entire passion in the mind of John. Death out of love for others is victory; the cross is coronation.

i) *18:1–27.* The first three scenes focus on the treachery of Judas (18:1–11). Then, after the central transition of both place and interest (18:12–14), the emphasis is rather on the denial by Peter (18:15–27). Jesus had been staying outside the city, presumably for safety; he returned to the temple only each morning. We know this from Mark 11:11–12, 15, 19–20, 27; 13:3. Those in the Sanhedrin who wished Jesus' death had already decided that it would be impossible to effect this during the festival lest it cause a riot (Mk 14:1–2; Mt 26:3–5; Lk 22:1–2; Jn 11:47–53). It was here that Judas stepped in and offered to pinpoint the exact whereabouts of Jesus on the night of the paschal supper which had to be eaten within Jerusalem itself. At the close of the bargain "he agreed, and sought an opportunity to betray him to them in the absence of the multitude" (Lk 22:3–6, and cf. Mk 14:10–11; Mt 26:14–16). This would also account for the mysterious and enigmatic nature of the instructions given by Jesus to two of the disciples on the whereabouts of the supper itself (cf. Mk 14:13; Lk 22:10 with Mt 26:18). Presumably the idea was to withhold from Judas the exact place of the supper. This would also explain his departure *during* the meal; only he waited long enough to learn where Jesus would be afterwards; then he left (Jn 13:30).

Notice the typical Johannine shift in vocabulary between 18:3: "So Judas, procuring a band of soldiers and some officers from the chief priests and the Pharisees, went there with lanterns and torches and weapons," and 18:12: "So the band of soldiers and their captain and the officers of the Jews seized Jesus and bound him." Once again the more specific "chief priests and Pharisees" has been converted into the much more general "the Jews." Annas was high priest in A.D. 6–15 and was followed by many other members of his house but only Caiaphas, his son-in-law, who ruled A.D. 18–36, is of interest to us here. Apparently Annas and Caiaphas, that is, the real power behind the throne and the actual high priest respectively, were the spearhead of the plot to kill Jesus. Their primary motive was self-interest. There had been no legitimate high priesthood since Antiochus IV Epiphanes

deposed Onias II, the legal heir of Sadoq who had been set up
as the hereditary high priest under Solomon in 973 B.C. Thus,
the Pharisees were constantly at loggerheads with the high
priest and his faction in the Sanhedrin, but they seemed to have
united against Jesus because he had severely threatened both
groups. The religious *status quo* to which the Pharisees were dedicated and the political and economic *status quo* with which the
Sadducees were involved were equally endangered by his activity.

The last three scenes (18:15–27) frame the witness of Jesus
before Annas with the first denial of Peter in 18:15–18 and the
two later denials in 18:25–27.

ii) *18:28–19:16.* We saw earlier that this section is a very
tightly constructed unity. Yet the same shift in vocabulary occurs
here also. In the dialogue with Pilate the accusers of Jesus are
first identified with, "When the *chief-priests and the* officers
saw him, they cried out, 'Crucify him, Crucify him!'" (19:6)
but in the very next verse, with exactly the same speakers involved, "*The Jews* answered him, 'We have a law, and by that
law he ought to die, because he has made himself the Son of
God'" (19:7). The same phenomenon occurs again a few
verses later. In 19:14, continuing the accusation before Pilate,
"Now it was the day of Preparation of the Passover; it was about
the sixth hour. He said to *the Jews*, 'Here is your king!'" Then,
in the next verse, "They cried out, 'Away with him, away with
him, crucify him!' Pilate said to them, 'Shall I crucify your
king?' *The chief priests* answered, 'We have no king but Caesar'"
(19:15). Once again it is clear that the term "the Jews" simply
means those in authority, especially the sacerdotal circles around
Annas, who instigated the death of Jesus.

At this point it might be well to pause for a moment and consider the usual presumption that there was a mob or multitude,
to some degree representative of the mind of Jerusalem, siding
with the authorities in demanding the death of Jesus. First of all,
the gathering of a mob was something about which Pilate was
extremely touchy (Josephus, *Antiquities* 18:3:1–2; 4:2). Second,
the evangelists repeatedly stress the fact that the ordinary people
were on the side of Jesus (Mk 11:18; 12:12, 37; Mt 21:45–46;
22:33; Lk 19:47–48; 20:19, 39; Jn 7:31; 8:30; 10:42; 12:19), and
that the plotters feared their intervention on his behalf. Against
a background of such difficulty this mob is not easy to explain.

There is absolutely no mention of it in John. There is no crowd or crowds cited during the proceedings before Pilate. There are of course "the Jews," but we have already seen what this means for John. In Luke, the crowd first appears without any explanation in 23:4. This does not help the problem of origin; they are simply there. We have no understanding of how the authorities who were seeking to avoid a crowd in Luke 22:2 suddenly find themselves with one in 23:4. Luke clearly understands the tradition as stating that there was a representative crowd or mob from Jerusalem accompanying the authorities to accuse Jesus. Three times Pilate declares Jesus innocent (23:4, 13, 22) and these declarations are made to the authorities accompanied by the crowds (23:4, 13). Luke has a Jerusalem crowd but he does not tell us whence it came; he merely records its presence and influence. Nor does Matthew particularly help in the solution of the problem. Once again the crowd is introduced, without any explanation, in 27:20. The question then still stands: Where in a city whose authorities fear the people (Mt 26:5) did they obtain the crowd found in Matthew 27:20? It is only in the narrative of Mark that the problem receives a possible solution. The pertinent text is as follows:

> Now at the feast he used to release for them one prisoner whom they asked. And among the rebels in prison, who had committed murder in the insurrection, there was a man called Barabbas. *And the crowd came up and began to ask Pilate to do as he was wont to do for them.* And he answered them, "Do you want me to release for you the King of the Jews?" For he perceived that it was out of envy that the chief priests had delivered him up. But the chief priests stirred up the crowd to have him release for them Barabbas instead (15:6–11).

It would seem that this text explains quite adequately the advent of the "mob." Its meaning is clear against the background of an occupied city. Barabbas and his companions had arisen against the Roman domination and killed either some Roman soldiers or Jewish quislings during the revolt. Thus, John 18:40 describes Barabbas as a *lēstēs*; and Jesus is crucified along with two *lēstai* (Mk 15:27; Mt 27:38, 44). This term does not mean a robber in our sense of the term, but rather an insurgent, a rebel, a guerrilla fighter against the occupation authorities. Barabbas and two followers were, then, to be crucified that day; "the crowd" came up to ask for the rebel's release according to the customary amnesty. There is absolutely no indication in Mark that they came up as a mob, or that they came up against Jesus, or that they were gathered by the authorities from the populace for this purpose. Indeed their first introduction, the italicized words, Mark 15:8, have no parallel in Matthew 27:16 or Luke 23:17. They arrived then to obtain the freedom of Barabbas. One could reasonably presume that they were friends or followers of the rebel leader and that they were a small band; neither the character of Pilate nor the use of the term "the crowd" in Mk 15:8 warrants the idea of a very large group, let alone that of a mob. They found themselves faced with a disappointment; there was now somebody else in prison. Pilate knew that Barabbas was more dangerous than Jesus and tried to release this latter to them. Strengthened by the promptings of the authorities who had brought Jesus before Pilate, they insisted on their original purpose: free Barabbas to them and let Jesus undergo crucifixion in his place. This would seem to be the picture which emerges with relative clarity from Mark. Later the tradition seems to have taken the crowd as being a mob from the populace, but this cannot be sustained elsewhere. We could state our conclusions under two points: the evidence explicitly and definitely points against any representative Jerusalem crowd shouting for Jesus' death; it is quite possible that the crowd before Pilate was interested primarily if not exclusively in Barabbas as a rebel hero and in Jesus only insofar as he became a threat to Barabbas' release. It is because of this fact that John simply ignores the crowd. In this regard it is also interesting to recall that Jesus' prophecy of his own death never mentioned any culpability outside that of the authorities; cf. Mark 8:31; 9:31; 10:32–34, and the parallels in Matthew 16:21; 17:22; 20:17–19; Luke 9:22, 44; 18:31–34. In summary, then, we are dealing with a plot by a group of highly placed officials who ask for Pilate's complicity in their design; the only others on the scene are those who come up to ask for the release of Barabbas.

The schematic balance of 18:28–19:16 in reversed parallelism depends on the division into seven scenes. This division is effected by Pilate's position "outside" or "inside" the Praetorium in which the dialogue between himself and the accusers takes place. We shall return to the meaning of 18:28, "Then they led Jesus from the House of Caiaphas to the Praetorium. It was early. They themselves did not enter the Praetorium, so that they might not be defiled, but might eat the Passover," later in Appendix I (p. 133 f). The theme of kingship and the nature of Jesus' dominion is the idea most stressed by John in this section. It appears in 18:33, 36, 37, 39 and in 19:12, 14, 15 but it is in the central scene of 19:1–3 that it is seen most fully. Jesus' kingship is not of this world but is rather a dominion of love. Its establishment is in the paradoxical vision of 19:1–3, where "The soldiers plaited a crown of thorns, and put it on his head, and arrayed him in a purple robe." This kingship is very much *in* this world but is not *of* this world; it is of God.

iii) *19:17–42.* The seven scenes of Act III center on the death of Jesus on the cross in 19:28–30. This scene is immediately preceded and followed by the vision of the Church in 19:25–27 (Mary and John) and in 19:31–37 (the thrust of the lance).

Recall the reversed parallelism between these seven scenes and those in 18:1–27. Pilate twice affirms by his inscription that Jesus is "King of the Jews" (19:17–22) just as Peter had twice denied him earlier (18:25–27). Jesus is stripped by the guards (19:23–24) as previously he had been struck by a guard (18:19–24). The point of the seamless robe is that the high priest's garment was also supposed to be such according to Josephus (and cf. Ex 31:10; Lv 21:10; Sir 50:11). Jesus is the true high priest whose sacrifice brings mankind from the realm of the unholy to that of the sacred and the divine, who transfers mankind from unconcern and hatred to concern and love.

In 18:15–18 Peter stood to deny Jesus (18:18) and in 19:25–27 Mary stands at the cross to complete her destiny.[19] This section must thus be seen as the companion passage to 2:1–11. Now is the time when the promise of that moment is to be fulfilled. Our thinking about Mary must begin with what Jesus himself said of her in Luke 11:27–28; "As he said this, a woman in the crowd raised her voice and said to him, 'Blessed is the womb that bore you, and the breasts that you sucked!' But he said, 'Blessed rather are those who hear the word of God and keep it!' " By this statement, Jesus denied that mere physical maternity,

---

[19] D. Unger, "The Meaning of John 19, 26–27 in the Light of Papal Documents," Mar 21 (1959) 186–221; C. P. Ceroke, "Mary's Maternal Role in John 19, 25–27," Mar Stud 11 (1960) 123–151.

awesome though it is in itself, was sufficient to render Mary blessed (*makaria*). Such blessedness consisted in commitment to the word of God spoken in Jesus. However, it was also in Luke 1:45 that Mary was addressed by Elizabeth with, "Blessed (*makaria*) is she who believed that there would be a fulfillment of what was spoken to her from the Lord." In other words, the divine maternity itself came to Mary as a word from God and only in her acceptance did the Word become flesh. Jesus' statement serves to warn us never to divide the divine maternity from the faith of Mary. The glory of her maternity is not just the physical fact itself; rather, this was effected in her only consequent and dependent upon her *fiat* which was the primordial and essential "yes" to the ultimate presence of God in Jesus. Mary's acceptance of the word was not just the first or even merely the greatest assent to the challenge of God. It was primeval affirmation and archetypal acceptance. Without her assent, no other assent before her or after her would have been possible. "The disciple whom Jesus loved" stands for all those who would come to faith in Jesus. They could only come to such life through the Church in which they are reborn within the community of love. But the archetype of the Church is Mary, for in her act of faith not only was the faith of all members of the Church most perfectly exemplified, but also it was this act which brought Jesus the Lord, the head of the Church, into existence. The faith of all the world looks to Mary as its archetype just as all life looks to Eve, "the Woman" of Genesis 3:20.

In the central scene of 19:28–30 Jesus dies, just as in the corresponding scene in 18:12–14 the warning of Caiaphas was recalled, "that one man should die for the people."

The description of the blood and water in 19:31–37 recalls the statement of 1 John 5:6–7:

This is he who came by water and blood, Jesus Christ, not with the water only but with the water and the blood. And the Spirit is the witness, because the Spirit is the truth. There are three witnesses, the Spirit, the water, and the blood; and these three agree.

There are probably layers of symbols hidden in the simple and apparently purely medical description of 19:34. Jesus' witness came in his entire Spirit-directed life, begun in water beside the

Jordan and consummated in blood upon Golgotha. And that of each Christian, likewise Spirit-guided, must begin in the water of baptism and continue through the blood of the Eucharist so that his whole life is lived as a continuing witness of love. The passage concludes with a double citation from the Old Testament: Exodus 12:46 in 19:36 and Zechariah 12:10 in 19:37. This double witness looks back to that of Jesus himself in 18:4–11 where he twice stated, "I am He."

After his death the fidelity of his disciples appears in 19:38–40 and contrasts sharply with the infidelity of Judas in 18:2–3. Then in 19:41–42 the seventh scene of Act III ends in a garden just as 18:1, the first scene of Act I, opened in a garden as well.

2) *The Resurrection* (20:1–10). In Appendix II (p. 139 f) we shall have to consider in more detail the postresurrectional apparitions of Jesus. Here we will consider only John. Mary Magdalene finds the empty tomb and tells the disciples. It would seem that John, presumably the unnamed disciple in question, hints that he alone immediately believed what had happened (20:8).

3) *The Ascension* (20:11–18). There are two "traditions" about the ascension of Jesus and these require some explanation.[20] The majority of the early Christian sources have absolutely no doubt that the resurrection involved the exaltation of Jesus to the glory of the Father. Yet they also keep a surprising silence on the mechanics of this exaltation. The greater number of texts presume the ascension and yet do not detail it; they speak of Jesus as exalted, glorified, in heaven, at the right hand of God, etc., and very often they do not mention the ascension itself at all. Other texts speak of it but in a theological rather than a historical and experimental manner. Only a few texts mention the ascension as an empirical phenomenon; for example, Acts 1:9 or Luke 24:51. In order to reconcile these "traditions" it seems necessary to distinguish in the mystery of the ascension two moments or modes. There is, first of all, a celestial exaltation, invisible but utterly real, whereby Jesus is suffused by the Spirit at the very moment of the resurrection. Indeed, this is the full implication of the resurrection itself. It is not just another case of Lazarus, as if Jesus had merely come back to life. This is clear in such a text as Romans 1:1–4. But this thinking would also be

[20] This is based on P. Benoit, "L'Ascension," *RB*, 56 (1949), 161–203 for which a summary appears in *TD*, 8 (1960), 105–110.

behind John 20:17, wherein the ascension of Jesus takes place on Easter Sunday, between the resurrection (20:1–10) and the gift of the Spirit (20:19–23). This "theological ascension" is actually drawing out the full understanding of the resurrection itself. The second aspect is a visible manifestation to assist the faith of the apostles whereby Jesus deigned to show in an external manner the spiritual reality of his presence in the glory of the Father by "ascending" from this earth. This tradition appears in both Luke and Acts. It is customary to reserve the name "ascension" for this latter visible manifestation; and in the liturgy we are accustomed, quite rightly, to distinguish ascension and resurrection chronologically. But it must be remembered that only in the Johannine tradition, where the resurrection involved both the immediate glorification (theological ascension) of Christ and also the gift of the Spirit can we make sense of the post-resurrection apparitions. John, therefore, gives us a fuller understanding of the mystery of the resurrection, which is much more than simply an empty tomb and Jesus alive again. The resurrection involves essentially the enduring efficacy and abiding presence of Christ in this world through the Spirit. If this were not true his resurrection would be just the same as that of Lazarus or any of the other people to whom God gave new life in the gospel.

4) *The Gift of the Spirit* (20:19–23). Notice how 20:19 insists that this event took place the same day. This is John's way of uniting resurrection — ascension — gift as one reality, one single divine event which is completed only in this totality. We saw already that the invisible, theological ascension was the immediate corollary of the resurrection in the Johannine tradition (20:17). In 20:22–23 the Spirit of the risen and ascended Christ is given to the apostles, also on Easter Sunday itself in the Johannine tradition. This, like the theological and invisible ascension, was the theological and invisible advent of the Spirit as promised in 16:7–9, but for after the ascension! However, in Acts 2:1–4 God gives the apostles, in merciful condescension to weakness and as an assistance to their faith, a visible, quasi-historical and experimental "advent" of the Holy Spirit. Just as there was a "double" ascension, so is there a "double" descent of the Spirit. But while one account, John, expresses the ultimate depths of reality, the other, Luke (Acts), is rather a sacramental for faith to understand the meaning of the event. Neither God nor Jesus is "up

there" somewhere; and neither is God's Spirit wind or flame. But we are human, and we meet each other and our God in symbol and sign. The gift of the Spirit inaugurates the mission of the community to continue that of Jesus; it is the power of God now operative on the world in the risen glory of Jesus' life and death (20:21). This mission means an all-out attack on sin and all that leads to it and stems from it, and most especially on that creeping unconcern which is its most prolific breeding ground (20:22–23). We recall from Mark 16:17–18 that this mission was also to include concern for all the pain of life because without such concern there is no love, and then there is no gospel because there is no kingdom.

5) *The Community of the Spirit* (20:24–31). The original Gospel of John closes with this scene: a vision of the future community of the risen Lord. The scene is set for "eight days later" (20:26), the following Sunday (cf. 20:19). On that day the risen Lord announces, "Blessed are those who have not seen and yet believe" (20:29). The community of faith, at any time or in any place after the end of that first archetypal generation, meets at its liturgical assembly on the Day of the Lord ("eight days later") and knows it is in solemn contact with its resurrected Master (cf. also Luke 24:13–35). The continuing community, blessed in its unseeing faith, is one of "eight days later," that is, one which meets its Lord on all the Sundays of all the years of all the future. Liturgy is the heart of its life.

The closing verses in 20:30–31 recapitulate the purpose of the writing. Only certain "signs," certain prophetic actions and their accompanying explanations, have been written down, but these have been given that "you may believe," or a better translation; "that you may continue in your belief that Jesus is the Christ, the Son of God, and that in believing you may have life in his name."

Appendix I: *On the Relative Chronology of the Passion.* The background to the last week of Jesus' life is the Passover feast which was celebrated at the full moon in the first month of the year, that is, the month of Nisan which would correspond to our March-April. On the tenth day, each family chose a one-year-old male lamb without blemish; on the evening of the fourteenth Nisan, which was already the start of the fifteenth Nisan by Jewish reckoning, this sacrificial lamb was eaten by a familial group large enough to consume the entire victim. Thus the paschal meal was eaten after sunset on the fourteenth, when it was already the start of the fifteenth Nisan by Jewish accounting.

i) The Problem. The Synoptics clearly state that the Last Supper which Jesus took with his disciples before his arrest was the paschal meal (Mk 14:12; Mt 26:17; Lk 22:7). But in John 18:28, after the arrest of Jesus, his accusers would not enter the Praetorium of Pilate to avoid defilement and so be able to eat the paschal meal. The discrepancy is clear: the Synoptics consider that the Pasch was eaten before the arrest, John presumes it was eaten by the authorities on the evening of the crucifixion. The difficulty has evoked many different explanations throughout the centuries. Actually, the events of the Last Supper as narrated in the Synoptics have been shown to fit very well against the background of the paschal meal, and so, in their own way, have many of the events in John 13–17. This intensifies the problem. There is no solution which has found agreement among a majority of scholars; there are difficulties against any one which has been proposed. It is very hard to accept the theory that the actual paschal meal was on the Friday evening after the crucifixion and that Jesus just "acted out" a passover meal at the preceding Last Supper in order to show the Pasch's completion in the eucharistic banquet, and that this "fiction" became fact in the oral period and so passed into the Synoptics. This theory solves the problem but would seem to presume much to much. Accordingly, it seems better to examine a more recent solution to the problem. This solution is still hypothetical, of course; it has been accepted by eminent scholars such as Vogt and Skehan, and opposed by others equally eminent; Benoit, for example. However, it has a foundation in extrabiblical fact and it solves the problem without raising greater ones. One might say that if this is not the answer, we do not know at the present moment what the answer is.

ii) The Proposed Solution.[21] Annie Jaubert of the Sorbonne

---

[21] A. Jaubert, *La Date de la Cène. Calendrier Biblique et Liturgie Chrétienne* ("Études Bibliques"; Paris, 1957). Summaries and critical reaction are given in *TD*, 5 (1957), 67–72; 6 (1958), 120–122; *NTA*, 4 (1959–1960) 285–287. Her reply is in "Jésus et la calendrier de Qumrân," *NTS*, 7 (1960), 1–30, of which an abstract is in *NTA*, 5 (1960–1961) 140. For other comment cf. L. Johnston, "The Date of the Last Supper," *Scr* 9 (1957) 108–115; P. W. Skehan, "The Date of the Last Supper," *CBQ* 20 (1958) 192–199; S. Smith, "The Holy Week Chronology: A New Approach," *IER*, 93 (1960) 223–236; R. E. Brown, "The Date of the Last

posits that since there were two liturgical calendars at the time of Jesus there were two possible methods of calculating the day on which the paschal meal was to be eaten:

First, the solar calendar of 364 days — this was a perpetual calendar and it had exactly fifty two weeks per year. It was divided into four quarters; each quarter had three months of which the first two had thirty days apiece and the third month had thirty one days. In this calendar there was an unalterable link between the numbered days of each month and the day of the week: for example, the first day of the year was always on a Wednesday (1st Nisan). The days, except the Sabbath, were referred to by number starting with our Sunday which was the "first day," etc. Thus a date such as "the sixth day of the fourth month" in this calendar would always be a known day of the week. This stable calendar must have had some system of compensating for the deficit of one and a quarter days per year with the solar system. Passed down in sacerdotal circles, its basic advantage was that the feasts always fell on the same day of the week every year. This calendar underlines the chronology of the Pentateuch, 1 and 2 Chronicles, Ezra, Nehemiah. Thus, the fourteenth Nisan, in the evening of which the Pasch was eaten, *always* fell on a Tuesday, "the third day of the week."

Second, the lunar calendar of 365 days — despite the existence of the other and older calendar, this was the official one, possibly from the time Palestine passed from under the Ptolemies to under the Seleucids. No doubt its adoption was seen by pious Jews as another intolerable example of Hellenization; it has even been suggested that it was this point which finally drove the Qumran group into the desert where they maintained the solar calendar in defiance of the official temple usage. This calendar was based on the moon and an intercalary month was added when needed to bring it into line with the sun.

Thus between these two calendars we would have fallen on a

Supper," *The Bible Today* 11 (1964) 727–732; "The Problem of Historicity in John," *New Testament Essays* (Milwaukee, 1965), pp. 143–167. While this theory is but a hypothesis it must be noted that alternative explanations are equally hypothetical and still the difficulty of Jn 18, 28 remains. For example, the last cited work is forced to the suggestion that Jesus "deliberately imitated many of the details of a Passover meal [except the lamb] to show the connection of the Eucharistic sacrifice to the historic deliverance of the Jews from Egypt on the first Passover" (p. 167).

discrepancy: in A.D. 30 and 33 the fifteenth Nisan would have fallen on a Saturday (Sabbath) in the official or lunar calendar; but it would have fallen (as always) on a Wednesday in the nonofficial or solar calendar.

It has long been known from the apocryphal books of *Enoch* and *Jubilees* that some Jewish classes were using this solar calendar in the second century B.C. Many fragmentary copies of *Jubilees* in its Hebrew original, and many sections of *Enoch*, especially the astronomical portions of it, in Aramaic original, were discovered at Qumran. Furthermore, the strictly sectarian documents of this group make it clear that this calendar was mandatory in the community. This means that at the very time of Jesus the Pasch was being observed at Qumran, and possibly in other Essene establishments as well, on the evening of the fourteenth Nisan, a Tuesday as always.

But we can advance the hypothesis a little farther. There is some positive evidence in favor of a paschal meal on Tuesday night, the solar fourteenth Nisan, as in the Synoptics, and the crucifixion on Friday afternoon, the lunar fourteenth Nisan, as in John 18:28 and 19:31. The following early texts are significant:[22]

a) *Didascalia Apostolorum.* This is a collection of moral and disciplinary precepts and represents one of the earliest attempts at legal codification. It dates from the latter part of the second century, from an unknown bishop in northern Syria. Of the three references to the event of Holy Week, the following is the fullest:

> After eating the Passover on Tuesday evening, we went to the Mount of Olives and, during the night, they took our Lord Jesus. The following day, Wednesday, he was kept in the house of the high-priest Caiaphas; the same day, the rulers of the people met and held counsel regarding him. The following day, Thursday, they led him to Pilate, the governor, and he was in Pilate's custody the night following Thursday. On the Friday morning, they accused him much before Pilate, and could prove nothing true, but brought forth testimonies against him, and demanded him of Pilate to put to death. They crucified him that same Friday (21, 14, 5–8).

---

[22]Full details on these sources and their historical background can be found in A. Jaubert, *La Date de la Cène* ("Études Bibliques"; Paris, 1957), pp. 79–91, from which these texts are taken.

b) St. Victorinus of Pettau (d. 304). This Austrian bishop does not depend on the preceding source and therefore witnesses to an independent tradition. He says:

> The man Jesus Christ, creator of all that we have mentioned above, was arrested by the impious on the fourth day. This is why we fast on the fourth day, because of his imprisonment . . . (*De Fabrica Mundi*, 49).

Once again the arrest takes place in the early hours of Wednesday, the fourth day of the week, the solar fifteenth Nisan.

c) St. Epiphanius (315–403). It has been argued that the preceding tradition was invented as justification for the custom of Wednesday fasting. This seems quite unlikely because *prima facie* the Synoptic record would seem to indicate a Thursday-night arrest and there would have to be very strong reasons for the arrival of a Tuesday-night arrest on the scene. There must have been strong tension between the two traditions — that of a Tuesday-night arrest and a Thursday-night arrest — as the following hybrid would indicate. In this text, after a Tuesday-night–Wednesday-morning arrest, the disciples join Jesus for the Last Supper *in prison* on Thursday night:

> At the ninth hour [3–6 p.m.] the Apostles were able to join Jesus in secret and He performed the breaking of bread with them in his prison (*Fragmentum* 17–20).

But the Cypriot bishop rejects this strange compromise and states elsewhere:

> We must fast on Wednesday and Friday up to the ninth hour because it was at the beginning of Wednesday that the Lord was arrested and on Friday that he was crucified (*De Fide*, 22).

d) *Book of Adam and Eve*. This is a Judaeo-Christian apocryphal work of the fifth or sixth century. Adam promises to sacrifice regularly on Wednesday and Friday and God replies:

> "Oh Adam, you have determined in advance the days on which sufferings will come to me, when I shall have become incarnate, that is, Wednesday and Friday" (A. Jaubert, *op. cit.*, p. 90).

It must be recalled that the value of these texts is enhanced by the difficulty in explaining the origin of a Tuesday-night paschal supper tradition when it seems to be directly opposed to the Synoptic tradition, which has Jesus apparently eating the Pasch on the night before he died.

In fact, all those Fathers who oppose the Tuesday tradition do so on exegetical grounds (for example, Irenaeus, Apollinaris, and Clement of Alexandria), since they claim it is against the New Testament teaching on the matter. They do not cite historical or traditional arguments.

In conclusion, we can trace the two traditions back to the second century. But while the Tuesday tradition shows no trace of its origin, unless it be fact itself, Thursday is always taken as the obvious understanding of the New Testament data. Possibly Tuesday is historical tradition, while Thursday is biblical exegesis.

Accordingly, it is now possible to look once more at the Gospel record in the light of this Tuesday-to-Friday passion chronology. The Synoptics or John do not give such an explicit Thursday-Friday sequence, as is often claimed. Expressions such as "when morning came" (Mt 27:1) might not necessarily have originally meant *next morning*. There are also indications of compression even as the narratives stand — Annas, Sanhedrin session(s), Herod Antipas, Pilate, etc. The discrepancy between the Synoptics and John is certainly solved in this theory; presumably Jesus used the nonofficial or solar calendar to stress the paschal nature of the eucharistic consecration. Thus, both Last Supper (Synoptics) and crucifixion (Jn) are seen against the background of the paschal sacrifice. To fit the large number of events into the period from late Thursday to midday Friday is almost impossible. However, this is no longer a problem in a late Tuesday to midday Friday chronology. Incidentally, it would also make Matthew 27:19 more sensible, unless the wife of Pilate was a late sleeper.

Before attempting to outline the events of the passion on the hypothesis of a Tuesday-to-Friday sequence we might recall the days of the last week of Jesus' life in the two calendars as follows:

Tuesday:	14th Nisan (solar)	
	MEAL	11th Nisan (lunar)
Wednesday:	15th Nisan (solar	
	PASCH	12th Nisan (lunar)
Thursday:	16th Nisan (solar)	13th Nisan (lunar)
Friday:	17th Nisan (solar)	14th Nisan (lunar)
		MEAL
Saturday:	18th Nisan (solar)	15th Nisan (lunar)
		PASCH

The events recorded in the four Gospel records would most likely be spread over the three days as follows:

Tuesday (evening-night). The paschal meal is eaten — using the solar calendar — and the Eucharist is instituted (Mt 26:17–29; Mk 14:12–25; Lk 22:7–30; Jn 13–17). Jesus is arrested on the Mount of Olives (Mt 26:30–56; Mk 14:26–52; Lk 22:31–53; Jn 18:1–11). Jesus is taken immediately to the house of Annas — Peter's denials take place here? (Jn 18:12–27 and cf. Mt 26:69–75; Mk 14:66–72; Lk 22:55–62). From Annas, Jesus is taken to Caiaphas and kept there the rest of the night — Tuesday-Wednesday (Mt 26:57–58; Mk 14:53–54; Lk 22:54; Jn 18:24).

Wednesday. The first or trial-session of the Sanhedrin meets in the early morning (Mt 26:59; Mk 14:35; Lk 22:66). False witnesses speak of Jesus' destroying the temple (Mt 26:60–62; Mk 14:56–60). The messianic admission of Jesus is given (Mt 26:63–66; Mk 14:61–64; Lk 22:67–71). Jesus is mocked and kept there overnight (Mt 26:67–68; Mk 14:65; Lk 22:63–65).

Thursday. The second or sentence-session of the Sanhedrin is held in the early morning, twenty-four hours after the preceding trial session (Mt 27:1; Mk 15:1a; Lk 22:66). Jesus is sent to Pilate and the interrogation begins (Mt 27:2–14; Mk 15:1b–5; Lk 23:1–5; Jn 18:28–38). Jesus is sent by Pilate to Herod Antipas (Lk 23:6–1). Jesus is sent back again to Pilate, and Pilate's wife has a dream as Jesus is retained in Pilate's prison overnight (Mt 27:19; Lk 23:11).

Friday. Jesus is again before Pilate; Barabbas is released and Jesus is condemned (Mt 27:15–26; Mk 15:6–15; Lk 23:13–25; Jn 18:39–40 and 19:4–16). Jesus is scourged, crowned, and mocked (Mt 27:27–31; Mk 15:16–20; Lk 23:11(!) Jn 19:2–3). Jesus is crucified as Jerusalem prepares for the paschal meal that evening — according to the lunar calendar (Mt 27:32–50; Mk 15:21–37; Lk 23:26–46; Jn 19:17–30).

Appendix II: On the Post-Resurrection Apparitions of Jesus. The different and sometimes conflicting accounts of the empty tomb and the post-resurrection apparitions of Jesus may be compared in Mark 16:1–20; Matthew 28:1–20; Luke 24:1–53; John 20–21; and 1 Corinthians 15:3–11. The following is a summary of the individual passages in question:

i) Matthew 28:1–20. Because of the problem with Mark 16:1–20 we shall begin with Matthew rather than Mark. Mary

Magdalene (cf. Jn 20:1, alone!) and the other Mary come to the tomb, but no mention is made of an anointing (28:1); an angel terrifies the guards but reassures the women (28:2–5), showing them the empty tomb and telling them to bring the news to the disciples that Jesus awaits them in Galilee (28:6–7); the women then meet Jesus himself and he gives them the same message for the disciples (28:8–10); the guards are bribed to explain the empty tomb (28:11–15); Jesus meets the Eleven in Galilee on a mountain (28:16); despite their initial doubts, they receive their universal commission from Jesus (28:17–20).

ii) *John 20–21.* We can look at the entire text of John 20–21 despite the problems of the relationship of 20 and 21 which will be discussed later. Mary Magdalene comes to the tomb and sees the stone dislodged (20:1); she tells Peter of this "theft" of the body (notice the "we" in 20:2) and he and John go to verify her statement (20:3–10); Mary remains at the empty tomb and meets Jesus, who gives her a message for the disciples (20:11–18); Jesus appears to them with the gift of the Spirit (20:19–23); the Thomas incident ensues (20:24–29); the conclusion to the Gospel is given (20:30–31); Jesus appears to the disciples in Galilee (21:1–14); Peter receives his commission (21:15–19); the question on the death of John arises (21:20–23); the conclusion to this extra chapter is added (21:24–25).

iii) *Mark 16:1–20.* Mary Magdalene, Mary the mother of James, and Salome come with spices to anoint Jesus (16:1); another chronological indication is given in 16:2 (a new incident?), and we shall discuss this later; they arrive at the tomb (16:3–4); a "young man" in the empty tomb gives them a message for the disciples, especially Peter, that Jesus awaits them in Galilee (16:5–7); they tell no one because of fear (16:8); the added section in 16:9–20 begins with a new chronological indication stating that Jesus appears "first" (prōton) to Mary Magdalene (16:9); others, however, refuse her credence (16:10–11); later he appears to two disciples as they depart from the city (16:12–13); finally, he appears to the Eleven at table, complains of their unbelief, and gives them their universal commission (16:14–18); the ascension and promise of assistance follow (16:19–20).

iv) *Luke 24:1–53.* Spices and ointments had been prepared before the Sabbath rest began (23:54–56); after the Sabbath

rest they (on 23:55 cf. 24:10) come to the tomb (24:1); entering the empty tomb they see two men who recall the prophecy
of Jesus on his death and resurrection while in Galilee (24:2–7);
the women are identified as Mary Magdalene, Joanna, Mary
the mother of James, and others, and these report to the apostles
but are met with disbelief (24:8–11); two disciples meet Jesus
at Emmaus (24:13–35); Jesus appears to the Eleven and con-
vinces their disbelief (24:36–43); he recalls how the Old Testament prophecies are fulfilled in himself (summary of kerygma
in 24:44–47); he promises them the Spirit and gives them their
mission (24:48–49); the ascension takes place (24:50–53).

v) *1 Corinthians 15:3–11.* The traditional nature of this
statement is clear in the schematic balance of the profession of
faith. The apparition to Peter balances the apparition to James:
the fact that he appeared after Peter to the Twelve is balanced
by the fact that he appeared after James to all the apostles; and
centrally placed, between a double "then," is the apparition to
the five hundred brethren. This is obviously an artistically
formed credal summary.

The following is suggested as a hypothesis to explain the
divergencies of these accounts. It is open to dispute, of course,
but it should be remembered that some explanation is demanded
for the discrepancies.[23]

First, the body of Jesus was hastily buried on the late afternoon of Friday with no time for proper embalming; it was
merely covered with a shroud and placed in Joseph's new tomb
(Mk 15:42–46; Mt 27:57–60; Lk 23:50–54; Jn 15:38); but the

---

[23] For the burial cf. E. Lussier, "The Holy Sepulcher," *The Bible Today,*
11 (1964), 734–742; R. Mercurio, "A Baptismal Motif in the Gospel Narratives of the Burial," *CBQ,* 21 (1959), 39–54; and on the shroud of burial
cf. E. A. Wuenschel, "The Holy Shroud of Turin," *AER,* 93 (1935), 441–
472; 102 (1940), 465–486; "The Shroud of Turin and the Burial of Christ,"
CBQ, 7 (1945), 405–437; 8 (1946), 135–178; C. J. McNasby, "The
Shroud of Turin," *CBQ,* 7 (1945), 144–164. The historical-theological
problem of the resurrection is considered in A. Dulles, *Apologetics and the
Biblical Christ* ("Woodstock Papers"; Westminster, 1963), pp. 45–60. With
specific reference to the postresurrection apparitions cf. J. H. Crehan, "St.
Peter's Journey to Emmaus," CBQ, 15 (1953), 418–426; R. Orlett, "An
Influence of the Early Liturgy upon the Emmaus Account," CBQ, 21
(1959), 212–219; E. F. F. Bishop, "The Risen Christ and the Five-hundred
Brethren," *CBQ,* 18 (1956), 341–344; E. L. Allen, "The Lost Kerygma,"
NTS, 3 (1957), 349–353; and especially C. F. D. Moule, "The Post-
Resurrection Appearances in the Light of Festival Pilgrimages," *NTS,* 4
(1957), 58–61.

women (Lk 23:55–56; cf. Mk 15:47; Mt 27:61) and Nicodemus (Jn 19:39) prepared the spices before sundown that Sabbath eve. Here it might be useful to look for a moment at the chronological data given at the start of this section in each record; it seems that there is an attempt to merge two chronological details, one mentioning the end of the Sabbath rest, i.e., the late evening of Saturday, and the other mentioning the early hours of Sunday morning itself.

And when the Sabbath was past . . . (Mk 16:1).

And very early on the first day of the week they went to the tomb when the sun had risen . . . (Mk 16:2).

Now after the Sabbath, toward the dawn of the first day of the week . . . (Mt 28:1).

But on the first day of the week, at early dawn . . . (Lk 24:1).

Now on the first day of the week Mary Magdalene came to the tomb early, while it was still dark . . . (Jn 20:1).

It would seem that the two times, Saturday at sundown and early Sunday morning of Mark 16:1 and 16:2, are gradually smoothed into one single chronological indication as we go from Mark to John.

Second, the women, having prepared the spices and ointments for full burial, came and anointed Jesus as soon as the Sabbath rest was over, i.e., after sundown on Saturday (Mk 26:1). This visit marked the second and complete burial according to Jewish customs of embalming and would be the event behind or underneath the narrations in Mark 16:2–8; Matthew 28:1–10; Luke 24:1–11; John 19:40–41. It was this event of the "full" burial which dropped from the tradition and became confused with Mary Magdalene's personal encounter with the risen Lord, so that it is then the women who, in Matthew, find the empty tomb and even see Jesus. The story of their not telling anyone of their discovery (only in Mk 16:8) would most probably be interpretation to account for their silence after the confusion had already taken place.

Third, Mary Magdalene returned to the tomb on Sunday morning; this would be the source of the second chronological indication in Mark 16:2. From the fact that she had also been among the anointing women (Mk 16:1; Mt 28:1; Lk 24:10; cf.

Jn 19:25), presumably arose the confusion of what happened to her and the others (the anointing) with what happened to her alone (the empty tomb and the vision). She found the tomb empty and reported to Peter and John who came and saw the tomb (Jn 20:1–10). Jesus appeared for the first time to Mary Magdalene as she stayed by the tomb, an obvious and appropriate reward for her fidelity and love, and gave her a message for the disciples (Jn 20:11–18; Mk 16:9; note the prōton, "first"). This seems to be the actual source of the tradition about the angel(s) who appeared to the women at the empty tomb (Mk 16:1–8; Mt 28:1–10; Lk 24:1–11). In Matthew 28 the angel (5–7) and then Jesus himself (9–10) appeared to the women and gave them the same message for the disciples. It is suggested that the message as recorded in Matthew 28 is the same one given to Mary Magdalene alone in John 20. The development of the tradition might have been as follows: Jesus appeared to Mary Magdalene alone and gave her a message for the apostles; later she is "expanded" in the text to include the women who had earlier accompanied her in anointing the body on Saturday evening; therefore, the women must also have seen Jesus and received the message; but since there is some doubt about the women having done so, the angel is introduced as the source of their witness. Thus, in this theory, there would be only one event, Mary's discovery of the empty tomb and the appearance of Jesus to her, behind Mark 16:1–8 = Mark 16:9; Matthew 28:1–8 = Matthew 28:9–10; Luke 24:1–11; John 20:11–18.

Fourth, there is a strong tradition of initial disbelief at the news of the resurrection, which would have come first, in this explanation, from Mary Magdalene alone (Mk 16:11, 13, 14; Luke 24:11, 41). Possibly it was this disbelief which necessitated the Jerusalem apparitions of Jesus (not in Mk 16:1–8, but cf. 16:12–14; nor in Mt, but in Lk 24:13–50 and Jn 20:19–29), in order to persuade them to go to Galilee. It does seem necessary to postulate a Jerusalem appearance to the Twelve to explain the specific insistence of John 20:19.

Fifth, the interval between the pilgrim feasts of Pasch and Pentecost found the disciples back in Galilee and Jesus appeared often to them there (Mt 28:16–20; Jn 21:1–23; but notice the lack of place in Mk 16:14). Luke deliberately omits all of the

Galilean period in order to concentrate on Jerusalem (cf. Lk 24:6; Mk 16:7; Mt 28:7).

Sixth, the external and visible ascension would most likely have taken place when they had returned to Jerusalem for the feast of Pentecost (Mk 16:19; Lk 24:50–51; Acts 1:9–11).

Accordingly, it is suggested here that there is *one*, no doubt incomplete, but basically harmonious, tradition of apparitions in Jerusalem, Galilee, and Jerusalem again. But some of the discrepancies were noted at an early stage and in attempting to harmonize them the records became merely more difficult to unravel later on.

11. Postscript

Read John 21:1–25.

There are very close contacts between this section and the rest of John, both in form, in that we have narrative and explanatory discourse intertwined so that each elucidates the other, and in content, in that the threefold denial of Peter (18:15–18, 25–27) is expiated by a threefold confession of love (21:15–19). In addition, the theme of the shepherd in John 10 is continued in John 21. In all probability this section stems from the oral catechesis of John and was appended by his own disciples who were schooled in both the form and content of his thinking.

The apparitions of Jesus in Galilee are deliberately linked with the two mentioned earlier in 20:19–23 and 20:26–29 by the "third time" of 21:14.

The event of the miraculous catch would have been an obvious homiletical story in the early community: without Jesus they catch nothing (21:5), but with Jesus they catch all fish. It has been suggested that this number, 153 (21:11), was that of the species of fishes distinguished by the Greeks, so the cipher represented all possible fishes. The incident is most likely that told also in Luke 5:1–10, and indeed the words of Simon-Peter in Luke 5:8 become much more understandable after his denials.

The incident of Peter's confession at Caesarea Philippi and his special mission does not appear in John, but recall 1:42 and 6:67–71. Moreover, the incident reported in John 21:15–19 does not seem to be a mere Johannine rephrasing of the incident in

Matthew 16:13–20. Rather it seems to be a clear statement that the function of Jesus in John 10 is to be transferred to Peter, and that this function as shepherd is associated with both love and death in John 21 as it was previously in John 10. Thus, Peter is made shepherd of the entire flock as the representative of Jesus; he is the center and efficacious symbol of its unity and its love. The question in 21:15 is a gentle and ironic reminder to Peter that he had claimed on the evening of the arrest that he would never fail Jesus even if all the others did (Mt 26:33; Mk 14:29). It would surely be incorrect to see in 21:15 a statement that Peter loved Jesus more than the rest of the Twelve did and so is put in a rank above them. However, having reminded Peter that his claim to love him more than all the others has not exactly proved correct, Jesus thereafter gives him the function of becoming the visible center of unity and focal point of the Twelve.

The narrative in 21:20–23 was written to offset a misunderstanding which may have caused some scandal at the death of John himself. Jesus had referred to John's being alive at his "coming," which would have meant of course the "coming" in judgment and salvation to the generation which had heard his preaching, but some had thought this meant that John would live to the end of the world. This would seem to be another misunderstanding of the "coming" of which Jesus had spoken so often. At the end of this added postscript the scribe-redactor of John 21 witnesses to the fact that this chapter also has Johannine authority behind it (21:24–25).

CHAPTER IV

Epilogue to the Gospel of Eternal Life

THE use of the term "Epilogue" is intended to be pedagogic rather than chronological. It is most likely that the Apocalypse was published before the final edition of the Gospel of John but both are the fruit of a long oral catechesis and also an extended literary process. It is instructive, however, to read Apocalypse today after one has studied the Gospel. It projects in hope the future of the community of love whose inauguration was the essential message of that Gospel. Apocalypse itself shows evidence of having been formed over a long period of time. With some degree of probability one main section may stem from the persecution of Nero (c. 65) and the other from that of Domitian (c. 95). This explains especially the changes in the theological outlook with regard to eschatology as the emphasis shifts from an imminent return of Jesus within his own generation to awareness that the resurrectional gift of the Spirit was already that return and one now awaits not return, but victory, not the second coming of the one who is gone but the climactic triumph of the one ever present among his people. The tension between these two views is, however, the tension in which each one of us finds himself. Each person meets Christ anew in his own generation and his eternal destiny establishes itself in that encounter, and thereby he participates for good or evil in the ongoing thrust of the people of God toward ultimate victory.

A. INTRODUCTION TO APOCALYPSE

One would show scant sympathy for a student who considered "Animal Farm" of little importance since it dealt with the

146

obvious absurdity of talking animals. One could only be tolerant toward the view that "Lord of the Flies" was an adventure story about young boys and therefore suitable reading only for such an audience. In more academic language, this would be a failure to appreciate and distinguish literary form. On another level, one accepts the black-and-white distinction of good and evil in the genre of the cowboy story and one does not expect or want meditations upon death and disaster in the middle of a murder mystery. The educated person knows and responds immediately and almost instincitvely to the literary genres or forms of his own experience and his own world. And yet, he may fail completely to understand the literary forms of an earlier generation or of a different mentality than his own. If a message of vital urgency is couched in such difficult forms, he may never discover its meaning let alone its importance. Of all the forms used in the Bible, that of Apocalypse is most alien to our thought processes. And yet no form holds a message more desperately vital to our age. When a generation pushes outward toward the stars, and cannot even be certain it will still be in existence when its latest satellite joins their galaxies, some vision of cosmic hope is surely its most immediate requirement. We need a voice of optimism but not of complacency, a word of hope but not of smugness. Is there a future without futility upon this planet? Is there a future at all for this earth? The answer is in Apocalypse.[1]

1. The Literary Form of Apocalypse

The word "apocalypse" is a literal transcription of the Greek *apokalypsis* which means an uncovering or revelation of what is hidden and secret. The revelation in question is usually of the future and of the unfolding of human history. The name has spread from the one New Testament book to all such literature,

---

[1] This type of literature is discussed in general by H. H. Rowley. *The Relevance of Apocalyptic* (London, 1947); S. B. Frost, *Old Testament Apocalyptic. Its Origins and Growth* (London, 1952); G. E. Ladd, "Why not Prophetic-Apocalyptic?" *JBL*, 76 (1957), 192–200; B. Vawter, "Apocalyptic: Its Relation to Prophecy," *CBQ*, 22 (1960), 33–46; M. J. Cantley, "Introduction to Apocalyptic," *The Bible Today*, 8 (1963), 500–504. With regard to the New Testament example of this genre cf. W. H. Quiery, "Opening the 'Closed Book' of the New Testament," *AER*, 143 (1960), 49–56; P. Fannon, "The Apocalypse," *Scr*, 14 (1962), 33–43. Cf. also M. Hopkins, "The Historical Perspective of Apocalypse 1–11," *CBQ*, 27 (1965), 42–47.

even that which preceded the New Testament in Israel. Apocalypse has been called "the child of prophecy" and this is a very apt description. But it also has another parent. One might say that its father was Prophecy and its mother Crisis. Apocalyptic writing was born in danger; it is prophecy for persecution.

a) From Prophecy to Apocalypse

This consideration of Apocalyptic as crisis-prophecy born of oppression and persecution is the first foundation for a proper understanding of the literary form.

In the preexilic period of Israel's existence, her prophets continually warned a proud, sinful, and self-confident nation that the future might well prove worse for Israel herself than for the pagan nations, and that she had better look to her own behavior. Their own vision held with absolute fidelity to the ancient and unconditional promises of Yahweh to Abraham:

> Now the Lord said to Abram, "Go from your country and your kindred and your father's house to the land that I will show you. And I will make of you a great nation, and I will bless you, and him who curses you I will curse; and by you all the families of the earth shall bless themselves" (Gn 12:1–3).

But they also knew with equal clarity the terrible "ifs" of the covenant at Sinai between God and his people, as Moses warned them:

> "And if you obey the voice of the Lord your God, being careful to do all his commandments which I command you this day, the Lord your God will set you high above all the nations of the earth. And all these blessings shall come upon you and overtake you, if you obey the voice of the Lord your God" (Dt 28:1–2).

> "But if you will not obey the voice of the Lord your God or be careful to do all his commandments and his statutes which I command you this day, then all these curses shall come upon you and overtake you" (Dt 28:15).

Looking at the increasing infidelity of the people of God, especially under the evil example of the monarchy, they knew a terrible day of wrath was approaching, but with a prophetic faith they foresaw what lay beyond the catastrophe for the purified remnant of God's people. This cataclysmic reckoning of God with his people, this "Day of the Lord," signalled in chronological vagueness with such terms as, "on that day," or "days are coming," etc., would be both judgment and salvation according to the dispositions of freedom it encountered. Thus one of the earliest of the preexilic prophets spoke emphatically of the judgment upon Israel:

> Woe to you who desire the day of the Lord!
>   Why would you have the day of the Lord?
> It is darkness, and not light;
>   as if a man fled from a lion,
>   and a bear met him;
> or went into the house and leaned with his hand against the wall,
>   and a serpent bit him.
> Is not the day of the Lord darkness, and not light,
>   and gloom with no brightness in it?
>   (Amos 5:18–20.)

But he also spoke of hope for those who had struggled through the darkness and into the light:

> Hate evil, and love good,
>   and establish justice in the gate;
> it may be that the Lord, the God of hosts,
>   will be gracious to the remnant of Joseph.
>   (Amos 5:15.)

However, in the exilic and postexilic period the prophets were in a very different situation. They were now called to offer hope and consolation to a vanquished and exiled people, to fan the flame of faith in the purified remnant of Israel. When they spoke of judgment, it was to the pagan and persecuting nations, and they talked of salvation to God's people as the elected remnant. The change is very clear in the book of Ezekiel. In 1–24 he inveighs against a Jerusalem doomed to destruction, but in 25–38 he speaks hope to a repentant people after that city's fall. Notice the difference between Ezekiel 24:20–21:

> Then I said to them, "The word of the Lord came to me: 'Say to the house of Israel, Thus says the Lord God: Behold, I will profane my sanctuary, the pride of your power, the delight of your eyes, and the desire of your soul; and your sons and your daughters whom you left behind shall fall by the sword.' "

And Ezekiel 25:3–4:

> "Say to the Ammonites, Hear the word of the Lord God: Thus

says the Lord God, Because you said, 'Aha!' over my sanctuary when it was profaned, and over the land of Israel when it was made desolate, and over the house of Judah when it went into exile; therefore I am handing you over to the people of the East for a possession. . . ."

This change in historical situation is the essential difference between preexilic prophecy and postexilic apocalyptical writing: the former spoke judgment on Israel and salvation to the remnant thereof, the latter spoke judgment on the persecuting world empires and salvation to God's people, now the chosen remnant.

But there is a second feature, which explains the form of Apocalypse rather than the content, and especially the esoteric nature which is so disconcerting to the modern reader. When, for example, Jeremiah spoke out against Jerusalem and its temple because of its lack of social justice despite liturgical and ritual exactitude (Jer 7 = 26), his words almost cost him his life. But to speak out against the great pagan and persecuting empires of the postexilic period could easily bring destruction on the entire people. Prophecy had to go underground and it appeared again as Apocalyptic. Just as the love songs of the Irish patriots, assuring their beloved of ultimate fidelity, were actually veiled vows of martial resistance to the foreign invaders of their country, so the use of symbolic figures, colors, numbers, etc., in Apocalypse revealed the message to the faithful and screened it from the oppressors themselves. Not with impunity could tiny Israel proclaim the destruction of the Seleucid dynasty (Dn), nor the infant Church announce the fall of Rome (Ap). This esoteric language is simply the imagery of the prophetic vocabulary burnished for battle as resistance literature.

b) The Message of Cosmic Hope

We are not dealing here with the hope of eternal life for the individual. This was quite sufficiently and frequently asserted in the Gospel itself; recall John 6 and 11. We are discussing hope for this world, on this earth, of this planet. Is this world merely a stage on which the individual works out his salvation, or is it also included in God's design? The prophetic view of the future "Day of the Lord" had always included a social dimension (Am 5:21–24; Is 1:10–17), a universal dimension (Is 2:2–4; 49:1–6;

Jon 4:11), and also a cosmic dimension (Is 35:5–7; Jl 2). This theme of the new creation, the cosmic dimension of Israel's future hope, appears again in the New Testament (for example, in Rom 8:19–23):

> For the creation waits with eager longing for the revealing of the sons of God; for the creation was subjected to futility, not of its own will but by the will of him who subjected it in hope; because the creation itself will be set free from its bondage to decay and obtain the glorious liberty of the children of God. We know that the whole creation has been groaning in travail together until now; and not only the creation, but we ourselves, who have the first fruits of the Spirit, groan inwardly as we wait for adoption as sons, the redemption of our bodies.

The function of Apocalypse is to consider the cosmic hope as such, and to project the future of the divinely given destiny of mankind in Genesis 1:26–28. Two hundred years ago, "the first things" seemed a closed and very simple book in which God had created everything a few thousand years before. It may well be that a few hundred years from now "the last things," seemingly equally closed and simple now, will be equally open and the future equally diverse for this earth. As individuals, we have no lasting abode here on earth, but God has here such an abode, for at least his interest with our earth is to be calculated by millions of years. We now ask what is the future of his earthly abode, for we know that even if we will soon be living in eternal existence with him, we will surely share his interest in that future.

The theological virtues are usually enumerated as faith, hope, and love, thereby accepting the sequence of 1 Corinthians 13:13 where Paul stated, "So faith, hope, love abide, these three; but the greatest of these is love." The sequence has love in last place for purposes of literary climax, and it is unfortunate that we have accepted this sequence as our official order since in almost all other cases Paul has the sequence, faith, love, and hope: this order makes it much easier to understand what these virtues mean to him and why there are three such and no more.

In many of his letters Paul immediately follows the introductory formula with a thanksgiving for the lives of his recipients. This appears as early as 1 Thessalonians 1:2–3:

> We give thanks to God always for you all, constantly mention-

ing you in our prayers, remembering before our God and Father your work of faith [*pistis*] and labor of love [*agapē*] and steadfastness of hope [*hypomonē tēs elpidos*] in our Lord Jesus Christ.

And as late as Ephesians 1:15–18:

> For this reason, because I have heard of your faith [*pistis*] in the Lord Jesus and your love [*agapē*] toward all the saints, I do not cease to give thanks for you, remembering you in my prayers, that the God of our Lord Jesus Christ, the Father of glory, may give you a spirit of wisdom and of revelation in the knowledge of him, having the eyes of your hearts enlightened, that you may know what is the hope [*elpis*] to which he has called you.

It also appears in 1 Thessalonians 5:8 and Colossians 1:4–5. The word *elpis*, which means "hope," is closely associated with *hypomonē* which means "patience, endurance" in such texts as 1 Thessalonians 1:3 and Romans 5:3–4. Thus, the triad also appears frequently as faith, love, and patience/endurance, for example, in 2 Thessalonians 1:3–5, in 1 Timothy 6:11, and in Titus 2:2.

One might see these virtues as fragmented moments or existential dimensions of Christian life. The first moment and enduring basis of all is faith; the continuing expression is love; and the future is grasped only in the enduring patience of hope. This hope is not just for my own eternal existence, for that is already contained explicitly in my faith. Rather, this hope looks out beyond my own existence to the ultimate destiny of the cosmos and of all creation (cf. Rom 8:24–25). This cosmic hope is for the ultimate victory of Jesus in which his people, totally dedicated to love, will have taken control of all the mighty forces of evolution and mold them to the service of each other's needs so that creation serves love as it was always destined to do. All of us present will long be with God before such a consummation, but our knowledge that God has a destiny for our earth as an enduring dwelling place ratifies and vindicates our concern for the cosmic process and its structuring toward concern and love. At this moment, we can only intimate about this future, but already the writings of men like Teilhard de Chardin recall us to our share while on earth in God's mysterious plan for its future. The great message of Apocalypse is that God's people, the community of faith in the presence of love, the society of acceptance and commitment to love, will not only endure despite all objection, all opposition, and all persecution, but will prevail and conquer in the very course of human history, where Christ has conquered before us and for us.

One reads and wonders at the closing words of Paul Tillich's address before the *Pacem in Terris* Convocation, February 18, 1965, in New York City:

> There is no hope for a final stage of history in which peace and justice rule. History is not fulfilled at its empirical end; but history is fulfilled in the great moments in which something new is created, or, as one could express it religiously, in which the kingdom of God breaks into history conquering the destructive structures of existence, one of the greatest of which is war. This means that we cannot hope for a final stage of justice and peace within history; but we can hope for partial victories over the forces of evil in a particular moment of time.

It would seem that the vision of Apocalypse offers hope beyond this and offers it, however vaguely, for this earth where God still dwells among his people. Ecclesiastes 5:2 said, "God is in heaven, and you upon earth; therefore let your words be few." If God is in heaven and we are alone on earth, then our words should be very few. But what if God has pitched his tent in the camp of his people (Jn 1:14)? Is the image, then, more like this?

> Then I saw a new heaven and a new earth; for the first heaven and the first earth had passed away, and the sea was no more. And I saw the holy city, new Jerusalem, coming down out of heaven from God, prepared as a bride adorned for her husband; and I heard a great voice from the throne saying, "Behold, the dwelling of God is with men. He will dwell with them, and they shall be his people, and God himself will be with them; he will wipe away every tear from their eyes, and death shall be no more, neither shall there be mourning nor crying nor pain any more, for the former things have passed away" (Ap 21:1–4).

It may seem paradoxical, but the security of this cosmic hope is strengthened by our own dawning awareness of the awesome power of unconcern and unlove on the personal, national, and international levels. The alternatives to love are becoming frighteningly obvious to us and the absolute necessity of incarnating the vision of Jesus in human society seems now a matter of urgent and impelling necessity. If love does not respond to human need in all its multifaceted anguish, that need will rise up to destroy our planet. Only the rule of concern structured into love can establish peace upon this earth for people and for nations. Apocalypse expresses this hope in the ultimate victory of love upon earth; beyond earth is not victory but reward, not conquest but repose, not triumph but rest.

2. *The Structure of Apocalypse*

An initial word on the "visions" of Apocalypse might be of assistance. What is the relationship between the visions constantly mentioned in this work and the carefully worked out literary framework? Did John see with his eyes, or have these images impressed miraculously on his imagination? The author is above all a seer, an ecstatic visionary. God grants to the seer in ecstasy some revelation of the future — a certain reality is impressed on his mind. It is this intellectual content, searing in its certainty and ineffable in its meaning, that the prophet must afterwards strive to express in merely human terms. Notice that no respect is paid to the fact that the *imagination* often balks at the visions portrayed; for example, what happens when one with a two-edged sword in his mouth starts to talk, or how does a lamb stand as if slain? John himself tells us that what he "saw" in ecstasy was "like . . ." (1:13; 4:6; 5:6; 15:2). John did not see these things with his own eyes or even with his imagination; what God revealed to his mind is expressed to us by these images and symbols, most of which are borrowed from earlier apocalyptic literature of the Old Testament, such as Ezekiel or Daniel. We might distinguish three stages in the making of our Apocalypse which could be characterized as follows: (a) the ecstatic experience or profound spiritual intuition impressed on the very depths of John's faith and John's consciousness; (b) the symbolic image which is built up in detail to express this intuition; (c) the literary unity in which these images and symbols are formed together into a consecutive literary work. Accordingly, what rules the description of the symbolic picture or scene is not whether the finished image is imaginable or even pleasing to the imagination. A beast with seven heads and ten horns is not easy to imagine. The point is whether the picture expresses as fully as possible all the content in the mind of the seer on that subject. Thus, the visionary tries to build up in his symbolic picture, detail by detail, the full expression of the divinely communicated theme. He adds things (blood, crown, sword), and colors (white, black, red), and numbers (seven, twelve one thousand), until the symbolic scene expresses to the mind, not the imagination, of the reader, the message of the author. Now the task is laid upon the reader. He must work laboriously back the opposite way to that in which the author himself worked: from the literary unity, back through the symbolic pictures, to the truth revealed by God. Bit by bit, one must break down the elements in the symbolic picture. Then, when all the elements are clear, he must see what is being taught in their unity. The main clues in this endeavor are the meaning of these images, numbers, and symbols in traditional Israelitic prophecy and apocalypse, and the purpose John had in using them for the Church in crisis. If one cannot do this the Apocalypse of John is a sealed book and, as such, a tremendous loss for both our faith and our hope.

From earliest tradition, Apocalypse was associated with the periods of both Nero (54–65) and Domitian (81–96) and their respective persecutions. It is quite likely that this ambivalence, and the great number of passages in the present Apocalypse which read almost like doublets, arise from the fact that an earlier Apocalypse written during Nero's persecution (around 65) was later widened and expanded into the present Apocalypse to offset an even worse persecution, that of Domitian (c. 95). When the Roman Empire first unleashed its full might against the infant Church under Nero it must have seemed the very end of everything, even of the world itself; surely now Jesus would appear upon the clouds in judgment upon the Roman eagles and in salvation for his persecuted faithful. But Peter and Paul died, and so did many others, and still the end of the world did not occur. The laws against the Christians remained on the books even during the period of imperial rivalry (68–69) and also under the Flavian rulers, Vespasian (69–79) and Titus (79–81). By this time, a more complete understanding of eschatology was possible. The end of the world was not imminent and the future remained undated. However, serene in faith and hope, John now declared that the Roman Empire, as a persecuting evil power, would be destroyed and the saints of God would prevail. We might term this "Roman eschatology." Rome, the great archetypal model of Satan's onslaught on God's people, would not overcome them. Furthermore, other empires and other nations would rise up against God's people again and again throughout history, and neither would they be able to conquer or destroy the community of love upon this earth. Indeed this community, in whose midst God dwelt, would finally overcome these forces of hate incarnated in whatever evil powers of earth. This victory is neither programed, dated, nor described; it is simply and serenely stated: love shall overcome upon this earth. That is hope; that is what Apocalypse is all about.

Throughout this work, but without going into more detail than is necessary in a book such as this, we will find a constant interweaving of the "Roman eschatology," God's judgment and salvation in one archetypal situation, and the "total eschatology," which is God's continuing judgment and salvation in all historical situations until the ultimate victory of love upon this earth of his creation. This "total eschatology" is usually depicted under the image of one gigantic final battle between good and evil. But in actual fact, this struggle is not single event, but continual process. The victory belongs to good, but it is in a war that lasts as long as human history. One feature requires special notice. In Apocalypse 2–3 we see that all is not well even within the church itself and the inclusion of this makes Apocalypse reminiscent of the preexilic prophets as well as the postexilic apocalyptists. There is no complacency in his optimism. The general outline of the work is as follows:

Introduction: 1:1–8.
Message to the Seven Churches: 1:9–3:22.
Announcement of the Day of the Lord: 4:1–16:21.
Advent of the Day of the Lord: 17:1–22:5.
Conclusion: 22:6–21.

B. EXPLANATION OF APOCALYPSE

1. Introduction

Read Apocalypse 1:1–8.

The passage in 1:1–3, 7–8 (cf. 22:6–13) is an introduction to the entire work, while 1:4–6, the standard epistolary opening of the New Testament letters, is more precisely that to the seven churches of Apocalypse 2–3, i.e., the symbolic plenitude of all Christian churches. God and Christ are coming in judgment and salvation upon the Roman situation as upon all future repetitions thereof. The battle between Rome and God (soon), and the great final battle between Satan and God (always), serve together as archetypal historical incident and enduring transtemporal image to state that all such evil forces will be overthrown and that God and his community will prevail.

2. Message to the Seven Churches

Read Apocalypse 1:9–3:22.

These are warnings against internal weaknesses within the community itself: not all trouble stems from without! By writing to seven ancient churches John shows that he writes symbolically to the whole Church at all times and in all places.

The vision in which John obtains his mission follows the usual literary structure of such visions in the Old Testament. The sequence is as follows: setting in time and place; the vision itself; fear; reassurance; the mission is given. Compare for example the stark simplicity of Jeremiah 1:6–10, or the highly ornamented account of Isaiah 6:1–13. John follows this same general form but with special references to the vision of Daniel 10. John's mission comes from Christ himself who appears both as priest (long robe) and king (golden girdle). His is eternal existence (white hair) and divine knowledge (eyes of flame). He cannot be moved (feet of bronze). He appears surrounded by the seven churches themselves (seven lampstands) and with complete power over them (seven stars in his right hand). Finally, the vision is one of mixed warning (two-edged sword) and joy (face like the sun).

After the mission-vision in 1:9–20, the letters to the churches of Ephesus (2:1–7), Smyrna (2:8–11), Pergamum (2:12–17), Thyatira (2:18–29), Sardis (3:1–6), Philadelphia (3:7–13), and Laodicea (3:14–22) follow immediately. The structure of these letters is very similar to that of 2 John and 3 John. These latter also address themselves to problems in the churches (one or two?) to which John was writing, problems either of jurisdiction (3 John) or even heresy (2 John). These two letters are composed of an opening address; praise, mentioning their good points; warning, mentioning their bad points; judgment, which speaks both of threats and of rewards; the promise of a future visit; and the final greetings. When we turn from these two letters to the seven in Apocalypse 2–3 we find a very similar structure. Each letter begins with the name of the church which receives the letter; then some aspect of Christ from the initial vision is mentioned; next follows praise for their good points; then warning against their bad points; then threats and rewards as judgment is passed; and finally the conclusion. The good points of the churches are usually summed up as moral virtue, constancy under persecution, and fidelity to truth despite a pagan environment. Their bad points involve the loss of moral virtue mostly owing to the effects of syncretistic pagan influences.

3. Announcement of the Day of the Lord

In this section (4:1–16:21) we find again the same traces of an earlier and later apocalyptic tradition. The inaugural vision of the scroll which is the seer's vocation to write appears both in 4:1–5:14 (later tradition) and 10:1–11 (earlier tradition). Then the day of God's reckoning is announced, both for Rome and for all such future situations until the end of time. This appears in the sequence of Roman (6:1–11), total (6:12–8:1), and Roman (8:2–11:19) eschatology (later tradition) and once again as Roman (13:1–14, 13), total (14:14–15:4), and Roman (15:5–16:21) eschatology (earlier tradition). Between these two statements is the conflict vision (12:1–17), placed centrally as it interprets the entire literary unity. The constant interweaving of the historical Roman situation and the general divine reckoning with all future kingdoms of hate and unconcern creates the excitement of the apocalyptic form in which abstract principle is embedded in, and exemplified by, a single, concrete, archetypal, and historical example.

a) The Scroll Vision

Read Apocalypse 4:1–5:14; 10:1–11.
There are two visions of the scroll in our present Apocalypse —

one in 4:1–5:14 (later tradition), and another in 10:1–11 (earlier tradition). At the earlier inaugural vision it was an angel who gave the scroll to John to keep and then to announce the Day of the Lord (10:1–11). The scroll represents John's message of doom against the pagan and persecuting powers.

In 4:1–5:14 there is a much fuller inaugural vision which actually stands now as the opening in the present final form of Apocalypse; the vision of Apocalypse 10 has been relegated to a secondary location in the final edition. This imagery is closely based on that of Ezekiel 1–3, the inaugural vision of the prophet Ezekiel. It opens with God (4:1–3) surrounded by his heavenly court (4:4–11) which is composed of all creation: God's people of both Testaments (twenty-four elders); the angelic hierarchy (seven torches); and the rest of creation in all its perfection of being (four living beings; cf. Ez 1–2). Next the scroll is introduced (5:1–4) and all creation is unable to unroll it until the lamb, the glorified Christ, approaches (5:5–7). He alone holds in his hands the destiny of the future for he alone has perfection of power (seven horns) and wisdom (seven eyes). Then all beings sing a mighty hymn of praise in three waves of song going out from the throne of God (5:9–10, 11–12, 13–14). The lamb is clearly divine (compare 4:11 with 5:12).

b) The First Announcement of the Day

Read Apocalypse 6:1–11:9.

This announcement of God's day of reckoning in both judgment (on evil) and salvation (for goodness) speaks first of Rome (6:1–8, 9–11), then of all such evil forces down the length of history (6:12–17; 7:1–8:1), and finally back again to Rome (8:2–9:21; 11:1–19). The present position of Apocalypse 10 breaks of course into this literary unity.

1) 6:1–11. The glorified Lord (white horse) will punish Rome with the standard Old Testament divine scourges of war (red horse), succeeded by famine (black horse), succeeded by pestilence (pale horse). This historical judgment on the Roman Empire (6:1–8) would be God's external sign of the salvation of those persecuted by evil, God's saints robed in the white of victory (6:9–11).

2) 6:12–8:1. The perspective now changes from the Roman

situation to that of all the future, symbolized and summed up as one mighty end-time battle between good and evil, one great divine act of judgment (6:12–17) and salvation (7:1–8, 1) on all of humanity. The Roman "end" is archetypal for all time, for it is the first onslaught on the infant Church from a great world empire and thus the first five seals (Rome) merge into the last two (all of future history).

The sixth seal (6:12–17) expands the promise of God's judgment beyond Rome unto all those who oppose at any time or at any place the teaching of love and concern which is that of God's saints. All of creation, summed up in seven areas — earthquake, sun, moon, stars, sky, mountains, and islands — will turn against those who so act, all of evil humanity, summed up in seven classes — kings, great men, generals, rich, strong, slaves, and free.

In 7:1–8:1 is a magnificent vista of the salvation of all the elect, the full number of all the saints of God, symbolized as the perfect number of the children of Israel. Just as the twenty-four elders, twelve plus twelve, of 4:4 represented the complete Israel of God, the community of both Testaments, so here the twelve times twelve times one thousand has the same connotation. In Apocalypse numbers have a symbolic meaning: seven indicates fullness, perfection, plenitude; three and a half indicates incompleteness, that which is abortive, short-lived, and so also does the cipher 1260, the number of days in forty-two months (reckoning thirty days to the month) and thus in three and a half years; six designates a deficit, almost seven but not exactly seven; eight, on the other hand, indicates superabundance, more than seven; 1000 means a multitude, a lot, a long time, or very many. Thus the numberless multitude of 7:9 does not contradict the precise numbering of 7:5–8.

The meaning of 8:1 is the silence which immediately preceded the unleashing of God's day (cf. Zph 1:7). This prepares the transition from the future vision of all of human history back to the historical and imminent destiny of the Roman Empire.

3) 8:2–11:19. Once again we revert to the Roman situation for both God's judgment (8:2–9:21) and salvation (11:1–19). The symbolism of seven angels (8:7, 8, 10, 12; 9:1, 13; 11:15) here replaces that of the seven seals (6:1, 3, 5, 7, 9, 12; 8:1), but both denote the control of judgment and salvation which rests in the hands of the glorified Lord.

The first four angels (8:7–12) strike only one-third of the world (earth, sea, rivers, heavens,) symbolizing judgment on Rome alone, not on all human history, as in 6:12–17. The fifth scourge (9:1–12) combines in one fearsome image of "warrior-locusts" (cf. Joel 2:2–11) the two greatest scourges of the ancient world, war and famine. The sixth angel now appears (9:13–21). The Euphrates was the eastern boundary of the empire and, like the American frontier, was the symbol and location of unrest, danger, and the permanent possibility of invasion. It is that across which the invaders must come, no matter whence they come! This goes beyond geography, of course. After the locusts come the horses, another mythoapocalyptic description calculated for terror. Once again they strike only a third of mankind, that is the Roman Empire itself. The horsemen combine the terrors of the infernal pit, the animal world, and the military world.

In the two sections on the downfall of Rome (6:1–8 and 8:2–9:21), it is stressed that only a part of the world is struck by this day of God's wrath, it is not the full day of wrath which will descend throughout history on any future people which emulates the example of Rome. Hence such terms as: "a fourth of the earth" (6:8); "a third of . . ." (8:7–12); "for five months" (9:5, 10). But notice also 9:20–21 where the rest of human history does not take warning from the fate of Rome but continues in immorality and idolatry.

In 11:1–19 the vista changes again to that of salvation, but still in the immediate context of Rome. The section in 11:1–13, 19 may have originally been an independent apocalyptic unit in its own right and it was placed here since it also speaks of salvation, as does the image of the seventh angel in 11:15–18.

While interpretations vary widely, it seems at least possible that this apocalyptic vision applies directly to the martyrdom of Peter and Paul. The effects of the death of the two great apostles must have been terrifying for the infant Church and John wishes to explain it within the plan of God for human history. Ezekiel 40–48 measured in vision the new temple of the new Jerusalem in order to signify all would take place as predetermined and pre-established by God. Here John wishes to say that all the slain of Nero's persecution were already "premeasured by God," that this too was within his design. The Roman Empire, however, would persecute only for the symbolic period of "three and one half" years (11:9, 11), that is, "forty-two months" (11:2), that is, "one thousand two hundred and sixty days" (11:3). This length of time is taken from the words of Daniel 7:25; 12:7 where the persecution of Antiochus IV Epiphanes lasted only three and one half years. Therefore, the persecution of Rome would be arrested while it was in midcourse by God, and throughout this period God would have two special witnesses against Rome. These two witnesses, symbolized by two olive trees or two lampstands, are Peter and Paul. This is modeled after Zechariah 4:1-4, 11-14 where they stood for Joshua and Zerubbabel, the sacerdotal and royal hopes for the postexilic restoration of Israel's past. Peter and Paul represent the center of hope in the priestly kingdom of the Church. They are described in terms taken from the description of Elijah and Moses from the Old Testament. In them, the entire prophetic, sacerdotal, and royal dignity of Israel of both Testaments comes to completion. When, at God's will, they have finished their witness, they are slain by Nero. All the nations prepare to make merry at their death but their rejoicing is abortive (11:9, 11). The conclusion of this vision of 11:1-13 appears in 11:19.

In 11:15-18, the trumpet of the seventh angel, is the prophecy of salvation for the elect of God persecuted and slain by the Roman empire.

c) The Conflict Vision

Read Apocalypse 12:1-17.

This chapter also shows traces of combination between an earlier vision of the conflict (12:7-12) and a later and much more developed one (12:1-6, 13-17). The purpose of the chapter is to give the theological basis for the great struggle of good against evil upon this earth. It was first visualized as the combat of Satan and his forces against Michael and his hosts (12:7-12), but in the more developed theology of later apocalyptic thought it is now a threefold attack by Satan against the woman — in her child (12:1-5), in herself (12:6, 13-16), and in her "other children" (12:17). The present position of Apocalypse 12 between the first or earlier (6:1-11:19) and second or later (13:1-16:21) announcement of the pending Day of the Lord's judgment and salvation makes of 6:1–16:22 a great triptych of which Apocalypse 12 is the central and interpretative panel.

John uses Mary, the woman (recall Jn 1:12–13; 2:1–4; 19:25–27), to incarnate in one symbolic and archetypal person his message of conflict.[2] Mary is mother of the child whom Satan attacks but who was taken up in resurrectional triumph from the first onslaught of evil, symbolized by the dragon (12:1–5). Secondly, she herself is the archetypal symbol of the Church because her faith-acceptance of the Word gave flesh to the final Word of God; she is thus the recipient of the onslaught which Satan unleashed upon the community of love through the Roman persecution. Mary in the wilderness for three and a half years symbolized the Church under the Neronic persecution (11:3), the second stage of Satan's attack (12:6). The third stage is all of human history and represents Satan's persecution of "the rest of her offspring." These are the faithful of all times and all places, "those who keep the commandments of God and their testimony to Jesus" (12:17). To dramatize this eternal conflict in visual imagery the dragon attacks the woman in three stages: in Christ, in the archetypal onslaught of the Roman Empire, and in all following persecutions of similar world powers of evil.

d) The Second Announcement of the Day

Read Apocalypse 13:1–16:21.

In the earlier edition of this work of consolation, composed for the situation of Nero's persecution around the year 65, the proclamation of divine reckoning had touched on Rome (6:1–11 and 11:1–13). In 13:1–16:21 is a later and more fully developed handling of this same theme. It appears in the same triple rhythm, bringing the earlier words up to date, and setting them against the wider and more terrible perspective of Domitian's at-

---

[2] Whether the woman is the feminine symbol for the people of God in the Old and/or New Testament or for Mary herself or for some literary combination of these is still quite disputed. For a summary of the debate and other opinions cf. B. J. LeFrois, "The Mary-Church relationship in the Apocalypse," Mar Stud, 9 (1958), 79–106, and TD, 7 (1959), 21–26; P. P. James, "Mary and the Great Sign," AER, 142 (1960), 321 329; N. D. O'Donoghue, "'A Woman Clothed with the Sun,'" Furrow, 11 (1960), 445–456; A. Feuillet, "The Messia born of the people of God," TD, 11 (1963), 10–11; J. E. Bruns, "The Contrasted Women of Apocalypse 12 and 17," CBQ, 26 (1964), 459–463.

tack on this community of love. The structure of 13:1–16:21 is thus very similar to that of 6:1–11:18. First of all both judgment (13:1–18) and salvation (14:1–13) are announced for the Roman situation; then judgment (14:14–20) and salvation (15:1–4) are proclaimed for all future situations throughout human history; finally, another announcement of the judgment upon Rome is given (15:5–16:21).

1) *13:1–14:3.* The image of judgment is based very closely on the imagery of Daniel 7 in which the evil empires of the world are portrayed as four beasts. Satan waited on the shore of the sea (12:17) to hand over evil power to the first beast (13:1), which represented the Roman Empire and especially the worship of the emperor as God. Out of the foaming and boiling unrest of humanity, symbolized by the surge of the sea, arises the blasphemous presence of the all-powerful (heads and horns symbolize the full list of the emperors and their vassals) empire which contains in itself all the evil of the Old Testament pagan empires in Daniel 7 (lion, bear, leopard). Despite internal strife, the beast emerges triumphant (13:3), but its activities are short lived (13:5; cf. 11:2–3; 12:6).

In 13:11 a second beast appears. John focuses on Satan (12:17), then on the Roman Empire (13:1–10), and finally on Nero himself (13:11–18), in whom the activity of evil takes its present incarnation. The second beast is the proximate and immediate presence of the first beast. The most likely interpretation of 13:18 is to see in it a cipher for the name "Nero Ceasar" by giving numerical value to the letters in which this would appear in Hebrew. Satan, the dragon; then the imperial worship of the Roman Empire, the first or sea beast; finally Nero, the second or earth beast, is the sequence of the development.

In 14:1–13 the vision changes once again from judgment to salvation. Over against the two beasts and their followers, who bear the beast's name on their forehead (13:15–17), stands the other mighty protagonist, the lamb, and his followers, who bear his name and that of God on their foreheads (14:1). The followers of the lamb are the full number of the elect (14:1 = 7:1–17). And once again it is a new song for their glorified being that they utter (14:3 = 5:9). They are specified as "virgins" but not in the sense that only consecrated virgins are in question. Just as all Christians of all time are "martyrs" for John (7:13–17), so all Christians are virgins. They are such not merely because they have avoided fornication (2:14) with the beast, that is the emperor-worship or idolatry, but because they have been engaged in the holy war of the Old Testament tradition for which celibacy was one of the required conditions (2 Sm 11:11).

2) *14:14–15:4.* The outlook widens again. The judgment upon evil expands to all the earth and the Son of Man destroys it with the sickle of his vengeance (14:14–20). Over against this is seen the salvation of those who have never bowed to idolatry, who have crossed the Red Sea and hymn their deliverance on the other side (15:1–4; cf. Ex 15).

3) *15:5–16:21.* The seven plagues (15:6), like the seven seals (6:1) and the seven trumpets (8:2), symbolize the announcement of God's settling of accounts with the Roman Empire in judgment and salvation. The first four plagues correspond closely to the first four trumpets. They strike earth, sea, rivers, and heavens in both cases. Despite these first punishments, Rome refuses to repent and God strikes directly at the throne. The fifth and sixth plagues represent internal and external turmoil for the Roman Empire. These disasters correspond to the locusts and the horses of the fifth and sixth trumpets. Once more the sixth plague, like the sixth trumpet, uses the Euphrates as the symbol of invasion. The death throes of Rome are described symbolically in 16:12–16. The Roman Empire and its vassals are assembled at Armageddon, that is, the Mountain of Megiddo. This was the vital pass which commanded passage from north to south in Palestine; where, for example, Josiah, king of Judah, tried in vain to stop Pharaoh Neco on his march north to aid the Assyrians in their last-ditch stand against the Babylonians (2 Kgs 23:29). Armageddon is thus a symbolic battlefield and also a symbol of defeat and mourning. The final plague shows Rome, called Babylon, in ruins against a symphonic background of apocalyptic orchestration (thunder, lightning, earthquake, and hailstones).

This passage finishes the announcement of the great day of judgment and salvation on pagan Rome and its martyrs on the one hand, and on all the opposing nations and their martyrs on the other (4–16). As announced by John, this judgment/salvation will be caused by the lamb. Its beginning is in the Christ-versus-Satan conflict and its continuation is in the combat of Satan's adorers, the followers of the beast, against God and the followers of the lamb. Its consummation is in the judgment/salvation of God upon Rome and upon all the nations.

4. Advent of the Day of the Lord

In order to heighten the efficacy of the prophetic proclamation, the judgment and salvation aspects of the day of God's reckoning are first announced as forthcoming (4–16), and then described in advent (17–22). In 17:1–22:5 we find once again the duality of judgment (17:1–18:24) and salvation (19:1–10) on the Roman situation, and also of judgment (19:11–20:15) and salvation (21:1–22:5) on all such future situations summed up in one gigantic end-time battle in which the forces of good utterly destroy those of evil. The Roman vision is always archetypal for the future.

a) The Day of Rome

Read Apocalypse 17:1–19:10

1) 17:1–18:24. Two images are here used for the Roman Empire at the time of the later apocalyptic writing. The present Rome is the harlot seated on the beast, the latest manifestation of the Roman Empire. The meaning of 17:8–10 is that Domitian (eighth emperor) is another persecutor, a Nero (fifth emperor) come back to evil life again. The writer places himself in the reign of Vespasian (sixth emperor). He says "five have fallen" (Augustus, Tiberius, Caligula, Claudius and Nero); "one is" (Vespasian, the sixth); "the other has not yet come, and when he comes he must remain only a little while" (Titus, the seventh, whose reign was shortest of all). "As for the beast that was and is not (i.e. Nero), it is an eighth (evil of Nero, the fifth Emperor has become reincarnate in Domitian, the eighth Emperor) but it belongs to the seven, and it goes to perdition" (Domitian, the eighth Emperor, really belongs to the seven in that he partakes of their fullness of evil and their punishment of perdition). The first image, that of the harlot seated upon the beast (17:1–7), is identical with the second image, that of the eighth king, Domitian, the present persecuting focus of blasphemous Rome (17:8–11). Rome will eventually fall devoured by her own vassal states (17:12–18).

The prophetic vision of Rome's fall follows in Apocalypse 18. The picture unfolds in three scenes: Rome is pronounced fallen (18:1–8); Rome is lamented in a triple dirge — by the kings (18:9–10), by the merchants (18:11–17), and by the mariners of the world (18:18–19). All is summed up in a concluding prophecy on the violence of her fall because of her blasphemous emperor-worship and her persecution of God's saints (18:20–24).

2) *19:1–10.* Corresponding as usual to this judgment-vision is the corresponding vision of salvation. All heaven rejoices because judgment has been passed on Rome and the martyrs reign with God. This reign of God is seen as the marriage of the lamb and his Church. The fall of Rome is the moment when God establishes his Church in full reign over the forces of evil. The lamb takes his bride, the Church, both the martyrs of Rome and all its members, all the saints. Rome's persecution only served to purify the bride's wedding garment.

b) The Day of All the Earth

Read Apocalypse 19:11–22:5.

If the message of consolation spoke only of the Roman part it would profit the ages but little. And if it spoke only of some distant future divine assessment it would be scant consolation in the midst of the anguish and ordeal of human history. But it deliberately mixes both perspectives together to make Rome the model for all such future events, and to assure history, through the image of one great and final battle between God and Satan, that love will finally prevail upon this earth. The mechanics of the victory are not given to us; possibly for the same reason that the mechanics of creation were not revealed to us. Once God gave us the heart of the matter, the past and the future could be fitted slowly into place as our faith and our experience upon this earth grew apace and grew hand in hand. We are God's people dwelling upon God's earth with God in our midst. Surely that is enough to work with. The beginning is wide open, save that it is the gift of God; the end is wide open, save that it is the victory of love.

1) *19:11–20:15.* The victory is assured because Christ, "clad in a robe dipped in blood," is the glorified presence of the cruci-

fied One in whom God continually confronts human history with the meaning of its own existence and the challenge to accept it as his word. He destroys the unconcern and unlove, the hate and persecution, not only of Rome, but of all such situations in the future (19:11–21).

The interlude in 20:1–10 is, of course, to be understood symbolically like all the other visions of this book. The period of human history will not always be one of conflict, but there will be lulls in the storm of fury, periods in which Satan is, as it were, bound, peace bought at the price of those who died in the last attack. These victims reign meanwhile with God while their brethren on earth await in their turn and in newer arenas the unleashing again of evil upon the earth.

The vision of 20:11–15 is of the judgment of vengeance which must meet all those who do not belong to the kingdom of God, in the community of love. No one at any place or at any time can escape this judgment. No one can avoid it.

2) 21:1–22:5. This passage contains the final and climactic image of the salvation of all those who belong to the community of love. This image is not a picture of heaven but rather of the community of love, the Church on earth as the perfect dwelling place of God and man and moving steadily toward the perfection of that bond. The details of the consummation are unknown but the accent is on the terrestrial rather than the heavenly: "And I saw the holy city, new Jerusalem, coming down out of heaven from God, prepared as a bride adorned for her husband" (21:2): "And in the Spirit he carried me away to a great, high mountain, and showed me the holy city Jerusalem coming down out of heaven from God, having the glory of God" (21:10–11), in both earlier and later accounts of ultimate salvation. Down here on earth God and Satan battle for man's wayward love and the victory of God, if victory there is to be, must take place on this earth. The end of the new creation is as open as was the beginning, but when earth becomes what God intended it to be it will merge at that moment with heaven: God's people perfectly at one with each other and with their God, forever.

This section, like so many others, is composed of an earlier apocalyptic work (21:1–8 and 22:3–5) and a later apocalyptic writing (21:9–22:2). In both cases the redeemed creation, the new Jerusalem, is seen in an image of ultimate victory as the bride (21:1–4 and 21:9–22). Then the inhabitants of the new Jerusalem are described first positively (21:5–7 and 21:22–26), then negatively (21:8; 21:7), and then again positively (22:3–5 and 22:1–2).

In 21:1–4 and 21:9–21, the Church is pictured as the ongoing community of love. It is a new creation since its love takes control of evolution's future and points it toward the good of all mankind. The community is seen as the dwelling place of God on earth, and as the perfect community of the elect, hence symbolic numbers ("twelve" in 21:12–14).

The inhabitants of this city of God upon earth and forever thereafter as the saints (21:5–7; 22:3–5; and 21:22–26; 21:1–2). No sinners can ever live therein; to the degree of their sin they have withdrawn from it and stand on their judgment (21:8; 21:27).

5. Conclusion

Read Apocalypse 22:6–21.

This conclusion reflects quite strongly the ideas in the opening words (1:1–3, 7–8), and like them, it stems from the earlier historical situation of the Neronic persecution when the community still thought in terms of an imminent return of the resurrected Lord in open judgment and salvation. The more complete understanding of John's later writings does not invalidate this way of thinking; it merely clarifies it. To the generation of those who stood against the might of Rome and to the pagan hate of Rome itself, Christ "came" in judgment and salvation. He "came" because he lives forever at the heart of human history and so "comes" to every generation until the consummation of the new creation, the perfect realization of the community of love. Every generation must say in its own term, "Come Lord Jesus." They must say it without fear, for perfect love casts out fear; and when love is perfect, Jesus has come most fully.

General Bibliography

THIS list contains some of the main books which the English-language reader might find useful for a wider investigation of the areas discussed in this study.

Bacon, B. W., *The Fourth Gospel in Research and Debate* (New Haven, 1918).

The work ranges over all the "anonymous writings attributed to the Apostle John" but especially the Gospel itself. This book is an example of what W. Sanday's book is opposing.

Bacon, B. W., *The Gospel of the Hellenists* (New York, 1933).

Discusses the Epistles and Gospel as the work of the Ephesian Elder, not the apostle John. This unknown elder represented the thought of the Hellenists who had left Jerusalem after Stephen's martyrdom and established themselves at Ephesus in Asia Minor.

Barrett, C. K., *The Gospel According to St. John* (London, 1955).

Unlike C. H. Dodd's work, this is a full commentary. There is an introduction and verse-by-verse notes on the Greek text — but without any text itself present. The author thinks of the entire Johannine literature as edited after the apostle's death by a number of his pupils, among whom the most brilliant and original was the writer of the Gospel; probably only sections of the Apocalypse are directly from the apostle himself. This position is toward the center of the two conflicting poles noted under J. Donovan and H. L. Jackson and debated since the turn of the century.

Brown, Raymond E., S.S., *The Gospel According to John* (i–xii) ("The Anchor Bible," 29; Garden City, N. Y., 1966).

This is the first volume on the Johannine literature in the "Anchor Bible" series. Written by a well-known American scholar, it is a translation of the first twelve chapters of the Gospel of John with an in-depth introduction and commentary.

Burney, C. F., *The Aramaic Origin of the Fourth Gospel* (Oxford, 1922).

An investigation into the original language in which the Gospel was written. The author seeks to demonstrate that the original was in Aramaic and that our Greek text is a translation from such a Semitic document.

Dodd, C. H., *Historical Tradition in the Fourth Gospel* (Cambridge, 1963).

This is a careful comparison of various areas where the three Synoptic Gospels and that of John converge. It argues that John represents an independent and parallel tradition to these other writings.

——— *The Interpretation of the Fourth Gospel* (Cambridge, 1953).

This book places the main ideas of the Gospel in close contact with the higher religion of Hellenism at the time of the writing and holds that its style of discourse and dialogue reflect their own pedagogical methods. Possibly the second half of the book, an investigation of argument and structure, is of more lasting value.

Donovan, J., *The Authorship of St. John's Gospel* (London, 1936).

A complete and thorough investigation of the authorship problem of the Epistles and Gospel. The writer argues for St. John as their communal author. The continuance of this debate on authorship, which dominated turn-of-the-century biblical scholarship (cf. H. L. Jackson), with both sides quite certain of their position, would tend to indicate that the truth must be somewhere in the middle. Neither the thesis, on the one hand, that St. John wrote all five works (like some modern author), nor the position, on the other hand, that he had nothing to do with any of them, was able to prevail in the debate.

Farrer, A., *A Rebirth of Images* (Glascow, 1949).

This book is an attempt to understand the Apocalypse as an integrated work with special concern for its cyclic patterns. It may possibly render the genre even more mysterious for the modern reader.

Guilding, A., *The Fourth Gospel and Jewish Worship* (Oxford, 1960).

Relates the fourth Gospel to the lectionary readings of the Old Testament in the Palestinian synagogues. The Gospel would be arranged almost as commentary on the three-year cycle of liturgical readings in use at its birth.

Howard, W. F., *The Fourth Gospel in Recent Criticism and Interpretation* (4th ed. rev.; London, 1955).

This is a survey of critical research in the twentieth century, as well as the author's own comments on many of the problems under discussion. The section from 1901–1930 is by the author; that of 1931–1953 in the revised edition is by C. K. Barrett.

Jackson, H. L., *The Problem of the Fourth Gospel* (Cambridge, 1918).

The author reviews all the main introductory problems of authorship, date, place, purpose, composition, structure, etc. The careful argumentation is generally critical of the simple exposition of the traditional view of Johannine authorship for the Gospel. This book, along with B. W. Bacon's *The Fourth Gospel* and W. Sanday's *Criticism*, shows clearly the critical preoccupations of the beginning of the century with more emphasis on the identity of the author than on the theology of his work.

Lightfoot, R. H., *St. John's Gospel* (Oxford, 1956).

An introduction and commentary which also indicates the change in critical interest since the early years of the century. Much less space is devoted to questions of authorship, etc., and much more to questions of content and theology.

Loenertz, R. J., *The Apocalypse of St. John* (London, 1947).

This is an analysis of the plan and structure of the writing with special attention to the cipher seven in the composition. It is written on the popular level and represents a useful introduction to a genre often strange to modern readers.

MacGregor, G. H. C., and Morton, A. Q., *The Structure of the Fourth Gospel* (London, 1961).

Applies statistical mathematics to the structure and composition of John. From such analysis the authors distinguish two sources and two stages of redaction in the final composition.

Sanday, W., *The Criticism of the Fourth Gospel* (Oxford, 1905).

This book consists of eight lectures on various subjects in the Gospel. It represents an appeal for more traditional views on various introductory problems, and appeared when such a position was not too popular; it defends the thesis that the apostle John wrote the Gospel.

Swete, H. B., *The Apocalypse of St. John* (London, 1906).

This is a full-scale commentary of magisterial proportions. It has introduction, the Greek text at the head of each page, and then a verse-by-verse commentary below.

Westcott, B. F., *The Gospel according to St. John* (London, 1919).

Like H. B. Swete's work, this is a complete commentary including both introduction, text, and verse-by-verse discussion. Position on introductory matters is usually conservative and traditional.

Scriptural Index

Genesis
1   13
1:1–2   50
1:1–13   50
1:14–31   50
1:26–28   13, 18, 41, 50, 62, 72, 94, 114, 151
2:1–4a   50
2:15   114
3:15   57
3:20   130
4–9   62
4–11   62
4:1   27
4:1–16   24
12:1–3   92, 148
17:17   92
21:6   92
28:10–17   56
49   108

Exodus
12:11   52
12:12–13   111
12:46   131
13:21   91
15   165
17:1–7   88
19–20   14
31:10   129
33   48
34:1   14
34:28   14

Leviticus
19:17–18   17
21:10   129

Numbers
20:8   88
21:9   64

Deuteronomy
2:14   71
6:4–5   17
6:20–23   45
18:15–22   117

26:5–9   45
28:1–2   148
28:15   148
33   108

Joshua
24   66
24:1–13   45
24:15   19

Judges
11:12   57

2 Samuel
7:14   96
11:11   165
16:10   57
17:23   111
19:22   57

1 Kings
11:41   36
14:19   37
14:29   37
17:18   57

2 Kings
3:13   57
17:24–34   66
23:29   165

Chronicles
35:21   57

Judith
   45

Psalms
33:6   13
69:9   61
71:15   22
82   99
82:2–4   99
98:2   22
105   45
105:41   88
118:22   55
147:18–19   14

Proverbs
2:4   7
8:22–26   45–46
8:22–36   45
8:27–30   46
8:31–35   46

Job
38:11   79
42:7   94

Ecclesiastes
5:2   48, 153

Sirach
1:1–8   46
1:1–10   45
1:9–10   46
1:11–30   46
24:1–4   46
24:1–7   45
24:5–7   46
24:8–34   46
44:1–
50:21   45
50:11   129

Wisdom
4:18–19   111
9:1–3   13
9:1–18   45
9:9a   46
9:9b   46
9:10–18   46
10–19   45
16   64
18:3–4   91
18:14–16   13, 111

Isaiah
1:10–17   60, 150
2:24   17, 150
6:1–13   157
6:9–10   106
9:1–2   91
28:16   55
35:5–7   151
40:3   52

40:11	98
42:6	91
46:13	21
48:12	79
48:21	88
49:6	91
49:1–6	150
53:7	52
56:1	22

Jeremiah

1:4–10	157
7	61
7:11	61
7:13–15	60
7:26	150
17:13	93
19:1–13	40
26	61
31:10	98
32:1–15	40

Ezekiel

1–3	159
24:20–21	149
25:3–4	149
34	98, 99
40–48	161
47:1–12	89

Daniel

	45
7	164
7:25	162
10	157

Hosea

6:6	60

Joel

2	151
2:2–11	161
3:14	84
3:17, 21	48

Amos

5:15	149
5:18–20	149
5:19–20	73
5:21–24	150
5:23–24	60
9:13	73

Jonah

4:11	151

Micah

6:6–8	60

Zechariah

4:1–4, 11–14	162
9:9	105
12:10	131
13:1	89
14:21	61

Zephaniah

1:7	160

1 Maccabees

4:36–59	99

2 Maccabees

1:1–2:18	99
10:1–8	99

Matthew

3:7–10	98
4:5–7	39
4:13	59
5:17	70
8:5–10	39
8:5–13	68
8:29	57
9:13	60
9:23	5
10:2–4	55
11:23	91
12:7	60
12:24	98
12:38–40	98
12:38–42	39
13:53–58	68
13:58	39
14:13–21	77
15:21–28	69
15:32–39	77
16:1a, 2–3	98
16:1b, 4	98
16:13–20	78, 145
16:21	128
17:1	5
17:22	128
19:3–9	93
19:29	89
20:17–19	128
21:12–13	59
21:21	120
21:33–46	12
21:42	55
21:45–46	126
22:33	126
24	119
24:3	5
25:14–30	24
25:31–40	94

25:31–46	25, 76
25:41–46	94
26–28	139
26:3–5	125
26:5	127
26:6–13	104
26:17	134
26:33	145
26:14–16	125
26:18	125
26:26	77
26:39	111
26:60–61	60
27:5	111
27:16	128
27:19	138
27:20	127
27:38, 44	127
27:39–40	60
28:1–20	139–144

Mark

1:1	38
1:16–20	54
1:21	59
1:21–22	69
1:24	57
1:27–28	39
1:29	54
1:35–38	5
1:36–38	54
2:1–3:6	107
2:23–28	76
3:16–19	55
3:22	98
5:7	57
5:37	5
6:1–6	68
6:5	39
6:30–44	77
7:24–30	39, 69
8:1–10	77
8:11–12	98
8:27–30	78
8:31	128
9:2	5
9:6–31	45
9:31	128
9:33–50	43
9:40	84
10:30	89
10:32–34	128
11:11–12	92, 125
11:12–14	40
11:15	125
11:15–17	40, 59
11:18	107, 126
11:19–20, 27	93, 125

11:20–21 40
11:23 120
11:27 125
12:1–12 12
12:12, 37 107, 126
12:13–17 93
13 119
13:1–3 93
13:3 5, 125
14–16 139
14:1–2 107, 125
14:3–9 104
14:10–11 112, 125
14:12 134
14:13 125
14:22 77
14:22–23 112
14:29 145
14:36 111
14:57–58 60
15:1 112
15:15 112
15:27 127
15:29–30 60
16:1–20 139–144, 140
16:17–18 133
20:31 38

Luke
1:45 130
2:41–50 57
3:7–9 98
4:16–30 60, 68
4:31 59
4:34 57
4:42–43 5
5:1–10 144
6:14–16 55
7:1–10 68
7:36–50 104
8:28 57
8:51 5
9:10–17 77
9:18–21 78
9:22, 44 128
9:28 5
10:25–28 17
10:30–37 25, 76
11:15 98
11:23 84
11:27–28 129
11:29–30 98
12:54–56 98
13:10–17 76
16 43
18:30 89
18:31–34 128
18:42 39

19:47–46 49
19:47–48 126
20:9–19 12
20:19, 39 126
21 119
21:7 5
21:38 92
22–24 139
22:1–2 125
22:2 127
22:3–6 125
22:7 134
22:10 125
22:19 77, 110
22:25–27 111
22:40 5
22:42 111
23:4 127
23:4, 13, 22 127
23:17 128
23:50–51 103
24:1–53 139–144, 140
24:13–35 133
25:51 131

John
1:6–8 64
1:6–8, 15, 19– 37 74
1:12–13 163
1:13 154
1:14 59, 113, 153
1:15 64
1:19–28 47
1:29–34 47
1:35–39 47
1:35–42 106
1:42 144
1:50–51 59
2:1–4 163
2:4 58
2:7–8 24
2:11 41, 69
2:18, 28 18
2:20 27
2:20, 26–27 29
2:20–21 20
2:23 69
2:26–27 27
3:1–13 90
3:7 18
3:3–5 48
3:11–24 27
3:14 91

3:17 96
3:22–30 47, 74
4:1–42 5
4:4 18, 29
4:6 154
5–6 154
5:12–13 95
5:21 18
5:22 96
6:64 112
6:67–71 144
7:6 58
7:30 58
7:31 126
8:15–16 96
8:20 58
8:30 126
9 39
9:1–3 72
10:11–18 55
10:41–42 47
10:42 126
11:47–53 107, 125
12:1 58
12:3, 7 90
12:19 126
12:23, 27 58
12:27 111
12:32, 34 91
12:42–43 90, 103
13:1 58
13:23–24 5
13:30 125
13:33 18, 92
14:3 92
14:16, 26 117
15:2 154
15:26 117
16:5–11 117
17:1 58
18–20 139
18:15–16 5
18:15–18, 25–27 144
18:28 134, 136
19:25–27 58, 163
19:31 136
19:38–39 103
19:39 90
20–21 139–144, 140
20:1–10 5
20:19–23 144
20:24–29 92
20:26–29 144
20:30 41, 59
20:31 30
21:15–19 55
21:20–23 5

The Acts
1:1	39
1:9	131
1:13	5, 55
1:18	111
2:1–4	132
2:22	38
2:33	91
2:41, 46, 47	107
3:1–4, 11	5
3:11	107
4:1–22	107
4:4, 33	107
4:11	55
4:13, 19	5
5:6, 10	102
5:13–14	107
5:17, 26, 28	107
5:31	91
6:8–8:3	107
8:4–25	62
8:12	107
8:14	5
8:14–17	5
9:31	107
10:38	38
12:1–24	107
18:24–19:7	64
21:20	107

Romans
1:1–4	131

1–2	71
5:3–4	152
5:6–8	117
8:19–23	151
8:24–25	152
9:33	55
10:11	55

1 Corinthians
11:17–34	83
11:23	112
11:24–25	110
13:13	151
15:3–11	139–144

Ephesians
1:15–18	152
2:20	55

Philippians
2:9	91

Colossians
1:4–5	152

1 Thessalonians
1:2–3	151
1:3	152
5:8	152

2 Thessalonians
1:3–5	152

Timothy
6:11	152

Hebrews
1:1–3	13

James
1:27	60

1 Peter
2:6	55
2:7	55
5:1–4	111

1 John
1:1	44
1:1–2	20
2:28–4:6	48
3:16–18	115
4:7–21	115
5:6–7	130

2 John
	158
7	18

3 John
	158

Apocalypse
5:6	92
12	57
21:1–4	113, 153
21:3	48
22:6–13	156

Subject Index

Action, symbolic, 59
Apparitions of Jesus after the resurrection, 139
Authorship, 2

Baptism, 48, 62, 95, 131

Catechesis, oral, 7
Community, 45, 53, 107, 111, 118, 133; of faith, 42, 115; of love, 15, 59, 90, 97, 114, 121, 156, 168
Conscience, 26
Creation, new, 49, 120

"Day of the Lord," 51, 149
"Day of Yahweh," 17, 61, 73
Decision, 78, 84, 90
Dialogue, 63, 112; into monologue, 108
Discourses of Jesus, 43

Eternal life, 15, 64
Eucharist, 77, 131
Evolution, 14, 18, 26, 41, 44, 47, 49, 53, 62, 67, 72, 74 f, 94, 109, 115, 152; divine, 76

Faith, 29, 39, 53, 64, 69, 83, 97, 101, 132, 155; community of, 42, 115
Fidelity, 22
Form Criticism, 35

Gentiles, 69, 105
Glorification, 58, 91

Historical Jesus, 36
Historicity of Gospel accounts, 32
Hope, 150, 155

Jesus, ministry of, 38; works and words of, 38
"Jews, the," 80, 85, 90, 95, 98, 103, 125, 126; the term, 72
John the apostle, 4; date for, 4; Gospel of, date for, 4; as poet, 6
John the Baptist, 47, 51, 62, 64
Judgment, 64, 96, 107, 150, 155; and salvation, 73, 84, 119, 156, 165

Kingdom, 17, 40, 69, 70, 95, 97, 108, 116
"Kingdom of God," 63
Kingdom of mercy, 74

Law, the, 71
Life, 47, 69, 88, 99, 100, 106, 109; liturgy and, 76
Light, 15, 16, 21, 23, 47, 90, 93, 99, 106, 109
Liturgy, 60; and life, 76
Love, 24, 40, 47, 62, 64, 90, 94, 100, 106, 108, 114, 117, 145, 152, 167; community of, 15, 59, 90, 97, 114, 121, 156, 168

Mark, narrative of, 127
Mary, 48, 57, 58, 129, 130, 163
Metahistory, 37
Miracles, 39, 100, 118
Monologue, 63, 112; dialogue into, 108

New creation, 49, 120

Oral catechesis, 7
Ordination, 110

Papyri, 4
Parallelism, 6, 16, 42, 46, 86, 128
Passion, relative chronology of, 133
Prayer, 120

Qumran, 4, 53

Revelation, 14, 23, 67, 78, 84, 96, 97, 147
"Righteousness of God," 21, 22

Sacrament, 18, 75, 114, 115, 122; of evolution, 27
Salvation, 64, 104, 107, 116, 150, 155, 160; judgment and, 73, 84, 119, 156, 165
"Sent, the," 53, 65, 121
Seven, 80, 95, 102, 119, 122, 123

179

Seven dialogues, 86, 101
Seven sign complexes, 42
Seven statements, 79
Seven times, 65
Seven-day span, 51
Signs, 57
Sin, 16, 31, 94, 133
Spirit, the, 29, 50, 89, 115; gift of, 66; and water, 63
Symbolic action, 59
Symbolic works, 40

Temple, 86; at Jerusalem, 59; new, 65

Unconcern, 16, 18, 24, 25, 62, 72, 133, 153

Water, 66, 88; Spirit and, 63
Wisdom, 45 f
Witness, 54, 74, 91
"Word of God," 13 f, 44 f
"World," 18, 113, 117